MILTON'S SECRECY

Literary and Scientific Cultures of Early Modernity

Series editors:

Mary Thomas Crane, Department of English, Boston College, USA
Henry Turner, Department of English, Rutgers University, USA

This series provides a forum for groundbreaking work on the relations between literary and scientific discourses in Europe, during a period when both fields were in a crucial moment of historical formation. We welcome proposals for books that address the many overlaps between modes of imaginative writing typical of the sixteenth and seventeenth centuries – poetics, rhetoric, prose narrative, dramatic production, utopia – and the vocabularies, conceptual models, and intellectual methods of newly emergent "scientific" fields such as medicine, astronomy, astrology, alchemy, psychology, mapping, mathematics, or natural history. In order to reflect the nature of intellectual inquiry during the period, the series is interdisciplinary in orientation and publishes monographs, edited collections, and selected critical editions of primary texts relevant to an understanding of the mutual implication of literary and scientific epistemologies.

Other titles in the series:

Poetry and Ecology in the Age of Milton and Marvell
Diane Kelsey McColley

Food in Shakespeare
Early Modern Dietaries
Joan Fitzpatrick

Hermaphrodites in Renaissance Europe
Kathleen P. Long

Renaissance Rhetoric Short-Title Catalogue 1460–1700
Lawrence D. Green and James J. Murphy

Milton's Secrecy
And Philosophical Hermeneutics

JAMES DOUGAL FLEMING
Simon Fraser University, Canada

Routledge
Taylor & Francis Group

LONDON AND NEW YORK

First published 2008 by Ashgate Publishing

2 Park Square, Milton Park, Abingdon, Oxon OX14 4RN
711 Third Avenue, New York, NY 10017, USA

Routledge is an imprint of the Taylor & Francis Group, an informa business

First issued in paperback 2016

British Library Cataloguing in Publication Data
Fleming, James Dougal
Milton's secrecy and philosophical hermeneutics. –
(Literary and scientific cultures of early modernity)
1. Milton, John, 1608–1674 – Criticism and interpretation
2. Secrecy in literature
I. Title
821.4

Library of Congress Cataloging-in-Publication Data
Fleming, James Dougal, 1968–
Milton's secrecy : and philosophical hermeneutics / James Dougal Fleming.
    p. cm. – (Literary and scientific cultures of early modernity)
Includes bibliographical references.
(alk. paper)
1. Milton, John, 1608–1674–Criticism and interpretation. 2. Milton, John, 1608–1674–Criticism, Textual. 3. Secrecy in literature. 4. Hermeneutics. 5. Knowledge, Theory of, in literature I. Title.
PR3592.S36F64 2007
821'.4–dc22
                                                                        2007012683

ISBN 13: 978-0-7546-6067-5 (hbk)
ISBN 13: 978-1-138-25969-0 (pbk)

For Cynthia
without whom not

Contents

Foreword		*ix*
Acknowledgements		*xi*
List of Abbreviations		*xiii*
	Introduction: Against Secrecy	1
1	Expressing the Conscience	31
2	The Armor of Intention	57
3	The Armor of Intension	93
4	Talking and Learning in Paradise	123
	Conclusion: Secrecy Again?	159
	Works Cited	*175*
	Index	*193*

Foreword

Among recent literary-historical commentaries, this one is somewhat atypical. For one thing, it is not historicist. It is not an attempt to situate a certain figure (in this case, Milton) with respect to certain discourses (in this case, Calvinism, casuistry, and Neoplatonism) in a certain time and place (in this case, seventeenth-century England). Rather, this book is an attempt to understand certain issues, here and now, that seem to be raised by that figure and those discourses in that time and place. The difference here is like the difference between analyzing a conversation, and participating in it. To analyze a conversation is to figure out how it works. To participate in a conversation, however, is to attend to its subject-matter. I have tried to follow some aspects of Milton's conversation with his contemporaries in the second way, rather than in the first.

The validity of such a move has to do with the nature of the conversational subject-matter. Here is another difference between this book and its recent analogues. This book is not empiricist. It is not an attempt to do a literary-historical version of social science (whether sociological, psychological, or economic). Rather, it is an attempt to do a literary-historical version of interpretative theory. Thus while I make some remarks about early-modern English social-psychology, for example, I am not making any claims about how the mind works, or about how it worked in seventeenth-century England. Instead, I am making claims about how the workings of the mind, as imagined and represented in some of Milton's texts and contexts, can help us to think about writing and meaning. I am making hermeneutic claims. Such claims, arguably, are of immediate and present concern precisely to the extent that historical work indicates fluctuation in their grounds of validity. For if historical inquiry indicates that interpretation itself changes in history, then we have to ask (right now) what we are doing when we are interpreting history.

Hermeneutic inquiry of this kind never departs from a concern with the same kind of inquiry that it is (or is trying to be). It is reflexive, not transitive. Its subject-matters are textuality, and the latter's components: intention, expression, and interpretation. Ultimately, the hermeneutic subject-matter is conversation itself. The strength of this approach is liberation from the inductive burden that empiricist projects must either shirk or bear. The weakness of the approach is its vulnerability to charges of tautology and insignificance. I will try to meet those charges by arguing that, if they can be levelled against this book, they can be levelled against Milton's books, too. His is the hermeneutic inquiry that prompts my hermeneutic inquiry. To be sure, Milton has other concerns in his various texts (religion, government, sexuality, etc.). But he always, or at least very frequently, has this one concern. Milton does not just deploy textuality in order to illuminate certain discourses. He also deploys certain discourses in order to illuminate textuality.

Perhaps it seems that textuality does not need to be illuminated. Perhaps it needs, rather, to be revealed – decoded, uncovered, demystified – by some theoretical method. Perhaps, too, it seems that the kind of inquiry I am describing (if it is to reveal anything) must be more-or-less deconstructive, and thus all-too-familiar. The second supposition is one that I will attempt to refute as it arises. Deconstructing textuality, I will argue, is precisely not an inquiry into textuality, but follows from the antecedent assumption that textuality offers nothing to inquire into. The first supposition, then, must be refuted as well. It is what this whole book attempts to refute. Textuality is not anything that needs to be, or can be, revealed by a method. It is, rather, something that involves us, as a skill or practice. It is always-already revealed. Milton's whole argument, his whole passionate claim, is that we must commit ourselves to textuality as the plenitude of understanding. The argument matters because we are free not to commit ourselves; free, instead, to propose that the plenitude hides a vacancy. This is the attitude of Milton's Satan, who sees in textuality only the secrecy that he holds in himself. *Milton's Secrecy* starts from Satan's reflexive and interminable suspicion. But to start is to depart. *In medias res.*

Simon Fraser University
Summer 2006

Acknowledgements

Like many, this book began as a dissertation. At Columbia University, where that beginning was, thanks are due to my advisors, Edward Tayler and David Scott Kastan; to Anne Lake Prescott and James Shapiro; to Joy Hayton; and to my peers and students. Further thanks, of the same academic kind, are due to everybody who has read, heard, or commented on any portion of this book as it developed (whether or not they knew they were so doing). These are too numerous to name. My research has been helped along by the staff of wonderful libraries. I gratefully acknowledge the financial support of the Social Sciences and Humanities Research Council of Canada (SSHRC). Thanks also to Yale University Press for permission to quote from the *Complete Prose Works of John Milton*.

At a personal level, the support of friends has been as persistent as the work on this book. Thanks to you all. My wife Cynthia has persisted even longer – from the very beginning before the beginning. Loudest thanks to her.

My children – Lucas, Dominique, and Sage – are thanks incarnate.

List of Abbreviations

Milton

Complete Prose	*CP*
Paradise Lost	*PL*
Paradise Regained	*PR*
Samson Agonistes	*SA*
The Works of John Milton	*Works*

Gadamer

Truth and Method	*TM*
Wahrheit und Methode	*WM*

Periodicals

English Literary History	*ELH*
English Literary Renaissance	*ELR*
Milton Quarterly	*MQ*
Milton Studies	*MS*
Renaissance Quarterly	*RQ*
Studies in English Literature, 1500–1900	*SEL*

Introduction

Against Secrecy

We assume that knowledge results from discovery. Evidence, gathered without prejudice, must be judged if it is to support a knowledge-claim. This judgment consists, typically, in a penetration of the evidence to reveal something non-evident. The essential, or the crucial, or the explanatory, or the probative is to be found beneath the surface, or among the details, or beyond appearances. It is somewhat difficult to recognize that we are talking metaphorically when we talk this way. It is very difficult to imagine any other way of talking. Yet we could, if we wished, trope the movement from data to knowledge differently – say, as construction, rather than as uncovering. It does not follow that our trope is wrong, only that it is a trope. Our commitment to discovery is a rhetorical choice with epistemological consequences.

For example:

1. all our knowledge is, ultimately, interpretative. This is an extremely uncontroversial proposal. It simply means that a passage from evident data to non-evident concept seems to be a necessary part of our knowing what we know. Further, such a process seems to be necessary no matter what kind of data we encounter – be it a flock of birds, a sudden pain, a collocation of words. Everything requires interpretation in order to be understood.
2. The study of interpretation – philosophical hermeneutics – is, therefore, a universal discipline.
3. The model of interpretation that obtains throughout the academy, and, indeed, throughout our culture, is closely in accord with the requirements and practices of modern natural science. The separation of data-collection from analysis, the epistemological impatience with appearances, the interpretative reduction of phenomena to their constitutive elements – all these are leitmotifs of inductive (or hypothetico-deductive) empiricism. With that generalization I do not mean to propose an hermeneutic genealogy, or (again) to question the efficacy or validity of the discovery-model. I do mean to suggest that there is something modern about the model. After all, science in our sense (as most scholars of the subject agree) emerged only several centuries ago. In its early phases, moreover, it included quite different assumptions from ours about the relationship between observation and knowledge. Some late-Aristotelian natural philosophers, for example, maintained that the truth of things was a matter of their surface

presentation.[1] My point is not that these scholars were right, but that they had not yet taken on our default hermeneutics. The discovery-model has not always seemed self-evident, but has emerged in history.

4. Modern knowledge is a function of secrecy. For the presupposition of discovery can only be that something is there to be discovered. This to-be-discovered can only be the not-yet-discovered. It can only be the covered; it can only be the secret. Discovery-interpretation consists in an apprehension of secrets (though how one knows they are there to be apprehended is a perplexing problem), followed by their revelation, precipitating knowledge. Secrets are the not-yet-known; the known is the formerly-secret. Interpretation, conceived as discovery, is the process of turning the one into the other.

We can, therefore, define as standard a modern hermeneutics of discovery. This is general enough, it seems to me, to subsume Paul Ricoeur's hermeneutics of suspicion, associated with the scepticism of Nietzsche, Marx and Freud; and Leo Strauss' theory of writing and reading as esoteric encoding and decoding.[2] Fetishized or hypertrophied, discovery becomes suspicion. Repeated or deferred, it becomes encoding-decoding. The one constant, unifying these advanced interpretative schemes with an unexamined cultural assumption, is that to interpret is to discover.

Evidently, the discovery-model is both plausible and powerful. Somewhat less evidently, it is also paradoxical. For the model makes secrecy the hiding-place of knowledge. But the hiding-place of knowledge, from the investigator's or would-be discoverer's perspective, is simply the place of knowledge. The place of knowledge is secret, from the investigator's perspective. But if the place of knowledge is secret, how is the investigator to find out where it is? How is he even to know where to look, or what for? More to the point: how is he to know *how* to look? Apparently, some fore-understanding or pre-judgment – prejudice – is necessary. But prejudice is exactly what the investigator is forbidden, on the model of impartial data-collection that provides a ground for discovery.[3]

Granted, the discovery-model does allow one kind of prejudice: the prejudice in favor of discovery, the prejudice in favor of secrets. But the prejudice in favor of secrets has its own destabilizing consequences. For one thing, the epistemic status of secrecy as the precondition of fact can produce an interpretative disease through an inductive logical fallacy. Since secrecy usually precedes knowledge, people have a tendency to infer (erroneously) that knowledge invariably follows secrecy. Accordingly, in conspiracy theory, official denials and exonerations – backed up, as it were, by absence

---

[1]   See David Freedberg, *The Eye of the Lynx: Galileo, His Friends, and the Beginnings of Modern Natural History* (Chicago, 2002), pp. 201–202, 233–234, 236–237, 325, 330, and 349–366.

[2]   See Paul Ricoeur, *Hermeneutics and the Human Sciences: Essays on Language, Action, and Interpretation*, ed. and trans. John B. Thompson (New York, 1981); and Leo Strauss, *Persecution and the Art of Writing* (Glencoe, IL, 1952).

[3]   See Hans-Georg Gadamer, *Truth and Method*, trans. rev. Joel Weinsheimer and Donald G. Marshall (New York, 2003), pp. 265–285. Hereafter cited as *TM*.

of evidence – simply support the theory. The academic version of this pathology is Foucauldianism, in which the most devastating bullets are always invisible.[4]

For another thing, secrets have a unique liminality and mercuriality. They are a volatile and evanescent hermeneutic fuel. Consider that the secret is what the investigator wants to uncover. It is in order to find out secrets, to come to know them, that he investigates. Now consider that the investigator, by definition, can never know any secrets. For as soon as he comes to know them, they cease to be secrets. There is no more certain index of discovery than an envelope stamped "top secret"; but effecting the discovery means annihilating the secret, turning it into mere knowledge. The latter, very surprisingly, turns out to be rather *disappointing* on the discovery-model. The thrill of the chase, insofar as it motivates the kill, can only be more delightful than the bagging and the eating.

There results a fetishization of secrecy. This features very largely in our culture at all levels. Readers and filmgoers reliably shell out money on anything with "secret," or "code," or their analogues in the title. Deconstructive philosophers, working the same vein, offer their work as an exotic "taste for the secret."[5] The latter is basically a taste for the discovery-model – in other words for the general hermeneutics of modern Western culture – with the twist of delay. But delay is itself an extremely common variant on our interpretative compulsions. Running into a friend on the threshold of a cinema, we may say, "Don't tell me; I don't want to know." Of course we *do* want to know – that is why we are going into the cinema – which makes our plea perverse. Yet we would be disappointed by the too-sudden arrival of the secret, even as we would be frustrated by its failure to arrive. In both modes, as seekers and avoiders of secrets, we are acting like good discoverers, good modern knowers.

And what of non-modern knowers? I have suggested in passing that the hermeneutics of discovery can be associated with the epistemological requirements of modern natural science. Since the latter emerged definitively only in the late seventeenth century, it would be reasonable to suspect some other hermeneutics before its emergence, and/or as a negative term against which it emerged. There is some evidence (which I will develop more fully later) to support this expectation. I have already alluded to the famous "doctrine of the signatures": isomorphism between a phenomenon's outward appearance and its essential nature. Also relevant is the emblematic tendency of early-modern culture, its overwhelming predilection for the homiletic and the symbolic.

Above all, though, I would note that in the Augustinian tradition that informed both Reformation and Counter-Reformation Christianity, secrecy tends to vitiate, rather than to invite, investigation. Overwhelmingly associated with the divine will,

---

4   See Stephen Greenblatt, "Invisible Bullets: Renaissance Authority and Its Subversion, Henry IV and Henry V," in Jonathan Dollimore and Alan Sinfield (eds), *Political Shakespeare: New Essays in Cultural Materialism* (Manchester, 1985), pp. 18–47; and Michel Foucault, *The History of Sexuality, Volume I: An Introduction*, trans. Robert Hurley (New York, 1990).

5   Jacques Derrida and Maurizio Ferraris, *A Taste for the Secret*, trans. Giacomo Donis (Oxford, 2001), pp. vii–viii and 1–92.

it is something into which the creature should not really look.[6] If he does look, he does not find anything out. Calvin writes that when events "seem fortuitous" – when they "bear on the face of them no other appearance" – we should strictly infer the opposite, the "secret stirrings of God's hand."[7] Evidence for randomness must be read as evidence for determinism: a very radical interpretative discovery, based on divine occlusion and omnipotence. But divine occlusion and omnipotence is also what this discovery discovers. The interpretation is not an occasion for Calvin to gain any new knowledge. It is, rather, an occasion for him to re-iterate what he already knows. This is far removed indeed from the modern discovery-model.

Now, many scholars have treated early-modern uses of secrecy, and their works constitute a large database for the issues I have raised.[8] All of these scholars, however, assume secrecy *per se* as trans-historically stable; and assume that early-modern interpretation works basically as modern interpretation does. In other words, they assume an early-modern hermeneutics of discovery. They may be right. That they may be wrong is a suggestion I will work out over the course of this Introduction. For now, I would like to establish the test-case of this book in the poetry and prose of John Milton (1608–1674).

Why Milton? He – or rather, scholarship on him – occupies a peculiar position with respect to the issues under consideration here. On the one hand, most Milton scholars work within an hermeneutics of discovery. They argue or assume, implicitly or explicitly, that studying the poet's work entails a search for hidden meaning. Thus Stanley Fish, summing up a lifetime's (extremely influential) post-structuralist work, speaks of a "*secret* difference" between Milton's "deep truth" and his "surface form."[9] Similarly, scholars of Milton's responses to seventeenth-century

---

[6]   See Howard Schultz, *Milton and Forbidden Knowledge* (New York, 1955).

[7]   John Calvin, *Institutes of the Christian Religion*, ed. John T. McNeill, trans. Ford Lewis Battles (Philadelphia, 1960), pp. 208, 210.

[8]   See Gisela Engel, Jonathan Elukin et al. (eds), *Das Geheimnis am Beginn der europäischen Moderne* (Frankfurt, 2002); William Eamon, *Science and the Secrets of Nature: Books of Secrets in Medieval and Early Modern Culture* (Princeton, 1994); Pamela O. Long, *Openness, Secrecy, Authorship* (Baltimore and London, 2001); Mario Biagioli, *Galileo's Instruments of Credit: Telescopes, Images, Secrecy* (Chicago and London, 2006); Lois Potter, *Secret Rites and Secret Writing: Royalist Literature, 1641–1660* (Cambridge and New York, 1989); Annabel Patterson, *Censorship and Interpretation* (Madison, WI, 1984) and *Reading between the Lines* (Madison, WI, 1993); James Loxley, *Royalism and Poetry in the English Civil Wars: The Drawn Sword* (London and New York, 1997); and Robert Wilcher, *The Writing of Royalism, 1628–1660* (Cambridge and New York, 2001).

[9]   Stanley Fish, *How Milton Works* (Cambridge, MA, 2001), pp. 46, 31, 58–59. See also Neil Forsyth, *The Satanic Epic* (Princeton and Oxford, 2003); Victoria Silver, *Imperfect Sense: The Predicament of Milton's Irony* (Princeton, 2001); Elizabeth Sauer, "The Politics of Performance in the Inner Theater: *Samson Agoniste*" as Closet Drama," in Stephen Dobranski and John Rumrich (eds), *Milton and Heresy* (New York, 1998), pp. 199–215; and R.A. Shoaf, *Milton, Poet of Duality: A Study of Semiosis in the Poetry and the Prose* (New Haven, CT, 1985).

English politics routinely assume or assert the importance of reading the poet's texts "between the lines."[10] Theorists of Miltonic uncertainty, a veritable sub-discipline, predicate entire books on Milton's intentional occlusion of his own intentions.[11] And historians of science argue that empirical currency "does not lie on the surface" of *Paradise Lost* – but is to be found, appropriately, in passages of the epic expressing epistemological and interpretative contempt for appearances.[12]

On the other hand, secrecy *per se* has never been treated as a sustained subject for Milton criticism.[13] Miltonists have assumed discovery as the hermeneutic path to their various subject-matters; but they have not, in any significant way, turned to hermeneutic discovery as a subject-matter in and of itself. That is odd, because secrecy and discovery have been treated as important subject-matters of scholarship on most other Renaissance literary heavyweights.[14] (Indeed, "secret" has proved as irresistible a keyword, throughout literary-historical academia, as in other cultural and intellectual areas.) Edmund Spenser (1554–1599) is, perhaps, particularly relevant. The prince of poets made his living as a governmental secretary. Etymologically and practically, a secretary is a repository of secrets, and it so happens that secrecy is a leitmotif of Spenser's poetry. This tropological chain leads scholars to a Spenser who works in and through the secrecy that joins his art to his career. Critically startling, this Spenser is also profoundly orthodox, an interpretative model made possible by,

---

[10] See David Norbrook, *Writing the English Republic: Poetry, Rhetoric, and Politics, 1627–1660* (New York, 1999), pp.163–164, and "The Reformation of the Masque," in David Lindley (ed.), *The Court Masque*, (Manchester, 1984), pp. 94–110; Sharon Achinstein, *Milton and the Revolutionary Reader* (Princeton, 1994); Warren Chernaik, "Books as Memorials: The Politics of Consolation," *Yearbook of English Studies* 21 (1991): 207–217; John Leonard, "'Trembling ears': the historical moment of *Lycidas*," *Journal of Medieval and Renaissance Studies* 21 (1991): 59–81; and I.S. MacLaren, "Milton's Nativity Ode: The Function of Poetry and Structures of Response in 1629," *Milton Studies* 15 (1981): 181–200.

[11] See Peter C. Herman, *Destabilizing Milton:* Paradise Lost *and the Poetics of Incertitude* (New York, 2005); Joseph Wittreich, *Shifting Contexts: Reinterpreting* Samson Agonistes (Pittsburgh, 2002); and John Shawcross, *The Uncertain World of* Samson Agonistes (Rochester, 2001).

[12] See Karen Edwards, *Milton and the Natural World: Science and Poetry in* Paradise Lost (Cambridge, 1999), p. 4; and Catherine Gimelli Martin, "'What If the Sun Be Centre to the World?': Milton's Epistemology, Cosmology, and Paradise of Fools Reconsidered," *Modern Philology* 99.2 (2001): 231–265. For a critique, see William Poole, "Milton and Science: A Caveat," *Milton Quarterly* 38.1 (2004): 18–34.

[13] The subject is treated in passing in John Rogers, "The Secret of *Samson Agonistes*," *Milton Studies* 33 (1996): 111–132; Dayton Haskin, *Milton's Burden of Interpretation* (Philadelphia, 1994), pp. 147–183; and Georgia B. Christopher, "The Secret Agent in *Paradise Regained*," *Modern Language Quarterly* 41.2 (1980): 131–150.

[14] See Theresa M. Krier, *Gazing on Secret Sights: Spenser, Classical Imitation, and the Decorums of Vision* (Ithaca, 1990); Richard A. Levin, *Shakespeare's Secret Schemers: The Study of an Early Modern Dramatic Device* (Newark, 2001); and William W.E. Slights, *Ben Jonson and the Art of Secrecy* (Toronto, 1994).

and illuminating, the transformations of secrecy.[15] Now Milton, too, was a secretary, for the prime decade of his working life. Milton's poetry, too, has "secret" as one of its keywords (as I will argue). And Milton is Spenser's self-appointed successor in the secret-ridden business of literature – where he occupies the office of Author, concealer and revealer of things. Yet there has never been a book about Milton's secrecy; yet Milton's secrecy looks, at first glance, promisingly intelligible.

I am going to argue that appearances, in this case, really are deceiving. In doing so, I hope to offer a new way of reading Milton, and a neglected way of thinking about early-modern literature. Milton opposes his master Spenser in many ways, but none more important than this: his writings are notable, not for their utilization of secrecy, but for their root-and-branch opposition to secrecy as a moral, political, and hermeneutic category. In his revolutionary and autobiographical polemics, Milton insists on radical openness. In his narrative and theological poetry, he correlates secret-keeping with damnation. Milton abjures hiddenness in himself and excoriates it in others, be they king (*Eikonoklastes*), priest (the anti-prelatical tracts), censor (*Areopagitica*), or devil (*PL*). A central imaginative project of the Miltonic corpus is the evisceration, inversion, and evacuation of secrecy.

Milton's secrecy, in short, is anti-secrecy. This is not just a motif, among many, of his interpretative engagements. As I have suggested, secrecy is the very category of interpretation – or at least of interpretation as discovery. The significance of Milton's (anti)secrecy, accordingly, is that it constitutes an attempt to confront and preclude the very hermeneutic structure – the very discovery-model of knowledge – that we have come to see as normative.

Sacred and Satanic

Milton's attempt begins with his use of the hermeneutic keyword. In the first invocation to *Paradise Lost*, the poet calls the Holy Spirit from the "secret top" of Sinai.[16] Milton's 18th-century editor Richard Bentley was alarmed by that phrase, emending it to the more decorous "*sacred* top." But the Spirit's mountaintop is (as modern editors observe) appropriately secret in the Latin sense of *secretum*, or "set-apart."[17] Secrecy, for Milton, is akin to sacredness. Milton's Almighty speaks from inside a "secret Cloud" (*PL* 10.32). He makes "high and secret judgments," and is

---

[15]   See Richard Rambuss, *Spenser's Secret Career* (Cambridge and New York, 1993).

[16]   John Milton, *Paradise Lost. A Poem in Twelve Books* (London, 1674), book 1, line 6. All further citations will be from this edition, abbreviated *PL*, and will be parenthesized by book and line number in the body of my text. Modern lower-case "s" replaces the long early-modern staffed variety throughout.

[17]   See Alastair Fowler (ed.), *John Milton:* Paradise Lost (London and New York, 1998), p. 58, n. 7; and William Kolbrener, *Milton's Warring Angels* (Cambridge, 1997), pp. 107–132.

"in some ways high, secret past finding out."[18] And of course holy fire touches the poet, in the Nativity Ode, from God's "secret altar" (28).[19]

Milton's usage is quite conventional. Calvin, for example, constantly emphasizes God's secrecy, making it a logical consequence of divine omniscience and inscrutability.[20] But this theological commonplace stands at the center of Milton's thought. "High Thron'd above all highth" (*PL* 3.58), Milton's God sees all, while remaining himself, insofar as he wishes, "invisible" and "inaccessible" (3.375, 377). This arrangement is not only a necessary, but a sufficient condition for God. "Secret" in this context can be considered Miltonic shorthand for his Arian theology and cosmology, its deity only *homosious* (of a similar substance), not *homoisious* (of the same substance), with even his nearest creation.[21] In the iota that demarcates the space of just-God – demarcates it from the divinely-derived cosmos, and even from the Son – a spot is defined which, alone in the universe, is truly secret. When Adam tells God, unnecessarily, "thou in thyself art perfet," he explains what he means by going on to add: "thou in thy secresie although alone" (*PL* 8.415, 427).

In his relation to the universe, Milton's God expresses his unique privilege. Like the proto-scientific alchemist Theophrastus Paracelsus, Milton posits "one first matter all" as the substratum of creation (5.472).[22] In this he differs from Scholastic natural philosophy, which considered matter inseparable from its essential form, and therefore relied on the ancient Greek system of irreducible elements (earth, water, air and fire). Dispensing with that system, as the sixteenth-century Scholastic Thomas Erastus complained, creates a problem for cosmogony (or theory of world-creation). For if everything is prime matter, and prime matter precedes creation, then one must account for creation itself "not through creation, but through separation [*non per creationem, sed per secretionem*]." This view, Erastus goes on, is "simply and absolutely impossible [*simpliciter absoluteque impossibile*]."[23] Milton, however, seems to consider it absolutely and simply necessary.

---

[18]   John Milton, *Complete Prose Works of John Milton*, eds Don M. Wolfe et al. (8 vols, New Haven and London, 1953–1982), vol. 3, p. 340; and vol. 2, p. 297. Except where noted, all further citations of Milton's prose will be from this edition, abbreviated *CP*, with references parenthesized by volume and page number in the body of my text.

[19]   Citations of Milton's shorter poetry will be from John Milton, *Poems, etc. upon Several Occasions* (London, 1673), parenthesized by line number in the body of my text.

[20]   Calvin, *Institutes*, pp. 229, 231, 233, 199, 207–208, 210, 212–213, 850, 922–923, 952, etc.

[21]   See Michael Bauman, *Milton's Arianism* (New York, 1986). For the cosmology and ontology of *PL*, see Walter Clyde Curry, *Milton's Ontology, Cosmogony, and Physics* (Lexington, KY, 1957).

[22]   For Milton's monism, see Stephen M. Fallon, *Milton among the Philosophers: Poetry and Materialism in Seventeenth-Century England* (Ithaca, NY, 1991); and D. Bentley Hart, "Matter, Monism, and Narrative: An Essay on the Metaphysics of *PL*," *MQ* 30.1 (1996): 16–26.

[23]   Thomas Erastus, *Disputationes de medicina noua Philippi Paracelsi* (Basil, 1572) pp. 4, 12.

When, in *PL*, the Son of God follows his father's instructions to create another world, he grasps his "golden Compasses" and proceeds to "circumscribe / This Universe" (7.227, 225):

One foot he center'd, and the other turn'd
Round through the vast profunditie obscure,
And said, Thus farr extend, thus farr thy bounds,
This be thy just Circumference, O World. (7.228-231)

Secretio makes unworld into world. Separating like from like establishes unlike and unlike.[24] The archangel Uriel, earlier in the poem, gives a very similar account of creation *per secretionem*, when nature stood "vast infinitude confin'd" (3.711). Only subsequently, according to Uriel, did the "cumbrous Elements" make their appearance (3.715). To be sure, *secretio* has cosmogonical warrant in the opening chapters of Genesis – a point that Milton is at pains to emphasize in the balance of his account (7.232–640). It is also, to be sure, consistent with the atomist materialism that re-emerged in seventeenth-century science, after centuries of disrepute.[25] That is to say, however, that *secretio* remains scientifically unorthodox, or at least non-traditional, in the period – and thus worthy of note. For Milton, an otherwise unitary non-world is made into a variegated world through *secretionem*. This *secretio* occurs, only and exclusively, through divine *fiat*. Therefore, the separateness or secrecy that the world infinitely manifests is always and only to be understood as a reminder and representation of that *fiat*. Created *secretio* explicitly denotes the *secretum* of the Creator.

In short, secrecy is a sole power and defining attribute of Milton's God. As such, it can never be appropriated, as attribute or power, by Milton's God's creatures. Neither should it be associated with them. In *PL*, the pendant to the "secret top" that so dismayed Bentley is the description of Adam's and Eve's bower in book four. This is "covert" (4.693), and "sequester'd" (4.706), it is "in close recess" (4.708), but it is not "secret." "*Pan or Silvanus*," Milton writes of the first parents' love-nest, never slept "in shadie Bower / More *sacred*" (4.705–706, my emphasis) – a line that seems to offer "secret," which would clearly be appropriate in the sense of "set-apart," only to substitute "sacred," which is both malapropos and (as I have argued) a Miltonic cousin of "secret." Similarly, when Raphael relates the creation of the earth, he describes as "sacred shades" the beauty of its trees – despite, one might add, the resulting allusion to the idolatrous groves of the Old Testament (7.331). The poetic quarantine of "secret" is especially striking because it seems so inconsistent with Milton's epic semiotics. This after all is a poet who calls on "the meaning, not the Name" (7.5), and who consistently demonstrates the innocence of Paradise

---

[24]   See Regina Schwartz, *Remembering and Repeating: Biblical Creation in* Paradise Lost (Cambridge and New York, 1988), pp. 11–12.

[25]   See William Newman, "The Alchemical Sources of Robert Boyle's Corpuscular Philosophy," *Annals of Science* 53 (1996): 567–585; and A.G. Debus, *The Chemical Philosophy: Paracelsian Science and Medicine* (New York, 1977).

through ostentatiously lapsarian keywords.[26] "Secret," though less evidently fallen than, say, "wanton" (4.306) and "Lapse" (8.263), is nonetheless more dangerous in Milton's paradise before it is lost.

True, the word "secret" is uttered in Milton's paradise before the fall – but only as tribute to God, denoting what unfallen creatures do not and must not seek. The archangel Raphael begins his account of the war in heaven by making clear that he does not wish to reveal "secrets of another world" – and will avoid doing so by "lik'ning spiritual to corporal forms," losing secrecy in translation (5.569, 573). Adam, asking Raphael to include an account of the world's creation, immediately adds that he asks "not to explore the secrets" of God's "Eternal Empire" (7.95– 96). Later, Raphael concurs that God "did wisely to conceal, and not divulge / His secrets to be scann'd by them who ought / Rather admire" (8.73–75). Admiration, a key concept, indicates the hermeneutic attitude that the unfallen Adam and Eve are supposed to take. This has nothing to do with ignorance. In one of the poem's most remarkable and volatile images, the disciplinary Adam is likened to a thirsty traveller, "whose drouth / Yet scarce allay'd still eyes the current streame, / Whose liquid murmur heard new thirst excites" (7.66–68). A plenitude of knowledge excites Adam, "yet sinless, with desire to know" (7.61). He is allowed, indeed encouraged, to drink and drink from this "streaming fountain," as Milton says in *Areopagitica* (*CP* 2.543), this Neoplatonic emanation of a truth that never runs out. However, Adam is not encouraged, or allowed, to think of his endless and even excessive learning as an uncovering of secrets. The trope of discovery, though not the activity of knowing, is banned from Paradise.

The exception that proves this rule is that discovery enters Paradise with Paradise's destroyer. On first entering the garden, Satan conceals himself in various animal shapes in order to sneak up on Adam and Eve, "unespi'd" (4.499). The suppressed comedy of the scene is that his targets are not hiding, and are not even aware (since Raphael has not yet warned them) that they should be watching for him. Satan, and Satan alone, has discovery as an hermeneutic norm. Later, in toad form, Satan infiltrates the first parents' bower – but starts up in his own shape, "discoverd and surpriz'd," when touched with Ithuriel's spear (4.814). Satan's discovery here is the corollary of his secrecy. True, Satan's self-concealments are often comically self-defeating. Among other things, he masquerades as a "stripling Cherube" (3.636); a cormorant (4.196); the aforementioned toad (4.800); mist (9.75); and, finally, a snake (9.76–785). The last of these impressions puts Eve's metaphorical rapist in the shape of an enormous phallus (9.494–504) – since snakes, we are told, went "erect" before the fall (9.501) – and thereby makes the point about them all: they are all, more or less, emblematic indicators of the very being, multiply grotesque, that Satan is trying to hide. In reality, he is small and immature (the cherub), greedy (the cormorant), ugly (the toad), and insubstantial and illusory (mist). Satan reveals himself, he does not hide himself, by

---

[26]   See John Leonard, *Naming in Paradise: Milton and the Language of Adam and Eve* (New York, 1990).

hiding. Yet this very self-defeat underlines his defining perversity as an utterly wilfull commitment to a secrecy that can never be his.

Indeed, when not applied to God in the poem, "secret" is simply *the* Miltonic keyword of Satanic sin. That is not only a rhetorical, but also a characterological observation. Satan's daughter and lover, Sin, speaks of the "secret amity" that links "things of like kinde / By secretest conveyance" (10.248–249). She reminds Satan of the "secret harmonie" in which their two hearts move (10.358). She has to remind him, because Satan tends to forget about her (a mental lapse the significance of which I will consider shortly). "I know thee not," he says at their first meeting in the poem (2.744); their second, though planned and predicted, is "unhop't" (10.348). Sin insists on a psychic connection between herself and Satan, and avails herself of secrecy-talk in order to explain this connection. She thereby indicates both what is wrong with secrecy, and what is wrong with Satan. Basically, secrecy is Satanic, and Satan is secretive. Above all, he is psychologically secretive, inward to the point of solipsism. It is from this inwardness that Sin first emerges, springing from Satan's head – "at th'Assembly," where he was engaged "in bold conspiracy against Heav'ns King" (2.749, 751) – to take "joy" with her parent "in secret" (2.765–766).

Psychological imperatives, then, are the upshot of Milton's "secret" poetics. The core problem of secrecy is that it names the configuration of apostasy: a breakdown of the conscience, such that the mind tries to seal itself from God. "No one should heedlessly slander anyone," Milton records in his Commonplace Book: "even if there be no one else, God is listening" (*CP* 1.390). Again, the idea is a (literal) commonplace, stressed by both Reformation and Counter-Reformation theologians, and the diligent poet is actually taking notes on Boiardo.[27] But Milton is quite obsessed with the idea of divine surveillance. In his self-defensive polemics, he repeatedly calls God to witness that he, Milton, never forgets God's witnessing. Absolute proof of moral integrity derives from this claim of theocentric exposure – or rather, this claim of a constant consciousness of theocentric exposure. For a subject who is always remembering that he is being watched by God is a subject who can do nothing that would displease or anger God. Such a subject can accrue no secrets; he can never forget that his secrets, to God, are not secrets. The importance of remembering this point, for Milton, indicates what is at stake in forgetting it: nothing less than attempting to be secret from God. And attempting secrecy from God (naturally the attempt must fail) means attempting a Godlike secrecy, the usurpation of a divine privilege.

This is exactly the disaster that Milton narrates in *Paradise Lost*. Satan's rebellion begins "in secret" (5.672), with a whisper to Beëlzebub, and consists in an attempt to set himself apart – from God, and like God. "The mind is its own place," says the adversary, most famously: "and in it self / Can make a Heav'n of Hell, a Hell

---

27   For the commonplace, see Jacques Revel, "The Uses of Civility," in Roger Chartier (ed.) and Arthur Goldhammer (trans.), *Passions of the Renaissance* (Cambridge, MA and London, 1989), pp. 167–206; and Anne Ferry, *The "Inward" Language: Sonnets of Wyatt, Sidney, Shakespeare, Donne* (Chicago and London, 1983), pp. 56–59.

of Heav'n" (1.254–255). That is a program for creaturely *apartheid*, copying God's kingdom (or so Satan hopes) by denying God's gaze. Of course, Satan can't be secret from God, because he can't be secret *like* God. Satan can't be secret like God, in turn, because he can't be like God. His mind can never be the *secretum* that God's mind, uniquely, is. Satan can and does, however, *want* his mind to be such a *secretum*. He succeeds in wanting to be like God by wanting his mind to be secret like God's. In this sense, Satan gets what he wants – but it does not follow that he wants what he gets. "My self am Hell" (4.75) is the corollary of "the mind is its own place." In his famous apostrophe to the sun, Satan's secrecy degrades into hermeneutic psycho-pathology. "In the lowest deep," he cries, "a lower deep / Still threatning to devour me opens wide" (4.76–77). Among other things, this is a cry of *interpretative* despair. There is always another secret to discover, under the secret that the secretive one discovers. Satan gets eternally to indulge his "taste for the secret" – but this is the very opposite of an hermeneutic feast. Nonetheless, endless secrecy is the choice that God leaves open to him, and the choice that Satan, compulsively, makes.

Eve, similarly, finds that the fall is a choice of secrecy. While the forbidden fruit is still settling in her stomach, Eve (thinks she) feels new "access" to a divine *sophia*, "though secret she retire," and immediately produces the corollary proposal that

> I perhaps am secret; Heav'n is high,
> High and remote to see from thence distinct
> Each thing on Earth; and other care perhaps
> May have diverted from continual watch
> Our great Forbidder, safe with all his Spies
> About him. (9.809–816)

The narrator comments, "nor was God-head from her thought" (9.790), and clearly Eve is fantasizing a Satanic usurpation of God's secrecy.[28] Of course it is only a fantasy. God still sees Eve; Eve is still seen by God. What has changed, however, is Eve's capacity for imagining this panoptic arrangement. Specifically, Eve has become capable of internally representing her relationship to God's omniscience, her placement within the universal field of his gaze, as a state of affairs from which she is potentially external. Indeed, she has become incapable of imagining this matter in any other way. To be seen, now, is to posit not being seen. To be open is to be, potentially, secret. Read back into creation, this hermeneutic tautology produces a representation of the universe as a cover, a fit-up job, for something that it is not. Heaven is still high; the angelic host still twinkles around the sun. But high now means remote, and the watchers now are spies. The hermeneutics of discovery attends the genesis of secrecy.

---

[28]   See Anne Barbeau Gardiner, "Milton's Parody of Catholic Hymns in Eve's Temptation and Fall: Original Sin as a Paradigm of 'Secret Idolatries'," *Studies in Philology* 91.2 (1994): 216–231.

This we have already learned from Milton's representation of Satan. His entrammelment in discovery, however, is not solely reflexive. Transitively, too, Satan's reaction to evidence – especially evidence of God's beneficence and power – is to assume, and insist on, whatever is non-evident. Thus Satan's paranoid argument for rebelling against God is that he, Satan, has glimpsed the little wizard behind the almighty curtain. The exaltation of the son, always-already at the right hand of the father, is for Satan nothing but ideological mystification, covering the imposition of "new Laws" (5.679). The evident truth that all angels were created by God must be met with the scientistic question "who saw / When this creation was?" (5.856–857) As the heavenly rebellion proceeds from disaster to disaster, Satan discovers success after success, lying under the interpretative surface. The rebels' defeat on the first day of heavenly battle is actually a glorious victory (6.418–424). The final expulsion to hell is the best thing that could possibly have happened (2.14–40). And, of course, the ongoing Satanic mission is to discover and bring forth non-evident "evil," in a quasi-alchemical transformation, from evident "good" (1.165).

Interestingly, the one tactical victory that the rebels gain during the heavenly war comes precisely, and explicitly, through *inventio* or discovery. "Deep under ground," Satan proposes after the first day's battle, he and his panting compeers will find "materials dark and crude" (6.478). With these they will be able to create cannon, "not uninvented" to the fallen mind (6.470), but a stunning "fraud" to the unfallen (6.555). Obviously in Milton's sights here is the late seventeenth century's new Baconian empiricism, which he also demonizes (literally) when the devils mine in hell (1.670–692), and when Tubal-Cain makes tools (11.603–611), and when Nimrod discovers bitumen (12.38–44). All are, to Milton's absolutely traditional loathing and contempt, "Inventers rare" (11.611) who have "with impious hands / Rifl'd the bowels of thir mother Earth / For Treasures better hid" (1.687–688).[29]

Satan's most daring and important use of hermeneutic discovery, however, is his claim that the Paradisal prohibition is not really a prohibition. Here, too, the devil appears as an empiricist (9.568–612) – though, to be sure, a very poor one, since (1) he has not performed the fruit-eating experiment that he relates to Eve, and (2) even if he had, a single procedure would not be enough to support his inductive claim. Nonetheless, Satan-in-the-snake claims to have made an experimental discovery, leading, as in heaven, to a radical interpretation: "God therefore cannot hurt ye, and be just," he tells Eve; "Not just, not God; not feard then, nor obeyd" (9.700–701). It turns out that God, *qua* God, can only want his prohibition of the fruit to be disobeyed. No doubt, Satan is projecting his own paranoid and manipulative fantasies. He is describing the sorts of lies that *he* would tell, if he were God. But that is to say that Satan's hermeneutics is the natural and devastating corollary of his psychology. Secret text and secret reader spring

---

29   Compare Edmund Spenser, *The Faerie Queene*, ed. Thomas P. Roche (London and New York, 1978), book 2, canto 7, stanzas 16–17; and Polydore Vergil, *On Discovery*, ed. and trans. Brian P. Copenhaver (Cambridge, MA, 2002), pp. 261–263, 313, and 485–491.

together into this world. Indeed, secrecy and discovery emerge as hermeneutic twins, and are rendered coterminous with interpretative activity by the effect of the fall.

At which point, the conundrum of Milton's secrecy begins to bite. For we have already seen that secrecy and discovery *do* appear coterminous with interpretative activity, in the sense that it appears more-or-less impossible to do, or theorize, interpretation without them. Thus Milton appears to be associating our interpretations with our fallenness – indeed, with the wilfull or Satanic persistence in fallenness that redeemable creatures must avoid or eschew. True, an historical qualification (as I have already suggested) may be available. It may be that interpretation equals discovery only in modernity. This qualification, however, can never be more than contestable – if only because interpretative activity, observed by us in any place or period, looks (on the very argument being offered) willy-nilly like discovery. Moreover, Milton himself stands on the cusp of modernity, and takes its emergent dynamics (or so it often seems) as his central concerns. In sum, there is no quick or easy way to avoid the conclusion that Milton is Satanizing our interpretative defaults.

Of course, this is the kind of thing that Milton does all the time. He constantly takes us to the limits of our capacity to understand – then turns to indicate and illuminate those limits, while indicting us (and himself) for inability to transcend them. This is a trick he performs (*inter alia*) with respect to time, language, and desire.[30] In Milton studies, the insight that results is known as the "devil's party" thesis, after William Blake's brilliantly Romantic comment that Milton was a "true poet" and therefore (as though by definition) "of the devil's party without knowing it."[31] In other words, the thesis is that Milton's interest is always in why we want what we can't have; always in the regret, the pain and irony, of our fallen finitude.

One can accept this insight, however, while noting that interpretation remains a special case within it. Interpretation is not just one thing among many that we are doomed not to be able to understand. It is, rather, the central cognitive and epistemological activity by which we understand, or do not understand, anything. After all, the devil's party thesis is basically about the limits of human understanding. It is about our inability to know, properly, what is lost on the far side of the fall. But all questions about what we can and cannot know devolve (as I noted at the outset) on questions of interpretation. Therefore, Milton's Satanizations of secrecy and discovery, insofar as these constitute the key terms of interpretation, occupy a unique and probative position within his overall system of Satanizations.

[30] See, respectively, Edward Tayler, *Milton's Poetry: Its Development in Time* (Pittsburgh, 1979); Stanley Fish, *Surprised by Sin: The Reader in* Paradise Lost (Berkeley, 1971); and Linda Gregerson, *The Reformation of the Subject: Spenser, Milton, and the English Protestant Epic* (Cambridge, 1995).
[31] William Blake, *The Marriage of Heaven and Hell*, in *Romanticism: An Anthology*, ed. Duncan Wu (Oxford, 1996), p. 80. See also A.J.A. Waldock, Paradise Lost *and its Critics* (Gloucester, MA, 1959), and William Empson, *Milton's God* (London, 1965); Fish, *How Milton Works*; Silver, *Imperfect Sense*; and Forsyth, *Satanic Epic*.

It follows that considering Milton's secrecy is not just another way of considering the devil's party thesis. It is, rather, a way of considering the limits, and the potential transcendence, of that thesis itself. If there is a way out of the fall, on Milton's view, it can only be the way of interpretative theory: the way of philosophical hermeneutics. It is a matter of unique urgency in Milton's work to consider why, and how, and with an eye to what alternatives (if any), secrecy and discovery become the subject-matter of that work.

Milton's Secrecies

In the first chapter of this book, I argue that Milton is motivated socially-psychologically. Working from the English Protestant notion of conscience, Milton constructs an ideal personality that is always-already outward and open. He thereby avoids the Satanic tendency toward infinite and compulsive self-discoveries. My argument in this chapter engages, and to some extent contradicts, both New Historicist and anti-New Historicist accounts of early-modern selfhood. It does so by engaging with Milton's own contradictions, particularly in his prose polemics and self-presentations. Sometimes, Milton excoriates his enemies for conserving their God-given apartness; sometimes, for violating that very apartness. I conclude that Milton's social-psychological ideal is neither an untenable denial of inwardness, nor an untenable insistence on inwardness. It is, rather, a paradoxical, but surprisingly stable, inversion of inwardness. This construct eventuates in its own textual manifestations – specifically, in *Lycidas* and in Milton's autobiographical prose – by way of formal proof, and naïve reification.

Chapters 2 and 3 treat Milton's drama as representations, and consequences, of the model established in Chapter 1. The Lady of *Comus* (1634) traces wild heaths as the embodiment of her chastity. If she cannot walk away when Comus enchants her "rinde," that is because she has retreated, in quasi-Satanic fashion, to her inward "minde." To be sure, both Augustinian tradition and modern assumption valorize a psychology of essential inwardness. I argue, however, that English Calvinism, Neoplatonism, and Stuart performatism all work to contradict this valorization. *Samson Agonistes*, then, at the other end of Milton's career (1671), gives answers to the questions that leave the Lady silent. Manifesting the secret of his hair before Philistine armies, Samson acts out the inwardness that is not his to hold. His erroneous turn to Dalilah is a closure, not a revelation, of his divine gift. By returning to exposure in the play's catastrophe, Samson achieves redemption, inverting his secrecy yet once more.

Samson's hair functions as a bridge, in my argument, to the second of Milton's anti-secret departments. This is semiotic-semantic. The usual assumption among Milton scholars, in accordance with objectivist traditions of language philosophy, is that Samson's outward and physical form is no more than a signifier of his inward and esoteric state. This assumption, I argue, is wrong. Referring to speech-act theory, Anglo-American semantics, and the philosophical hermeneutics of

Hans-Georg Gadamer, I argue that the whole point of (Milton's) Samson's hair is a set toward the external. Against the twin esoteric reductions of mental intentionality and semantic intensionality (sic), Milton sets an exoteric ideal of utterance and semantic incarnation. The result is a view of language as fundamentally, and pragmatically, meaningful – and of meaning as a property of texts in the world, not of the minds that project texts into the world.

My fourth and final chapter articulates the hermeneutic ramifications of such a view. These are summed up in a key Gadamerian term: dialogue. Returning to *PL*, I distinguish between the deconstructive interminability that characterizes some recent accounts of the poem, and the pragmatic productivity that it seems really to be about. The focus of Milton's epic, I argue, is not God's unknowability, or his creatures' interpretative uncertainty, or the analogous uncertainty of the poem's readers. Rather, the poem's focus is in the irrelevance of these concerns to the hermeneutic activity (dialogue) that the poem represents. The significance of this point is twofold. First: dialogue, the hermeneutic matrix, is not merely the means by which *PL* comes to be about things. It is also what *PL* is, ultimately, about. Second: if dialogue is primary, minds are not. Therefore, Satanic solipsism is completely off the mark – as is any other attempt to derive meaning solely from mental intention. "The mind is its own place" is an erroneous slogan, not only as a matter of degree, but as a matter of kind.

In the end, I am arguing that Milton's work is hermeneutic – in the broad, philosophical, Gadamerian sense of that word. Milton's is an attempt, not just to understand certain things, but also to understand what understanding is.[32] Only through that theoretical attempt can critical or referential understanding be secured. The question of interpretation, clearly, is central to this sort of hermeneutic work. Yet if interpretation is always a matter of secrecy and discovery – if we know, in advance, what interpretation is – then the hermeneutic inquiry into understanding is, as it were, finished from the start. Understanding will always be a matter of discovered secrets, if interpretation is always a matter of discovering secrets. The difficulty of this view is not only that it heuristically prevents hermeneutical inquiry, but also that it leads to the very hermeneutic paradoxes that I outlined at the beginning of this discussion. Those paradoxes, moreover, are exactly the ones within which Milton's Satan welters and agonizes. In short, secrecy and discovery must be rendered hermeneutically optional if there is to be any hope in Milton, or in understanding, at all.

In the remainder of this Introduction, I will broach the possibility of hermeneutic hope, in two main ways. First, I will expand on the very brief remarks I have already

---

[32] See *TM*, pp. xi–xxxviii and 291–341; Gadamer, *Philosophical Hermeneutics,* trans. and ed. David E. Linge (Berkeley, 1976); Joel Weinsheimer, *Philosophical Hermeneutics and Literary Theory* (New Haven, CT, 1991); and pp. 43–50 below. Some Milton criticism talks of "hermeneutics," but only in non-Gadamerian senses. See Haskin, *Milton's Burden* (despite his citation of Gadamer); and Gale H. Carrithers and James D. Hardy, Jr., *Milton and the Hermeneutic Journey* (Baton Rouge, 1994).

made about situating Milton's anti-secrecy in its historical context. Second, I will expand on my theoretical remarks, vis-à-vis Gadamer's work.

The Renaissance Exoteric

Milton is not alone as an early-modern enemy of secrecy. Socially, secrecy is highly problematic in the period. It is the unobservable subjectivity where vices are at home. Its epithets – like the English "policy," or the German *Practick* – are familiar and hated.[33] There is evidence for a period synonymy of "secrecy" with "privacy," no doubt as a material consequence of cramped domestic arrangements.[34] But this is to say, from the other way around, that being set-apart is unusual and alarming in the period. An early-modern "right to privacy" would be something like a right to secrecy.

Nowadays, of course, we recognize just such a right. Derrida has recently spoken for the usual view: "the demand that everything be paraded in the public square," he complains, "and that there be no internal forum is a glaring sign of the totalitarianization of democracy... if a right to the secret is not maintained, we are in a totalitarian space."[35] These remarks would have been shocking in the sixteenth and seventeenth centuries. True, the increasing acceptance of Machiavellianism and neo-Stoicism, over the course of the period, did allow a quasi-orthodox discourse of secrecy. By the late 1630s, an English country gentleman like Sir William Drake can take it for granted that "a man should never produce his opinion and judgment," and that "the most crafty, faithless and audacious men...are those that rule the world."[36] Drake's grim axioms, however, are drawn from his private journal, and logically rule out the public discussion of his adherence to them. Secrecy allows Drake to distinguish his private from his public persona – exactly the move that his culture views (publicly at least) as a social and political anathema.

The one exception to this rule, and the one that illuminates and proves it, involves the political arbiter. As Linda Gregerson has recently shown, early-modern secrecy is the unique and defining political privilege of subjects without subjection.[37] The great European monarchies, centralizing power throughout this period, signified

---

[33]   See Valentin Groebner, "Invisible Gifts: Secrecy, Corruption and the Politics of Information at the Beginning of the 16th Century," in Engel and Elukin (eds), *Das Geheimnis*, pp. 98–110.

[34]   See Ferry, pp. 8 and 55–59; Orest Ranum, "The Refuges of Intimacy" in Chartier and Goldhammer (eds), *Passions of the Renaissance*, p. 212; and Sissela Bok, *Secrets: On the Ethics of Concealment and Revelation* (New York, 1982), p. 9.

[35]   Derrida and Ferraris, *A Taste for the Secret*, p. 59.

[36]   Kevin Sharpe, *Reading Revolutions: The Politics of Reading in Early Modern England* (New Haven and London, 2000), p.129. For Neostoicism, see Adriana McCrea, *Constant Minds: Political Virtue and the Lipsian Paradigm in England, 1584–1650* (Toronto, 1997).

[37]   See Linda Gregerson, "The Secret of Princes: Sexual Scandal at the Tudor Court," in Engel and Elukin (eds), *Das Geheimnis*, pp. 130–141.

and secured that power through princely sequestration.[38] The resulting panoptic arrangements are almost quaintly awesome: Louis XIII tests his council through the *technē* of a little curtain; the lunar Elizabeth, "she who never sleeps," supervises Spenser on his wedding-night of all nights.[39] Yet here, too, in the prince's necessary vantage, early-modern culture is uncomfortable with secrecy. The fear and loathing of apartness is routinely displaced onto courtiers, who are hated (as Bacon puts it) because they "come to the knowledge of more secretes" than others.[40] Meanwhile, the necessity of state secrecy, whether given Machiavellian or Lipsian justification, is also often explained as a matter of proto-Hobbesian compulsion. It is always because the neighboring court is so naturally and viciously secretive that one's own court, against its better instincts, must maximize *arcana imperii*. Thus Bacon describes cabinet or secret councils as "a remedy worse than the disease," while associating them with the Italian and French monarchies. Raleigh cites foreign affairs as the sole legitimate arena of secrecy – precisely because it is among foreigners (i.e., non-Englishmen) that one encounters masters of the art.[41]

Indeed, in England, under the early Stuarts, the alienation of secrecy seems to have become a core matter of policy. As Kevin Sharpe has demonstrated, James I consistently defined his public probity as a revelation of all his private secrets. Charles I, if anything, took this moral exhibitionism more seriously than his father.[42] The point here is not whether the early Stuarts actually revealed their secrets, or whether, in claiming to do so, they were hypocrites or fools. The point is that they claimed to do so, and thereby defined a socio-political discourse. Not even the English king, who is in principle right to be secretive, has an unproblematic right to his secrets except as things that must be shown.[43]

Here, however, we re-encounter secrecy as a paradox. It is a paradox that early-modern Europe feels peculiarly. Basically, to show a secret is not to show a secret. It is to show something that used to be a secret, until it was shown. The result, under an hermeneutic commitment to secrecy, is an infinite regress. For the

---

[38]   See Jonathan M. Elukin, "Keeping Secrets in Medieval and Early Modern English Government," in Engel and Elukin (eds), *Das Geheimnis*, pp. 111–129.

[39]   See Robert A. Schneider, "Disclosing Mysteries: The Contradictions of State in 17th-Century France," in Engel and Elukin (eds), *Das Geheimnis*, pp. 159–178; and Spenser, *Epithalamion,* in *The Yale Edition of the Shorter Poems of Edmund Spenser,* ed. William Oram et al. (New Haven and London, 1989), l. 374. All further citations of Spenser, excluding the *Faerie Queene*, will be from this edition.

[40]   *The Wisdome of the Ancients, written in Latine by the Right Honourable Sir* Francis Bacon *Knight*, trans. Sir Arthur Gorges (London, 1619), p. 52.

[41]   See Bacon, "Of Counsel," in *The Essayes or Counsels, Civill and Morall*, ed. Michael Kiernan (Oxford, 1985), p. 65; and McCrea, *Constant Minds*, p. 64.

[42]   See "Private Conscience and Public Duty in the Writings of James VI and I" and "Private Conscience and Public Duty in the Writings of Charles I," both in Sharpe's *Remapping Early Modern England: The Culture of Seventeenth-Century Politics* (Cambridge, 2000), pp. 151–198.

[43]   See Jonathan Goldberg, *James I and the Politics of Literature: Jonson, Shakespeare, Donne and their Contemporaries* (Baltimore and London, 1983), pp. 55–141.

secret that constitutes and validates meaning can never be apprehended in a way that would constitute and validate meaning. There must always be a deeper secret to seek, if we are to continue our interpretative engagement. Alternatively, there must be other secrets somewhere else, allowing us to commence new engagements. In post-modern thought, the upshot of this paradox is Derrida's secretive "taste" – for the secret as such, as the not-yet-revealed, as the joy of interpretative promise that must be lost when it is fulfilled.[44] In pre-modern thought, the ground of this paradox is the Aristotelian doctrine of occult qualities, which generate and essentialize all apprehensible phenomena, while being themselves, by definition, absolutely inapprehensible.[45] Thus for Derrida, secrets can never be found – and therefore we must eagerly and incessantly search after secrets. For Aristotle, or for a late-Renaissance Aristotelian such as Alexander Ross, secrets can never be found – and therefore we must not waste our time seeking after secrets.[46] Obviously the difference between the two positions is epistemologically diametrical, and yet their hermeneutic result is identical. Secrets, *per se*, cannot be revealed. How, then, can the early-modern discomfort with secrecy be exorcized? How can early-moderns show that they are showing their secrets?

Bacon begins to explain how. In his *Wisdom of the Ancients*, Bacon describes a mythographic paradox: "*There is found among men,*" he writes, "*a two-fold use of Parables, and those (which is more to be admired) referred to contrary ends; conducing as well to the foulding up and keeping of things under a vaile, as to the inlightning and laying open of obscurities.*" The meanings of the ancient allegories are "*hidden and involved,*" but so very clearly hidden and involved that they signify themselves: "*they shew, and as it were proclaime a parable afar off.*"[47] Bacon is claiming (1) that the ancient fables are secretive signs that conceal meanings while indicating that concealment, and (2) that he, Bacon, has found out the meanings and will now reveal them for the public good. The fables themselves, in this process, would seem to be have been rendered irrelevant – dissolved into so many aphorisms

---

44   See Derrida and Ferraris, *A Taste for the Secret.*

45   See Keith Hutchison, "What Happened to Occult Qualities in the Scientific Revolution?" in Peter Dear (ed.), *The Scientific Enterprise in Early Modern Europe: Readings from* Isis (Chicago and London, 1997), pp. 86–106; and Ron Millen, "The Manifestation of Occult Qualities in the Scientific Revolution," in Margaret J. Osler and Paul Lawrence Farber (eds), *Religion, Science and Worldview: Essays in Honor of Richard S. Westfall* (Cambridge and New York, 1985), pp.185–216.

46   See Ross, *Arcana microcosmi, or, The hid secrets of man's body discovered* (London, 1652). Despite his title, Ross typically argues as follows: "Now the reason why we feel the moisture of the brain, but not its frigidity, is, because there is nothing to hinder the tact from discerning its moisture, being in a soft substance ... but the tact is hindred from dicerning the frigidity of the brain, because of the veins and arteries within it, containing warm blood and spirits" (p.15). The brain is cold with an unpalpable coldness. This is an occult quality: totally determinative of a given phenomenon, even though, or rather because, it is totally undiscoverable.

47   *Wisdome,* Preface.

of the great instauration. Yet Bacon insists that the ancient parables remain necessary as parables, and are marvellously reinscribed by being correctly interpreted. Discovering their meanings, turning them into knowledge, does not annihilate, but establishes, the ancient secrets as secrets. Their allegorical form has come down to us not "*aduentitially, and as it were by constraint,*" but "*naturally and properly.*" They must be "*absolutely receiued, as a thing graue and sober, free from all vanitie, and exceeding profitable and necessary to all sciences.*"[48]

Much pre-Enlightenment natural philosophy is like the *Wisdom of the Ancients* in its estimation of what is "*profitable and necessary to all sciences.*" While modern scientific hermeneutics typically involves revealing (and thus destroying) secrets, its early-modern analogue frequently involves manifesting (and thus reifying) them. The distinction is rendered meaningful by a double rhetorical move. On the one hand, the period's natural-philosophical authors routinely demonstrate their knowledge through a discourse of print-culture. On the other hand, and in the same books, the same authors insist that what they are demonstrating is secret.[49] Thus Cornelius Agrippa, while publishing his *De occulta philosophia libri tres,* insists that occult philosophy is something that should not be made public.[50] Girolamo Ruscelli, in his *Secreti nuovi,* reveals the existence of a scientific academy that is demonstrated to be occult (he explains) by being revealed.[51] And hundreds of other *professore de' secreti* publish arcane knowledge as though it remains arcane – indeed, as though they establish or prove its arcaneness by publishing it. In 1582, Jacob Wecker arranged all the known technical and some non-technical arts in a Ramist compendium. Wecker included things (like the trivium) that had never been obscure, and things (like common love-potions) that had been well-known for many years. All are "*Secreta*" in Wecker's classification, and his work, which went through many editions, is called the *De secretis libri XVIII.*[52]

Bacon suggests that there is no necessary opposition between secrecy and openness: "even things which are thought to be secret," he notes, "have an open and public nature in other cases."[53] Girolamo Cardano writes that "if secrets are divulged and made common, they lose their beauty and dignity…Thus the ancient physicians hid their compositions, even giving them beautiful names, so they might possess them as secrets."[54] At first glance, Cardano seems to be describing a familiar binary of secrecy and openness. A secret that counts as such cannot be revealed, while a

---

[48] ibid.

[49] See Eamon, *Science and the Secrets*; and Long, *Openness, Secrecy, Authorship*, pp.154–174.

[50] I take my discussion from Long, pp. 157–161; and Eamon, pp. 280, 114.

[51] Eamon, pp. 148–149.

[52] Eamon, p. 276. See Wecker, *Eighteen Books of the Secrets of Nature … now much Augmented and Inlarged by Dr R. Read* (London, 1660).

[53] *The New Organon*, eds Lisa Jardine and Michael Silverthorne (Cambridge, 2000), p. 73.

[54] Cited in Eamon, p. 280.

secret that is revealed no longer counts. Cardano trots out the binary, however, as part of an argument for revealing all known secrets in a universal encyclopedia (à la Wecker). Meanwhile, the "ancient physicians" of Cardano's account "possess" their secrets, "as secrets," in a manner completely outside the esoteric binary – the very manner that Cardano is constructing as a cognitive ideal. The Aristotelian Julius Caesar Scaliger attacked Cardano on these grounds, claiming that the Italian polymath was illogically attempting to have his secrets and show them too. Cardano, however, had the ready and pithy reply that "a secret is not a secret because it is hidden; *it is a secret because it is worthy of hiding.*"[55]

That idea of a secret as something worthy of hiding, but recognized and used as a secret precisely by being unhidden, seems to me important to several well-known areas of early-modern culture. Take, for example, the English court masques. In Carew's *Coelum Brittanicum*, the god Momus enters wearing "a long darkish Robe, all wrought over with ponyards, Serpents tongues, eyes and eares, his beard and hair partly coloured, and upon his head a wreath stucke with Feathers, and a Porcupine in the forepart."[56] Why ponyards? Why a parti-coloured beard? Why, for goodness' sake, a porcupine? I really don't know; but I do know exactly how I, as a member of the masque audience, could find out. I would look in the handbooks of Cartari, Conti, and other Renaissance iconographers. I would read Carew's immediate source, Bruno's *Spaccio de la bestia trionfante*. Perhaps I would check Burton's *Anatomy of Melancholy*, where Momus is theorized. My point is that, after research, any spectator of the masque would be able to explain the god's costume – but it would not follow that the spectator would take no further interest in Momus. That is not the way Momus is supposed to work. Momus would become, instead, what the ancient myths are for Bacon: a secret fully rendered by being understood in detail; a textualized *arcanum* which can be transparent, and yet arcane. He is a secret that walks the stage, talks to the audience, etc. As such he is an extremely typical masque persona.

Similar personae are, of course, also found in some High Renaissance and Baroque visual art. In the Farnese palace at Caprarola, for example, is a large wall-painting of Mercury and Minerva with their arms around each other's shoulders. A second glance reveals that the two gods are actually joined at the shoulder, and that a single pair of legs pokes out below their tactful drapery. Below the prodigy is the label EPMAΘHNA.[57] In looking at the Hermathena – and this is my rather underwhelming point – we are very obviously looking at something very strange. Yet the strangeness is entirely explicable. Mentioned by Cicero, theorized by Ficino, the

[55]   ibid. My italics.

[56]   Thomas Carew, *Coelum Brittanicum*, in *Thomas Carew: Poems 1640, together with Poems from the Wyburd Manuscript* (Menston, England, 1969), p. 213. Further citations from this edition, parenthesized by page number in my text.

[57]   The picture is reproduced in the supporting pages to Elizabeth Mcgrath, 'Rubens' Musathena," *Journal of the Warburg and Courtauld Institutes* 50 (1987): 233–245. It is also online at http://www.italica.rai.it/rinascimento/iconografia/prot_1060.htm

Hermathena is an item in the iconographic handbooks. As Richard Linche explains in his translation and revision of Cartari, the figure represents "a composed medling and entermixing" of eloquence (Mercury) and wisdom (Minerva). Because "a kind of Sympathie and concordance" naturally obtains between them, "the Ancients have thought fit to conioine the Statues of this god and goddesse together."[58] We might think that the painter, Federico Zuccari, exceeds decorum in his physical fusion of the gods: Bartholomeus Spranger's 1585 "Hermathena" shows Mercury and Pallas cooperating but distinct, and Rubens, who is fond of this figure, takes the same tack.[59] Antiquarians, for that matter, insisted that Cicero's Hermathena had just been an herm with a bust of Minerva on it, and that its whole symbolic *frisson* was an effect of faulty philology.[60] All such learned and sophisticated Hermathenae, however, are interpretative penetrations and demystifications of the sources. Zuccari's, by contrast, is a literal reading. He paints a conjunction of Mercury and Minerva because that is what his texts describe. The image that results is exceedingly perverse – but perverse because it is exceedingly unrecondite.

By now it will be clear that, in talking about anti-secrets, I am talking (in part) about the emblematic tendency of Renaissance culture. I am describing this culture's impulse toward making meaning symbolically available, through a highly formalized and standardized hermeneutic process. The emblems that exemplify this process are notoriously difficult to define, but usually consist in an image accompanied by a motto and a poem. Typically, the image is mysterious; the motto, gnomic; the poem, sententiously and completely explanatory. The overall effect is of something like a unified sign, supporting, in the classic theory, a "dual function of representation and interpretation."[61] The prominent emblem scholar Michael Bath has challenged the usefulness of this view. Bath observes that any sign "involves" both representation and interpretation, and suggests that an emblem, like any other artifact, requires interpretation on some external basis: it "assumes an educated reader who recognises the genealogy of its topos, or who can at least supply the

---

[58]   See Cicero, *Letters to Atticus*, ed. and trans. D.R. Shackleton Bailey (6 vols, Cambridge, MA, 1999). vol. 1, p. 123; and Richard Linche, *The Fountaine of Ancient Fiction* (London, 1599), pp. 133–134.

[59]   Spranger's Hermathena can be seen at http://www.vol.cz/RUDOLFII/galerie.html. See also Hansoon Lee, *Kunsttheorie in der Kunst: Studien zur Ikonographie von Minerva, Merkur und Apollo im 16. Jahrhundert* Frankfurt am Main, 1996), pp.105–35. Rubens includes conjunctions of Hermes and Minerva on the Banqueting House ceiling and elsewhere. See Mcgrath, "Rubens' Musathena."

[60]   Mcgrath, "Rubens' Musathena," p. 242.

[61]   See Peter M. Daly, *Literature in the Light of the Emblem*, (Toronto and London, 1998), pp. 42–58; and Daniel S. Russell, "Perceiving, Seeing and Meaning: Emblems and Approaches to Reading in Early Modern Culture," in Peter M. Daly and John Manning (eds), *Aspects of Renaissance and Baroque Symbol Theory, 1500–1700* (New York, 1999), pp. 77–92.

missing context of its classical use."[62] But this describes a literary-historical, not a readerly task. The reader of an emblem no more needs to know its cultural origins than I need to know diachronic linguistics in order to write this sentence. There is not supposed to be anything "missing" from an emblem at all. Emblem art, on the contrary, consists in manifestation. An emblem incorporates a conundrum within (what is supposed to be) an entirely sufficient interpretative context, explaining and resolving the conundrum while leaving it available for appreciation and meditation. The result is a transparent mystery, neither enigmatic nor factual, but a tension of both; synchronically perceived, yet not mutually annihilating.

I wish to call this kind of thing "exoteric secrecy." For short, I will simply say "exoteric." By exoteric I do not just mean "apparent" or "open" – non-esoteric. I do mean that; but I also mean, and more importantly for my purposes, anti-esoteric – the term of an hermeneutic inversion. Admittedly, we are accustomed to thinking of much Renaissance culture (including some of the areas I have cited here) as esoteric. Hierogylphs, decans, olympian mysteries and arcane allegories proliferate in the period's art and literature. Agrippa, Paracelsus, Bruno and other magi fill their teaching with elaborate gestures of reticence and selectiveness. I believe that I have already dealt, in part, with such gestures. They do indeed proclaim arcaneness – but very loudly, and through mass mechanical reproduction. This is a highly performative esotericism, if it is an esotericism; it is a bump and grind of secrecy, hardly the way to hide anything.

Similarly, I would argue that the period's semiotic mysteries are, in many cases, not esoteric, but exoteric. They make secrets manifest, as though from metamorphic depths. The seventeenth-century hermeticist Michael Maier proposed that the Egyptian hieroglyphs had been invented by learned men, during a time of chaos and breakdown, in order to preserve knowledge. But the way to preserve knowledge was to put it in forms beyond the interpretative reach of the unlearned; but the forms would be useless unless they signalled the presence of knowledge, somehow, in themselves.[63] In Bacon's phrase, the hieroglyphs had to *shew, and as it were proclaime a parable afar off.* Like the emblems, like Momus, and like the Hermathena, the hieroglyphs had to be overtly secret, obviously strange.

It seems to me that an absolutely natural and not wholly terminological distinction obtains between this kind of secrecy, which I am calling exoteric, and esoteric secrecy, which conceals itself as secret. The distinction is something like the distinction between a ciphered message and a coded one. Cipher is formed when a non-linguistic and/or non-lexical syntagma stands for a lexical and/or linguistic one. For example, the imperative "flee" might be ciphered into an homophonic rebus, and represented by an image of a small blood-sucking parasite. Code, on the other hand, is formed when one linguistic and/or lexical syntagma stands for another: for example,

---

[62]   Michael Bath, *Speaking Pictures: English Emblem Books and Renaissance Culture* (London and New York, 1994), p. 32.

[63]   See Don Cameron Allen, *Mysteriously Meant: The Rediscovery of Pagan Symbolism and Allegorical Interpretation in the Renaissance* (Baltimore, 1970), pp. 118, 122.

the imperative "flee" might be encoded by a simple rule of orthographic expansion, and represented by the sentence "fools like early evenings." Either technique is a way of conveying secret meaning, but whereas the ciper is overtly secret, the code is covertly so.[64] An image of a flea in the middle of a diplomatic dispatch, say, demands further attention – whether or not that attention turns out to be warranted. The sentence "fools like early evenings" in the same dispatch, however, does not – at least not in the same way. It does not make sense to collapse the one example into the other, and call both kinds of non-evident meaning "esoteric."

Such a collapse is, however, effected by the canonical modern theorization of "esoteric" and "exoteric," in the hermeneutic work of Leo Strauss. Still highly influential in Milton studies (and beyond), Strauss observes that pre-modern history is a welter of gross censorship and ignorance. He therefore hypothesizes that significant thinkers, throughout this sorry epoch, must not have said or written what they really meant. Reading their work, accordingly, entails a search for hidden meanings. Since all reading can be understood as involving such a search, Straussianism conserves its special version by positing two coterminous but entirely different texts: outer, or "exoteric," and inner, or "esoteric." By "exoteric" Strauss simply means open or apparent or obvious – and therefore, as though by definition, not really meaningful. By "esoteric" he simply means hidden or encoded or latent – and therefore, again as though by definition, irresistibly meaningful. Code is the model here, but is being claimed as hermeneutically universal. Thus the Straussian plebs receive nothing, insofar as they only receive the exoteric or outer text. Straussian patricians, on the other hand, receive everything, insofar as they correctly perceive the outerness of the outer text. For they then can search for the inner text, its esoteric meaning. And esoteric meaning, on Strauss' code-model, is simply meaning.[65]

The model is a powerful one, in part because it tends to be self-validating. If you assume that a text is encoded, you will invariably be able to provide some decoding. But that way lies paranoia and incontinence. Indeed, the obvious conundrum of Straussian theory is how esoteric readers are to perceive something that is, by definition, not indicated. Absent an independent codebook, and secure knowledge that it is being used, readers can only find the inner text on the basis of signs in the outer text. But if the outer text signifies the inner text, it is no longer distinct from the inner text. But if the outer text does not signify the inner text, it no longer gives access to the inner text. There is no clear way to bridge, or even find, this gap. Accordingly, Straussian decoders spend most of their time on the outer text, arguing for the validity of their method through a pre-interpretation of traces. Meanwhile, they must move on to another text as soon as their decoding is done, because they have completely identified the work of interpretation with the esoteric penetration.

We are right back to the fundamental paradox of secrecy. Indeed, Strauss' theory establishes a kind of hermeneutic primitivism, strongly recalling the primal scene

---

[64]   See Potter, *Secret Rites*, p. 38.
[65]   See Strauss, *Persecution*, pp. 14–35.

of modern Western knowledge. This, Frank Kermode has argued, was set when an obscure first-century teacher gave a class for his twelve pupils at the beach. The teacher distinguished between the twelve and everybody else on the basis of their access to his, the teacher's, knowledge. To the twelve he told and would always tell the meaning of his stories, but to the multitude he told the stories only, "that seeing they may see, and not perceive; and hearing they may hear, and not understand."[66] Kermode's central topos, in his classic work *The Genesis of Secrecy*, is St. Matthew's revision of St. Mark's "[so] that" (*hina*), which Matthew turns into the more ecumenical but quite antithetical "because" (*hoti*). "Because seeing they see not, and hearing they hear not" (Matt.13:13), Matthew's multitude must be shown and told in the concrete and colorful terms that suit it. The story thus becomes one of Christ's pitching his parables to the defects of his hearers, rather than using parables, as in Mark, to hoodwink them.[67] Yet hoodwinking, for Strauss, and (I think) for most of us, seems more-or-less identical with impressive hermeneutic procedure.

Matthew suggests another possibility. The transition from Mark to Matthew, from *hina* to *hoti*, reverses the Straussian penetration from the exoteric to the esoteric. Instead, it offers a *transformation* of the esoteric into the exoteric. This transformation, in turn, entails a retheorization and revaluation of the exoteric. For Matthew's *hoti* does not mean that Christ's parables are merely obvious or unproductive or unmeaningful. Neither does it mean that the parables are transparent or homiletic – that the multitude sees through them to their essential teaching. Neither, finally, does it mean that the fable is divorced from teaching, or that, as in *hina*-hermeneutics, the multitude is left to wander home with a parabolic souvenir that it does not understand. *Hoti* means, rather, that parabolic meaning is to be understood as a kind of meaning in its own right; which does not require, but would indeed be destroyed by, reduction into the kind of propositional learning assumed by *hina*. The many accept Christ's parables, without analysis, without penetration. The claim of *hina* is that they are, therefore, consigned to outer darkness. But the claim of *hoti* is that they are already in the light, because the parable constitutes precisely an externalization and hypostatization of the interpretative process they do not know how to perform – of the secret, as I would put it, that they do not know how to discover.

My historical proposal is that the Renaissance is not limited, as our own period's culture seems to be, to a model of interpretation based on discovery. That is not to say that the Renaissance *lacks* our model. Quite the contrary: it is to say that in tandem and perhaps in conflict with an esoteric (or *hina*-) hermeneutics of discovery, the Renaissance has an exoteric (or *hoti*-) hermeneutics of anti-discovery. Interpretation, on this hermeneutics, is not just a matter of reducing the forms of data into their essential propositions. It is, rather, a matter of understanding data in and through the

---

[66]   Mark 4:12. I cite King James Version throughout. Hereafter parenthesized by book, chapter and verse in body of my text.

[67]   Kermode, *The Genesis of Secrecy: On the Interpretation of Narrative* (Cambridge, 1979), pp. 30–31.

forms that are proper to it. To adopt Neoplatonic metaphors, exoteric interpretation is as much about clothing knowledge as about undressing it. In Straussian terms, it is as much encoding as decoding. Exoteric secrecy presents the Renaissance subject with data raised into arcaneness, while avoiding – indeed, annihilating – the anti-social and anti-theological implications of the esoteric. The exoteric option, I wish to argue, provides an historical opening for Milton's secrecy.

From God to Gadamer

No doubt such an option remains difficult to understand. Yet it enjoys theoretical support from Hans-Georg Gadamer, the major modern philosopher of interpretation.[68] Gadamer's extrapolations from Heideggerian scepticism have been far less influential (at least in literary studies) than the rival extrapolations of Franco-American postmodernism.[69] In my opinion, this is a great shame, the great lost opportunity of postmodern theory. Where Derrida, say, remains in hock to the traditional categories he subverts – deriving the whole *frisson* of his philosophy from their assumed indispensability – Gadamer thinks much more freely and productively about these categories. To take an example particularly relevant to the hermeneutics of discovery, and its possible alternatives: scientific objectivity, under deconstruction, can only yield to an all-embracing and relativizing interrelation with subjectivity. This is a direct negative consequence of objectivity itself; to demonstrate that relativization follows from the deconstruction of the objectivity/subjectivity binary is simply to demonstrate the importance of the binary. It is also, incidentally, to demonstrate the vacuity of

---

[68]   Gadamer's magnum opus is *TM*. The standard German edition is *Wahrheit und Methode: Grundzüge einer philosophischen Hermeneutik* (Tübingen, 1990). Hereafter cited as *WM*. Commentaries include Georgia Warnke, *Gadamer: Hermeneutics, Tradition and Reason* (Cambridge: Polity, 1987); and G.B. Madison, *The Hermeneutics of Postmodernity: Figures and Themes* (Bloomington and Indianapolis: Indiana UP, 1990), pp. 106–124. See also *Gadamer's Century: Essays in Honor of Hans-Georg Gadamer*, eds Jeff Malpas, Ulrich Arnswald, and Jens Kertscher (Cambridge, MA, 2002); and *The Cambridge Companion to Gadamer*, ed. Robert J. Dostal (Cambridge and New York, 2002).

[69]   See Diane P. Michelfelder and Richard E. Palmer (eds), *Dialogue and Deconstruction: The Gadamer-Derrida Encounter* (Albany, 1989); Robert Sokolowski, "Gadamer's Theory of Hermeneutics," in Lewis Edwin Hahn (ed.), *The Philosophy of Hans-Georg Gadamer* (Chicago, 1997), pp. 223–236; Francis J. Ambrosio, "The Figure of Socrates in Gadamer's Philosophical Hermeneutics," in Hahn (ed.), *The Philosophy of Hans-Georg Gadamer*, pp. 259–274; Ronald Beiner, "Gadamer's Philosophy of Dialogue and Its Relation to the Postmodernism of Nietzsche, Heidegger, Derrida, and Strauss," in Bruce Krajewski (ed.), *Gadamer's Repercussions: Reconsidering Philosophical Hermeneutics* (Berkeley, 2004), pp. 145–157; and Jens Kertscher, "'We understand differently when we understand at all': Gadamer's Ontology of Language Reconsidered," in Malpas, Arnswald, and Kertscher (eds), *Gadamer's Century*, pp. 135–156.

deconstruction, which can only ever succeed in re-demarcating the concepts within which it supposedly provides freedom – albeit a freedom theorized as "play."[70]

Play, as it happens, is profoundly theorized by Gadamer, with genuinely liberating consequences for objectivity/subjectivity. Beginning *Truth and Method* with a theory of the artwork, Gadamer works, first of all, from the ontology of play. The latter, he notes, is not play to those who are engaged in it; the one position that is (so to speak) out of bounds for players of a game, insofar as they are to play the game, is "it's only a game." Play must be serious, if it is to be play. Ontologically speaking, this means that play does not consist in an encounter between an object – the game – and subjects – the players. For the players, once they are players, have no subjectivity to bring to (or withhold from) the game; and there is no game for the players to come to (or not come to), until they have already forfeited their ability to apprehend and objectify the game. The game arises, precisely and exclusively, through disappearance of the players' subjectivity in the attempt to play the game. It is an engrossing, total, and transformative phenomenon that arises through the attempt of all parties to produce just that phenomenon. Moreover, it is quite clear that the game, so described, can only be identified as *hermeneutic experience*: the experience of meaning, the actualization of knowledge, the engagement of minds with matter and with mattering.[71]

Extrapolating from his game-theory to his art-theory, then, Gadamer founds an hermeneutics outside the conventional logic of objects and subjects. Always, his emphasis is on knowledge as an involving experience (*Erfahrung*), such that the non-involvement presumed by scientific hermeneutics cannot account for the emergence of knowledge. Gadamer's primary target is "aesthetic differentiation," the Kantian assumption at the core of the Enlightenment attitude that Gadamer calls, pejoratively, "aesthetic consciousness." Aesthetic consciousness is, more or less, the ideological notion that there is a category of art. Aesthetic differentiation is the hermeneutic principle that art involves mutual and several objective/subjective alienations: observer against observed, representation against represented. It is the viewer considering the artwork as an object from which he is removed, and the artwork referring to its subject-matter as the reality from which it is removed. Of course, objective/subjective alienation is the mode of all interpretation, under the hermeneutics of discovery that supports modern natural science. But science, supported by Enlightenment rationalism, is exactly the ideology (Gadamer contends) that produces and defines aesthetic consciousness.[72]

Moreover, while scientific ideology defines science as the field of objects in which subjects discover knowledge, it defines art – non-science – as the field of objects in which subjects discover only non-knowledge. Beauty, pleasure,

---

[70]   See Derrida, "Structure, Sign and Play in the Discourse of the Human Sciences," in Richard Macksey and Eugenio Donato (eds), *The Structuralist Controversy: The Languages of Criticism and the Sciences of Man* (Baltimore and London, 1972), pp. 247–264.

[71]   *TM*, pp. 101–110.

[72]   *TM*, pp. 81–100.

diversion, culturedness – these are the trivial and unintellectual quantities that aesthetic consciousness consigns to the aesthetic. It is intriguing to note that aesthetic consciousness, operating on an hermeneutics that defines knowledge as the discoverable, and the discoverable as knowledge, thereby proves, as though despite itself, the existence of a field where the said hermeneutics does not apply: namely, the field of "art," where one discovers only that there is not much to discover. Aesthetic differentiation thus reveals itself as incoherent, unable to make sense of the phenomenon that it supposedly describes. For it supposedly describes art; that is what aesthetic consciousness is about. Yet all it can say about art is that there is not much to say about it.

Against aesthetic differentiation, Gadamer poses "aesthetic non-differentiation."[73] This ontologizes art, not by the discovery of nothing, but not by discovery at all. Gadamer proposes that the artwork, once removed from its predetermination by scientific ideology and aesthetic consciousness, reveals itself as the non-differentiation of object and subject. By non-differentiation, it is important to note, he means neither identity nor differentiation. In working out this tricky idea, Gadamer pays particular attention to the artistic relationship between a representation and what it represents. Aesthetic identity, he writes, is typified by the mirror-image, in which "the entity itself appears," but only as long as the entity itself is present. Aesthetic differentiation, on the other hand, is typified by the copy, which "must always be regarded in relation to the thing it means," and "tries to be nothing but the reproduction of something and has its only function in identifying it." Aesthetic *non*-differentiation, however, is typified by the picture, which "is not destined to be self-effacing, for it is not a means to an end." Instead, "the picture itself is what is meant" – but precisely "insofar as the important thing is how the thing represented is presented in it." The pictorial relation between representation and represented is based in the sovereignty of the former, but directed toward the augmentation of the latter. "The picture affirms its own being," yes – but only "in order to let what is depicted exist." The picture draws us to itself, addressing and engrossing us, in order to reaffirm and contribute to our experience of the depicted.[74]

Thus the representational relationship, on the model of the picture, is neither between different entities, nor between different temporal or spatial moments of the same entity. It is, rather, an ontological modulation of the same entity (the experience of the depicted). This modulation, in turn, guarantees the epistemological and hermeneutic status of representation *per se*. After all, on the model of aesthetic differentiation, the only significant use of a representation is when one is unfamiliar with what it represents; either because the representation shows some previously-unknown aspect of the world, or because it holds something back, harbors some secret. Turning to the representation, one discovers the secret, or the previously-unknown aspect – and subsequently one has no further use for the representation (other than the trivial

---

73   *TM*, p. 117.
74   *TM*, pp. 138–139.

pasttimes of aesthetic consciousness). On the model of aesthetic non-differentiation, by contrast, the significant use of a representation begins when one is *familiar* with what it represents. One turns to a representation, not to discover what one did not know – indeed not to discover anything – but to *re-cognize* what one already knows. This recognition, moreover, is an event of understanding. Art yields, not pleasure, but knowledge; a knowledge based, not in discovery, but in recognition.

Let us recall Milton's Satan, wailing at the sun. He refuses to recognize (as I have said) even the manifest truths that he recognizes. He sees that he has only himself to blame for his downfall (4.42–57). He explains that he cannot be forgiven because he cannot ask for forgiveness (4.79–104). He wishes that he had been, in heaven, a creature different from the one he was (4.58–61); but acknowledges that, even if he had been, he still would have become as miserable as he is (4.61–63). All Satan's introspective honesty, all his appalling perspicuity, eventuates in nothing more than a reflexive exclamation – his famous "me miserable!" (4.73) – and an inexcusable determination not to see what he in fact sees. "Evil be thou my Good," he concludes (4.110), nailing his colors to the inverted mast of radical discovery. His cause is lost, and badly lost, and he deserved to lose it, and he can only lose. He sees all this, and says all this – and then decides to go for broke anyway. He takes, but expels, the cure of recognition; and turns back in puke and fear to the junk of discovery.

Satan chooses discovery over recognition. Gadamer chooses recognition over discovery. He argues from an aesthetic non-differentiation that is foreign to aesthetic consciousness, to an hermeneutics of recognition that is foreign to the hermeneutics of discovery. Gadamer's hermeneutics of recognition subsumes the hermeneutics of anti-discovery.[75] Recognition entails an epistemological experience of the obvious – an experience that can only be perfected by iteration and re-iteration. We are better able to experience, Gadamer notes (with Jimi Hendrix) when we are experienced.[76] Experience, in turn, entails an interpretative involvement that we can trace right back to Gadamer's ontology of the game. The knowledge that comes from recognition has the character of a choice to play, of a decision and projection. Moreover, it is only because we know or cognize something that we can re-cognize it. Playing again is the privilege and expression of knowing how to play. It follows that we do not always have to be looking for new and hidden games. Rather, we have to play the games of which we are manifest members.

---

[75]   For the hermeneutics of recognition, see *TM*, pp. 113–114; James Risser, *Hermeneutics and the Voice of the Other: Re-Reading Gadamer's Philosophical Hermeneutics* (Albany, 1997); Gadamer, "Text and Interpretation," in Michelfelder and Palmer (eds), *Dialogue and Deconstruction*, pp. 21–51; and Gadamer, "Reply to Stanley H. Rosen," in Hahn (ed.), *The Philosophy of Hans-Georg Gadamer*, pp. 219–222. In the latter essay, Gadamer opposes his position to Straussian discovery. On the same point, see Beiner, "Gadamer's Philosophy of Dialogue"; Joel Weinsheimer, "Meaningless Hermeneutics?" in Krajewski (ed.), *Gadamer's Repercussions*, pp. 158–166; and *TM*, pp. 294–295 and 532–541.

[76]   *TM*, pp. 346–362.

"Sollicit not thy thoughts with matters hid," says Raphael to Adam (*PL* 8.167). This is also Milton's advice for us. His hermeneutic strategy is to "distinguish between 'secret gaze' and 'open admiration'."[77] Such a strategy is as difficult to effect as it is to understand. Yet for that reason, it attracts Milton – and us. Milton's exotericism is what makes Milton Milton. The attempt to explain Milton's exotericism is what makes up this book.

---

[77]   Schwartz, *Remembering and Repeating*, p. 57.

Chapter 1

Expressing the Conscience

A very influential claim of postmodern literary theory has been that texts are constructed by societies and readers, as much as they are by individual authors. This claim, however, has had little effect on Milton studies.[1] Miltonists today are profoundly committed to their eponymous author, treating his life and times as a necessary adjunct of his work.[2] Psychoanalytic studies remain prominent in the field, along with less technical psychobiographies.[3] Skinnerian analyses of the poet's politics, in recent years a dominant critical strain, routinely pass from discussing his texts to reconstructing his thoughts.[4] Finally, work on the Miltonic "self," though postmodernistically dressed, is basically the post-postmodern re-emergence of traditional biographic criticism.[5]

Why so much Milton, so much sought in his extra-textual existence? The usual explanation involves his intra-textual presence. "If any author is in his texts," we are

---

[1]   See Seán Burke, *The Death and Return of the Author: Criticism and Subjectivity in Barthes, Foucault and Derrida* (Edinburgh, 1998); and Joseph Wittreich, "'Reading' Milton: The Death (and Survival) of the Author," *Milton Studies* 38 (2000): 10–46.

[2]   See J. Michael Vinovich, "Protocols of Reading: Milton and Biography," *Early Modern Literary Studies* 1.3 (1995): 1–15.

[3]   See William Kerrigan, *The Sacred Complex: The Psychogenesis of* Paradise Lost (Cambridge, MA, 1983); John Shawcross, *Milton: The Self and the World* (Lexington, KY, 1993); Nancy Armstrong and Leonard Tennenhouse, *The Imaginary Puritan* (Berkeley and Los Angeles, 1992), pp. 27–46; John Rumrich, *Milton Unbound: Controversy and Reinterpretation* (Cambridge, 1996); Gregerson, *Reformation of the Subject*; Marshall Grossman, *The Story of All Things: Writing the Self in English Renaissance Narrative Poetry* (London, 1998); Claudia Champagne, "Adam and his 'Other Self' in *Paradise Lost*: A Lacanian Study in Psychic Development," in William Zunder (ed.), *Paradise Lost* (New York, 1999), pp. 117–135; and Kathleen M. Swaim, "'Myself a True Poem': Early Milton and the Reformation of the Subject," *MS* 38 (2000): 66–95.

[4]   See David Armitage, Armand Himy and Quentin Skinner (eds), *Milton and Republicanism* (Cambridge, 1995); Barbara Lewalski, "How Radical Was the Young Milton?" in Dobranski and Rumrich (eds), *Milton and Heresy*, pp. 49–72; David Norbrook, "The Politics of Milton's Early Poetry," in Annabel Patterson (ed.), *John Milton* (London and New York, 1992), pp. 46–64; and Annabel Patterson, "'Forc'd fingers': Milton's Early Poems and Ideological Constraint," in Claude J. Summers and Ted-Larry Pebworth (eds), *"The Muses Common-Weale": Poetry and Politics in the Seventeenth Century* (Columbia, MO, 1988) pp. 9–22. For Skinner's historical originalism, see James Tully and Quentin Skinner (eds), *Meaning and Context: Quentin Skinner and His Critics* (Cambridge, 1988).

[5]   See Volume 38 of *Milton Studies* (2000), especially the Introduction by Albert Labriola.

told, "Milton is in his."[6] To be sure – from *The Reason of Church Government* (1642) to the *Second Defense of the English People* (1654), from the pastoral lament for *Lycidas* (1638) to the invocations of *Paradise Lost* (1674) – Milton often seems to project his own experience as the matter of his writing. A poet, this poet said, "ought himself to be a true poem" (*CP* 1.890). Autobiography, or at least a commanding self-referentiality, comes in as the scansion of his integrity. It will not do, however, to say that Miltonists are therefore compelled to write biographically author-centered or biographic criticism (which I will abbreviate as "biocriticism"). After all, author-centeredness is exactly what is supposed to enable post-authorial decentering. It is because Spenser writes about his experiences in Ireland that we can make him a mouthpiece for nascent imperialism. It is because Shakespeare expresses intimate knowledge of brothels that we can hand his sonneteer's pencil to early-modern gender discourse. Textual presence, not absence, is what fixes canonical Authors with hermeneutic functions – making them "guest" (in Barthes' oft-quoted phrase) where they formerly were "host." If Milton is more "in" his texts than other authors are, we ought to find it easier, not harder than usual, to contain him.

Explanations from external evidence are also unsatisfactory. "More is known about Milton," states Thomas Corns (classically), "than about any earlier canonical writer. Among his younger contemporaries we find Marvell, a figure in public life for several decades, but his biography is much less well documented. Compared with Milton, John Dryden seems a ghostly shadow." Because there is so much relevant archival information, so well-prepared by earlier scholars, Corns considers that "it is easy to write about Milton": "the pieces" of biocriticism "stand ready for the game."[7] Corns' observations are elegant, but, again, somewhat beside the point. While it is true that a large pool of Milton documents exists, these cannot form an hermeneutic imperative to Miltonic biocriticism. After all, a good theoretical case can be made against literary interpretation from life-documents *tout court*. The documentary turn rests on an antecedent assumption that the turn itself is necessary. Biocriticism determines archivalism, not the other way around.

In this chapter, I will offer a new account of Milton's autobiographical projections. My main texts will be the pastoral *Lycidas* (1638), and the polemical "Defenses" of the 1650s. The former provides perhaps the classic example of a Milton text that turns out (allegedly) to be about its author. The latter supplies much of the biographical background for this and all other biocritical readings. The resulting work, clearly, conforms to the hermeneutics of discovery: one reads the texts to uncover Milton "in" them, and/or to penetrate them and arrive at the pre-textual level of biography and psychology. I will

6   Stephen M. Fallon, "The Spur of Self-Concernment," *MS* 38 (2000): 220–242; 220.

7   Thomas Corns, "'Some Rousing Motions': the Plurality of Miltonic Ideology," in Thomas Healey and Jonathan Sawday (eds), *Literature and the English Civil War* (Cambridge and New York, 1990), p.111. For the playing-pieces, see J. Milton French (ed.), *The Life Records of John Milton* (5 vols, New Brunswick, 1950); William Riley Parker, *Milton: A Biography*, ed. Gordon Campbell (2 vols, Oxford, 1996); Robert Fallon, *Milton in Government* (University Park, PA, 1993); and Gordon Campbell, *A Milton Chronology* (New York, 1997).

offer readings, instead, that conform to the hermeneutics of recognition (see pp. 25–9). That is to say, I will not claim to be uncovering anything latent in these texts, or in their relations to authorial/historical contexts. Rather, I will claim to be illuminating things that are already manifest in these texts, and/or in their contextual interrelations. Further, and as the hermeneutic justification for my own procedure, I will claim that the texts in question are themselves about this kind of illumination.

My core literary-historical claim will be that Milton's self-presentational texts are casuistical representations. By that I do not just mean that the poet speaks his mind, but that he speaks and effects his mind as an exoteric textualization of the seventeenth-century English Protestant conscience. The latter, as I am at some pains to point out, is structured in such a way that it produces imperatives toward exactly such textualization. Milton's self-presentations, responding perfectly to these imperatives, produce him as social-psychological exemplar, and hermeneutic wonder. His mind-texts do not just give us insight into his conscience; they are his conscience, which is always-already mind-text. That, at least, is the claim that the texts make, and that the relevant period discourses, under Milton's handling, support.

Exoteric Casuistry

According to the seventeenth-century theory of conscience, or casuistry, each Christian mind is really two minds wrapped up in one. The Puritan casuist William Perkins gives the usual etymological account: to "know," Latin *scire*, "is of one man alone by himself." *Conscire*, however, is "when two at the least know some one secret thing; either of them knowing it together with the other." *Conscientia*, therefore, is immutably dialogic, "a science or knowledge joined with another knowledge: for by it I conceive and know what I know."[8] Of course, many late-modern theorists assume a divided psyche as normative, and to that extent the early-modern conscience may seem surprisingly familiar. What makes it unfamiliar, however, is its explicit theocentrism. The knowledge that is not our knowledge, but is joined to our knowledge, is divine. Jeremy Taylor explains that God "hath given us *Conscience* to be in Gods stead to us," as his "Vicar," his "Watchman," and his "deputy."[9] Perkins, following Calvin (who, as usual, follows Augustine and Paul), goes so far as to prove God's existence by *conscientia*, which is nothing less than "a little God sitting in the middle of men's hearts."[10] As divine "guardian," as "keeper" and "guide," conscience reads to the mind from an innate library of the moral law.

---

[8]   Perkins, *A Discourse of Conscience*, in Thomas F. Merril (ed.), *William Perkins 1558–1602: English Puritanist* (Nieuwkoop: B. De Graaf, 1966), pp. 7–8. See Camille Wells Slights, *The Casuistical Tradition in Shakespeare, Donne, Herbert and Milton* (Princeton, 1981), pp.16–17. Calvin gives the etymological account of *conscientia* at *Institutes*, p. 848.

[9]   Jeremy Taylor, *Ductor Dubitantium, or The Rule of Conscience In All her General Measures* (London, 1666), Book 1, p. 2.

[10]   Perkins, *Discourse*, p. 9; Calvin, *Institutes*, pp. 184, 282.

This is called *synteresis*, and guarantees ethical judgment – or at least it would, if human beings retained their unfallen capacities.[11] Unfortunately, fallen corruption guarantees misreadings of *synteresis*; for which, nonetheless, the mind is entirely responsible.[12] When we err, conscience puts on another of its aspects, becoming God's "Notarie," his "monitor," and his "tribunal."[13] Haled before our "sense of divine judgment," we are utterly without excuse, because our mind's own mind is "a thousand witnesses" against us.[14]

Conscience, then, is a moral and religious psychology of mental doubling and theocentric exposure. Each human mind is mind-plus-mind, the second term mirroring God's mind. "Conscience" names both the second mind, and the overall structure. That terminological slippage is crucial. Early-modern people are *examined by* conscience, in the sense of an immanent but alien judge that disciplines the psyche. They also, however, *examine* conscience, in the sense of the very psyche that receives discipline from the judge. Theocentric dialogism becomes homocentric paralogism: the notion that the mind is objectively checked means that the mind must subjectively check itself. Yet that checking can only be identified as a function of the conscience; which means that when one searches one's conscience (in the typical phrase), conscience itself is what does the searching. Meanwhile, the mind can only produce its checking function by first of all checking that its checking is working properly – otherwise it is in danger of coming under an erring conscience. But to check in that manner is precisely to assume the checking function, conscience, while starting down the road of an infinite regress (as the checking must be checked, and that checking must be checked, etc.).

In short, the theory of conscience is bewilderingly tautological, while demanding attention to its tautologies as a matter of devotion and salvation. The one thing that must never be allowed to occur in the system is any failure of its equations – any difference, if you like, between mind-as-mind and mind-as-conscience. For difference would be redolent of sin (how else could it occur?), and would produce more sin, insofar as it interfered with the mind's correct representation of itself as conscience. Yet even the mind's need to avoid difference from conscience is, *ipso facto*, nascent difference from conscience.

Clearly, what the theory of conscience needs is some allowable decentering, rendering it both un-neurotic and experientially applicable. Counter-Reformation casuists provide just such decentering, managing "cases of conscience" through

---

[11]   Calvin, *Institutes*, pp. 367–368. See also William Ames, *Conscience with the Power and Cases thereof* (London, 1643), pp. 4–6.

[12]   Slights, *Casuistical Tradition*, pp. 12–13.

[13]   Richard Kilby, *The Burthen of a Loaded Conscience* (Cambridge, 1608), pp. 85–86.

[14]   Calvin, *Institutes*, p. 848, quoting Quintilian. Compare Henry Stubbes, *Conscience the Best Friend Upon Earth* (London, 1678), pp. 8–11. See also Peggy Muñoz Simonds, "Some Images of the Conscience in Emblem Literature," in Stella P. Revard, Fidel Rädle and Mario A. Cesare (eds), *Acta Conventus Neo-Latini Guelpherbytani: Proceedings of the Sixth International Congress of Neo-Latin Studies* (Binghamton, 1988), pp. 314–330; 317.

several kinds of equivocation. The first, probabiliorism, holds that in a choice between two objects or actions, the moral subject should choose the one that seems more acceptable to conscience. This is the moderate standard on which most casuistry devolves; it is an attempt to gauge the problem of conscience, and to give full credit for the good-faith attempt. On a given Friday, for example, one must not eat meat, but perhaps one has no other food. The probabiliorist will allow the prohibition against meat-eating to be broken, because not breaking it (and as a result starving) would be inconsistent with the law of charity. No such solutions are good enough for the second equivocation, probabilism, which teaches that the moral subject may choose an object that seems *less* acceptable than its alternative to conscience. The probabilist would probably extend the probabiliorist argument about meat-eating to all Fridays, while reproducing the violation of prohibitions as a special way of keeping them. Deconstruction is not the word: after enough sophistical somersaults, the High Renaissance probabilist can prove that flesh is fish because it is flesh.[15] (On second thought, perhaps deconstruction is the word.)

A third equivocation, Nicodemism, has specifically to do with religious persecution. Taking his cue from the eponymous Pharisee, and secret Christian, the Nicodemite conformed outwardly, but dissented inwardly. He went to church in one faith while remaining secretly true to another; he said "yes" or "no" under questioning, while meaning "no" or "yes" in his heart. Such a performative strategy could be either orthodox or subversive in a period that demanded spiritual obedience, but often settled for physical and political passivity. And it led back, not only to an apocryphal gospel, but also through Erasmus and Jerome to St. Peter and St. John (Galatians 2:11–14; John 3:1–21).[16]

None of these options was entirely kosher in seventeenth-century England. Probabilism, associated with Jesuits, was energetically despised. Probabiliorism was the default standard – but not the admired one. That was tutiorism: the strictest possible casuistry, demanding a conscience "void of offence both toward God and toward man."[17] The standard in its English form can be traced to Calvin, who is absolutely inimical to fudging or dissembling in spiritual matters. To be sure, nobody is clearer than the Genevan about the antinomies of his position. There is a "smoldering cinder of evil," he writes (his word is *fomes*, kindling wood), even in the regenerate; yet the Lord forbids us (he insists elsewhere), "even to be kindled."[18] "Let even the most perfect man descend into his conscience," and he will discover the incredible difficulty of avoiding "the terrors of hell."[19] But the difficulty of descending, for Calvin and his followers, simply proves the absolute necessity of descending.

---

[15]   Slights, *Casuistical Tradition*, pp. 9–10.
[16]   See Perez Zagorin, *Ways of Lying: Dissimulation, Persecution, and Conformity in Early Modern Europe* (Cambridge, MA, 1990).
[17]   Taylor, *Ductor*, book 1, p. vii; Slights, *Casuistical Tradition*, pp. 15–16.
[18]   Calvin, *Institutes*, pp. 602, 422.
[19]   Calvin, *Institutes*, p. 765.

An illuminating distinction opens here between the Genevan and the Lutheran traditions. The Lutheran conscience is a power of the flesh, not in direct contact with God.[20] Believing otherwise, for Luther, would constitute a theology of glory, a fantasy of creaturely access to *arcana dei*.[21] The fantasy, moreover, would be a recipe for continual despair (rather than temporary and productive *Anfechtung*), since "even the most pious Christian conscience can only believe that God is angry toward sinners."[22] One can only become frustrated, Luther says, in striving for "a conscience which is as pure and good as the will requires."[23] But to this one can only imagine Calvin responding, in Luther's vernacular, "*na und?*" ("and your point is — ?") As I have indicated, he makes similar statements, while roundly approving what the German calls unbearable. "Painful," we should always remember, is a term of praise among the orthodox Reformed. For Calvin, and for a broad spectrum of Calvinistic opinion, the painful paradoxicality of a casuistical standard is exactly what recommends it.

A similar logic dictates the Genevan hatred of Nicodemism. Calvin himself polemicized against Nicodemites, using the term as a pejorative designation for covert Protestants who overtly conformed to Rome. On the Genevan view, no excuse can be admitted for this sort of dissembling – least of all the complaint that one might like to avoid martyrdom. Secret Protestants are kept in their secrecy, Calvin insists, by love of the world. In refusing to come out (as we now might say), these merely-inward Protestants are doing less than "half their duty."[24] For "the church is built up solely by outward preaching," the "prophesying" that William Perkins called an "engine" against heresy.[25] True, "the inward renewal of the mind" is what bears "true conversion of life."[26] We do not want to be like those popish flagellants who "pant after many witnesses" by praying in the marketplace.[27] But men who are not prepared, indeed eager, to make their faith public and open "know not what it is" to pray in secret at home.[28]

Thus Calvin sees confession to one's fellow men as *a fortiori* proof of one's direct confession to God. For "he who embraces this confession in his heart and before God will without doubt also have a tongue prepared for confession, whenever there is need to proclaim God's mercy among men; and not only to whisper the secret of his heart to one man and at one time, and in the ear" – the esoteric Catholic model that Calvin excoriates – "but often, publicly, with all the world hearing, unfeignedly

---

[20]   Randall C. Zachman, *The Assurance of Faith: Conscience in the Theology of Martin Luther and John Calvin* (Minneapolis, 1993), p. 21.

[21]   Zachman, *Assurance*, p. 36.

[22]   Zachman, *Assurance*, p. 69.

[23]   Zachman, *Assurance*, p. 86.

[24]   Zagorin, *Ways of Lying*, p. 74.

[25]   Quoted in James S. Baumlin, "Willam Perkins's *Art of Prophesying* and Milton's 'Two-Handed Engine,'" *MQ* 33.3: 66–71.

[26]   Calvin, *Institutes*, p. 623.

[27]   Calvin, *Institutes*, p. 891.

[28]   Calvin, *Institutes*, p. 892.

to recount both his own disgrace and God's magnificence and honor": the exoteric model that Calvin approves.[29] Public silence becomes a sign of private hypocrisy. A truly secret sincerity would have to proclaim itself everywhere. This is the ethical corollary of the moral commonplace that a true obedience obtains "in the absence, as well as in the presence of lookers on."[30]

Luther, again, differs sharply and interestingly. For the German, the inward life of faith can be indifferently expressed. No liturgical or social gesture is absolutely compelled, or absolutely proscribed, as long as one's spiritual work proceeds. But the orthodox Genevan tendency is to insist that inner truth be continuous with, and gloriously manifested in, outward performance. It is recusants who say one thing publicly and mean another privately. It is antinomians who see no need to articulate their conversion.[31] Calvin strongly emphasizes, for example, the Pauline doctrine that temporal laws bind the conscience (if only for the sake of God).[32] That is why an oath like the 1640 Etcetera ("I do approve the doctrine and discipline or government established in the Church of England ... without any equivocation or mental evasion, or secret reservation whatsoever"[33]) is formally orthodox in Calvinist terms. It is also why the refusal of anti-episcopalians to take such an oath – which would bind them to "archbishops, bishops, deans, archdeacons, *et cetera*" – is equally orthodox. Among painful but non-sectarian English Protestants, uttering without intending is simply unacceptable.

But this is because the converse – intending without uttering – is also unacceptable. I do not propose to decide which comes first in these casuistical priorities: the chicken or the egg, the intention or its expression. I do propose, on the contrary, that a general result of the Calvinist view is a practical inseparability of intention and expression. Now, the theoretical separability of these semantic moments, by a long and ever-living tradition – which I will consider in later chapters, but which will, I hope, simply sound familiar for now – inevitably devolves on the priority of intention. What people mean has (almost) always been separable from, and subordinate to, what they meant to mean. Utterance, hedged by immanence (using the latter term, as I usually will, in its psychological sense), gives semantic authority to the latter. But Calvinist casuistry denies the hedging, and therefore redistributes the authority. The result is an effective reprioritization of expression.

The painful conscience, in a word, is exoteric (in my sense). It is a secret that must be shown; a truth that must be performed. As such it suggests, from more recent rhetorical theory, the speech-acts of (among others) J.L. Austin and John Searle, as

---

29   Calvin, *Institutes*, p. 634.

30   Ames, *Conscience with the Power*, p. 55.

31   See Calvin, *Institutes*, p. 373; Zagorin, *Ways of Lying*, pp. 68, 227; Zachman, *Assurance*, pp. 8–13; and Jonathan Wright, "The World's Worst Worm: Conscience and Conformity during the English Reformation," *Sixteenth Century Journal* 30.1 (1999): 113–133.

32   Calvin, *Institutes*, p. 848.

33   See David Martin Jones, *Conscience and Allegiance in Seventeenth Century England: The Political Significance of Oaths and Engagements* (Rochester, 1999), p. 273.

well as the latter's (mis)construction by Jacques Derrida.[34] Austin began his thinking from statements, like "I promise" or "I lament," that seemed to accomplish what they said. These he called "performatives," distinguished from merely propositional "constatives," and used to blur the ancient distinction between speech and action.[35] Derrida objects that Austin's "performatives" are really special cases of play-like or (Austin's term) "parasitic" performances – utterances that precisely do *not* accomplish what they say.[36] Derrida's claim comes under his standing proposal that iteration = alteration. The sign (allegedly) is constituted by the "trace" of *différance*, and is therefore always-already differentiated from itself.[37] It follows that one cannot repeat "I promise" without failing to repeat "I promise," and therefore necessitating theatrical recuperation of the utterance. Austin, therefore, was wrong (Derrida says) to distinguish performative iteration from parasitic citationality. For the iteration is always-already citationality, and the performative can never attain the perfect or ideal or untroubled repetition that is (allegedly) presupposed by Austin's theory.

Derrida's argument is capricious, and (strangely) quite metaphysical. Yet on both grounds it has affinities with seventeenth-century conscience-theory. There too, the perfect iteration of mind as conscience would seem to propagate the trace of its own impossibility. There, too, Austinian performative would seem to be predicated on parasitic performance, such that the exoteric enactment – "I call God to witness," for example – must take the quasi-theatrical form of the dissembling it denies. In short, the Derridean critique of Austin and Searle seems to put my historical work in a theoretical bind. For I am arguing that the seventeenth-century English Protestant conscience generates an Austinian logic of definitive iteration. This is the logic, I hope to show, that structures Milton's self-presentations. At the same time, however, I am arguing that the same English Protestant theory of conscience manifests a Derridean sense of iterative interminability. The "once more" of mind-as-conscience becomes "yet once more ... and once more," and so on. Exoteric utterance is esoterically subverted, as indicated by its need to repeat itself *ad infinitum*.

Yet a very general difference obtains between post-structuralism and seventeenth-century English casuistry. Simply put, the latter field is not troubled by the conundra that trouble it. English Protestant casuists are either accustomed or delighted to find themselves thinking in circles, and/or to emphasize the dangerous identity of correct and incorrect repetition. They have, therefore, a kind of homeopathic immunity to deconstruction: they think through paradox, but without the commitment to classical logic that finds paradox paradoxical.[38] In this respect, casuistry is a major support for the

---

34   See Jonathan Culler, *On Deconstruction* (Ithaca, 1982), pp. 110–134.

35   See J.L. Austin, *How to Do Things with Words* (New York, 1965).

36   See Jacques Derrida, "Signature Evènement Contexte," in *Marges de la Philosophie* (Paris, 1972), pp. 365–393.

37   See Derrida and Ferraris, *A Taste for the Secret*, pp. 67–68.

38   See Don Cameron Allen, "Milton's 'Comus' as a Failure in Artistic Compromise," *ELH* 16 (1949): 104–119; Rosalie Colie, Paradoxia Epidemica: *The Renaissance Tradition of Paradox* (Princeton, 1966); William Kolbrener, *Milton's Warring Angels*; and Leo Damrosch,

post-post-modern scepticism that has recently been expressed by Renaissance scholars like R.V. Young and Richard Strier. For these scholars, an initial agreement between early- and post-modern fields leads only to an eventual and general disagreement.[39] The effect seems to occur because the early-moderns, coming before the Enlightenment, do not know how to think in Enlightenment terms; while the post-moderns, despite their best efforts, do not know how not to. Searle points out that post-structuralist epistemology has much in common with that of logical positivism – a highly ironic inheritance.[40] And indeed, deconstruction bases its ludic subversions on a positivist standard of absolute distinctions and ideal non-contradictions. Such a standard can only illuminate the strangeness of early-modern *discordia concors*, which knows Derrida's logical reduction only as an error it must avoid.

The same goes for Lacanian psychology, which also bears some superficial relevance to casuistry. Numerous recent studies have read Milton re: Lacan, with particular reference to the latter's "mirror stage."[41] According to this developmental precept, the human subject necessarily experiences itself as a represented other. Like an infant recognizing itself for the first time – but doing so only via that other baby in the mirror – the subject is always-already alienated from itself. As I have already intimated, *conscientia* could be read as an analogue of this model, just as Milton's mirror-episodes (notably Eve-as-Narcissus in *Paradise Lost* book 4) have been read as Lacanian representations. Yet one can only compare Lacan with casuistry by subtracting the latter's theocentrism; which is rather like comparing Judaism with Christianity by subtracting the latter's Christ. The procedure achieves a nominal identity of terms, but only by evacuating their significant content.

Moreover: *analogy* between disparate ideas and specific theoretical precepts may be the very opposite of rigorous theoretical application. "In the *Phaedrus*," writes Linda Gregerson, "the Other is the memory of the god one served in a prior life. In *The Faerie Queene* and in Paul's epistle to the Corinthians it is the face glimpsed darkly through a glass. In *Paradise Lost* it is mediated godhead in all its guises: in the tutorial hand of the Creator, in the voice of an angel and, both before and after the Fall, in the lineaments of a human companion."[42] Gregerson's ostensibly Lacanian

---

God's Plot and Man's Stories: Studies in the Fictional Imagination from Milton to Fielding (Chicago, 1985), p. 4.

[39] R.V. Young, *Doctrine and Devotion in Seventeenth-Century Poetry: Studies in Donne, Herbert, Crashaw, and Vaughan* (Rochester, 2000); Richard Strier, *Resistant Structures: Particularity, Radicalism, and Renaissance Texts* (Berkeley, 1995).

[40] See John Searle, "The Word Turned Upside Down," *The New York Review of Books* (October 1983): 12–16; and "Literary Theory and its Discontents," in Dwight Eddins (ed.), *The Emperor Redressed: Critiquing Critical Theory* (Tuscaloosa and London, 1995), pp.166–198. See also Reed Way Dasenbrock, *Truth And Consequences: Intentions, Conventions, And The New Thematics* (University Park, PA, 2001), p. 23.

[41] See Gregerson, *Reformation*; Grossman, *Story*; and Champagne, "Adam and his 'Other Self'."

[42] Gregerson, *Reformation*, p. 158.

paradigm is little more than an inventory of general dialogisms. Lacan is hardly the first theorist to note the importance of the not-I for identity-formation; it would be difficult to find anybody, from Charles Taylor back to Augustine, who does not. That Lacan called himself an Augustinian simply proves my point: he and his followers are repeating truisms of an ancient tradition, without thereby demonstrating the particular value of their repetitions.

Above all, we must recognize that Lacanian theory is the exact opposite of what I am calling exoteric casuistry. Lacan says that the mind always propagates another mind, and that the idea of psychic unity is therefore false. Difficult though it may be for us to understand, the seventeenth century has a diametrically-opposed theory: that the mind always propagates another mind, and that the idea of psychic unity is therefore true. Casuistical representation reflects and manifests this ideal – not as its prop, but as its proof.

Lycidas, Italy, and Milton Biocriticism

At this point I would like to turn to a canonical piece of Milton biocriticism, in hopes of demonstrating how the idea of a casuistical representation both responds to and differs from it. I am referring to *Lycidas*, Milton's pastoral elegy of 1638, and to the familiar reading that makes the poem's ending into a biographical and political beginning. At issue are the elegy's last eight lines:

> Thus sang the uncouth Swain to th'Okes and rills,
> While the still morn went out with Sandals gray,
> He touch'd the tender stops of various Quills,
> With eager thought warbling his *Dorick* lay:
> And now the Sun had stretch'd out all the hills,
> And now was dropt into the Western Bay;
> At last he rose, and twitch'd his Mantle blew:
> Tomorrow to fresh Woods, and Pastures new. (186–193)

That passage sits very oddly (as most readers notice) with the famous beginning of the poem: "Yet once more, O ye Laurels, and once more, / Ye Myrtles brown, with Ivy never sear, / *I* com to pluck your Berries harsh and crude" (1–3, my emphasis). *Lycidas* opens, and has continued up to this point, in a highly affective first-person voice. The poet has delivered himself of musings and expostulations ("Ay me, I fondly dream!" [56]), and emphasized the personal connection between himself and the dead shepherd ("we were nurst upon the self-same hill," etc.) (23). The pastoral world surrounded him; we saw it through his eyes. Now, without warning, "he" is a figure in a story. The pastoral world is placed in a frame. In there live singing shepherds; out here live all of us. And among "us" appears to be reckoned, finally, the poet who imposes the frame.

This biocritical argument goes back, in general terms, to Tillyard. His proposal that *Lycidas* is "really about Milton" has since been made by many scholars in many ways, and can I think quite safely be called a standard reading of the poem.[43] In recent years, another standard has been to read *Lycidas* as political allegory, and these two strains have been brilliantly and influentially combined by J. Martin Evans.[44] Evans asks us to recall that, before 1638, Milton's actions and writings suggest learned vocation, and (at least relative) socio-political seclusion. Milton seems not to have maintained residence at Cambridge for a period after his degree, as was customary. He did not enter the church, as most young men of his abilities and qualifications were expected to. And he did not, arguably, commit to love and sex (though debated, the "vow of chastity" remains a staple of Milton biography).[45] Instead he retired to his father's suburban and country houses, where he spent five years in isolated study and poetic effort. According to Evans Milton represents this period (with a glance at Cambridge) in the regretted pastoral idyll of the elegy: "Under the opening eye-lids of the morn, / We drove a field," etc. (26–27).

The drowning of the clergyman and minor poet Edward King, however, presents a turning-point, for Evans, in Milton's conception of his own life and work. King's death gives Milton occasion to realize that poetry for its own sake – in Virgilian pastoral terms, "the homely slighted Shepherds trade" (65) – is powerless against the furies of this world. The crypto-Popish Laudian bishops are ravaging the "hungry Sheep" (125). The shepherd who wants to defend the fold – who wants to *do* something, rather than just waiting for "th'abhorred shears" to slit his "thin spun life" (75, 76) – will have to stop lying around in Arcadia. And it is this realization, this revolution in Milton's ideas of selfhood and vocation, that underwrites that extraordinary closing shift from "I" to "he" in the elegy. The poet turns away from himself *qua* "uncouth Swain," and leaves that self behind, in a receding aesthetic realm.

On this brilliant biocritical reading, Milton before the moment of *Lycidas* is a poet on the road to Damascus. After it he is a pastor, or perhaps a poet-pastor, ready and willing to minister to his country's flock. "The hungry Sheep look up, and are not fed" (125); the poet-pastor will feed them, and not with "lean and flashy songs" (123). As Evans puts it, the Milton of 1638 is about to "abandon that part of himself represented by the swain, with his devotion to retirement, chastity, and poetry." In the next few years he will get married, commence his two decades of public life in

---

[43]   See Parker, *Milton,* p. 164; Barbara K. Lewalski, *The Life of John Milton: A Critical Biography* (Oxford, 2000), pp. 76–86; Russell Fraser, "Milton's Two Poets," *SEL* 34 (1994): 109–18; and Stella P. Revard, *Milton and the Tangles of Neaera's Hair: The Making of the 1645 Poems* (Columbia, MO, 1997), pp. 163–165. For the Tillyard tradition, see C.A. Patrides (ed.) and M.H. Abrams (fwd), *Milton's* Lycidas*: The Tradition and the Poem* (Columbia, MO, 1983).

[44]   See Evans, "*Lycidas,*" in Dennis Danielson (ed.), *The Cambridge Companion to Milton* (Cambridge, 1999), pp. 39–53; and "The Road from Horton," in *The Miltonic Moment* (Lexington, KY, 1998), pp. 71–116. See also Timothy J. O'Keefe, *Milton and the Pauline Tradition: A Study of Theme and Symbolism* (Washington, 1982).

[45]   See John Leonard, "Milton's Vow of Celibacy: A Reconsideration of the Evidence," in P.G. Stanwood (ed.), *Of Poetry and Politics: New Essays on Milton and his World* (Binghamton, NY, 1995), pp. 187–202.

London, and establish himself as "one of the principal champions of the Puritan and Parliamentarian cause." He will march out of his classical Arcadia to the Christian "wars of truth."[46]

Evans' analysis is as persuasive, re: *Lycidas*, as it is paradigmatic of the biocriticism that dominates Milton studies. Yet two objections arise. The first, theoretical, concerns the kind of artifact that is addressed by literary criticism. Presumably this is a text of some kind (a linguistic syntagma), or some non-textual object (a culture, a movie, a rock) treated as a text (i.e., "read"). The latter option, needless to say, has been very popular in recent decades, and one can imagine analyses of *Lycidas*-as-authorial-conversion that would theorize it as a materialist hybrid. Evans, however, offers no such theorization. He simply finds the significance of the conclusion to *Lycidas* in authorial biography. To be sure, biographical values for author-centered literary interpretation are eminently available, whether in the commonsensical theory of Samuel Johnson, or in the Romantic intentionalism that leads from Schleiermacher to E.D. Hirsch. Yet, as Gadamer might insist, making sense of a text in terms of its author's subsequent life means making a sense that the text cannot have had when it appeared – because the author's subsequent life, by definition, had not yet happened.[47] That much goes for what the author meant by the text; if we turn to what his readers saw in it, the problem becomes more severe. Clearly, if the 1638 readers of Milton's elegy for King needed Milton's biography in order to understand the poem's conclusion, then most of the poem's readers, by definition, did not understand it. Conversely, if Milton wrote that conclusion as transparent only to his own hopes and plans, then he wrote himself a self-indulgent and reflexive memo.

The second objection, factual, augments the theoretical. Although it requires extended statement, the brief point is as follows: Milton did not, in 1638, turn to any "wars of truth." The wars were certainly there, and were more than metaphorical. In July 1637 there were riots in Edinburgh over the introduction of a Laudian prayer book. In March 1638, the Scottish clergy signed a National Covenant opposing Laud's reforms. Scottish defiance would lead in 1639 to the First Bishops' War; the battle for the hungry sheep was about to begin for real. By May 1641, Milton would have joined up, with the publication of his first pro-presbyterian and anti-episcopal pamphlet (*Of Reformation*). He would write and publish similar pamphlets until episcopacy was dead and buried; he would then go on, to other issues and other tracts, all in an engaged and perceptibly leftward vein. In short, there is a manifest turn in Milton's life and work to a progressive, public mission – in 1641. But not in 1638. In that year, I repeat, Milton did not walk out of Arcadia to put on the Protestant armor of God. He walked, instead, onto a ship at Dover; and, just a month or two after the Scottish Covenant, left England for a year-and-a-half-long tour, via France, of Catholic Italy.

[46]   Evans, "*Lycidas*," p. 52.
[47]   See *TM*, pp. 55–80.

Milton's continental sojourn has been a perennial subject of biocritical debate. The usual question is whether there is anything to debate.[48] But even those who shrug off the topic of Milton in Italy must admit, I think, a disjunction with the conversion-moment of *Lycidas*. Evans presents Milton's journey as a first turn to the public world, and in a sense I suppose it is – but only in a minor sense. If, in the moment of *Lycidas*, the poet has "cast off the old man"; if in reading the elegy we have witnessed a "rebirth" [49]; then it is surely rather disappointing to find the new man going promptly on holiday. And while it is easy to understand Milton's attraction to the Italian humanist past, it is hard to ignore, in his immediate biographic context, the all-too-human present. In Barberini Italy, as W.R. Parker puts it, "vice was practised openly": "courtesans were honored by all men with respectful salutations."[50] The English visitor became the dedicatee of an obscene sonnet sequence while in Florence, from a poet (Malatesti, "bad texts") whose notebooks were burned as immoral after his death.[51] In Rome, at the Palazzo Barberini, Milton attended a singing recital by the reputed mistress of two cardinals, and subsequently addressed three poems to her.[52] The poet of *Lycidas*, 1638, had been dubious about sporting "with *Amaryllis* in the shade" (68). The zealot of the anti-prelatical tracts, 1641, would abhor "mixed dancing" and all the "luxurious and ribald feasts of *Baal-peor*" (*CP* 1.589). Between these two positions there is a *prima facie* moral continuity: we could draw a line between them, and declare part of this subject mapped. But we can't, because Italy, chronologically, is directly in the way. And to this series there is a *prima facie* moral discontinuity.

Confessional discontinuity is also quite evident. Milton's journey took him, as he later put it, into "the very stronghold of the Pope" (*CP* 4.619). That belligerent phrase comes from the Cromwellian *Second Defense of the English People* (1654), in which the regicidal government's Latin Secretary accounts for his Italian sojourn as a showing of the Protestant flag. But Milton does not mention, in that account, his private audience with the Cardinal Francesco Barberini; he does not mention that, like any other visiting Englishman, he dined at the Jesuit College in Rome.[53] Instead, he claims that the Jesuits wanted to kill him, for speaking too freely in matters of religion. There is indeed some evidence that Milton spoke his mind in Italy, and

---

[48]   See Thomas N. Corns, "John Milton: Italianate Humanist, Northern European Protestant, Englishman," in Mario di Cesare (ed.), *Milton in Italy: Contexts, Images, Contradictions* (Binghamton, NY, 1991), pp.1–8. Compare Suzanne Woods, "'That Freedom of Discussion Which I Loved': Italy and Milton's Cultural Self-Definition," in di Cesare (ed.), *Milton in Italy*, pp. 9–18; Diana Treviño Benet, "The Escape from Rome: Milton's *Second Defense* and a Renaissance Genre," in di Cesare (ed.), *Milton in Italy*, pp. 29–51; and Edward Chaney, *The Grand Tour and the Great Rebellion: Richard Lassels and "The Voyage of Italy" in the Seventeenth Century* (Moncalieri, 1985), pp. 244–245.

[49]   See Evans, "*Lycidas*," p. 52.

[50]   Parker, *Milton*, p. 181.

[51]   John Arthos, *Milton and the Italian Cities* (London, 1968), p. 27.

[52]   Campbell, *Milton Chronology*, pp. 64–65.

[53]   Parker, *Milton*, pp.173 and 1228–1229; Campbell, *Milton Chronology*, pp. 62–63.

was disliked by some of the *literati* for a Protestant prude. But Milton's Italian friends, after all, were neither liberal nor Nicodemist Catholics. As A.M. Cinquemani points out, one (Buonmattei) was "a committed and active churchman," another (Dati) "a defender of the Catholic state and opponent of Protestantism," and yet another (Coltellini) "a censor of the Roman Inquisition and author of perhaps forty religious works."[54] In *Lycidas*, Milton has just attacked the English bishops for being incompetent, selfish, and unqualified: they "scarce themselves know how to hold / A Sheep-hook, or have learn'd ought els the least / That to the faithfull Herdmans art belongs!"(119–121) In Italy, by symmetrical contrast, he lavishes praise on "the most excellent (*praestantissimum*) Cardinal Francesco Barberini," "whose great virtues and regard for what is right ... are always present before my eyes"[55] – Barberini, who won a cardinal's cap at age twenty-six on the qualification of being a papal nephew, and who ministered to the hungry sheep of Rome with elaborate palaces and private entertainments. In *Lycidas*, the only thing worse than the greedy Laudian bishops is the darkly Popish "Woolf with privy paw," who "daily devours apace" (128–129). But directly after publishing that allegation, Milton leaves the sheep behind and heads for the wolf's lair. If *Lycidas* is the poet's emergence from a lukewarm Protestant Arcadia, Italy seems to be his entry, forthwith, into a Catholic School of Athens.

My goal here is not to demonstrate anything about Milton's biography. On the contrary, my goal is to demonstrate that Milton's biography can demonstrate nothing about the ending of *Lycidas*. For the hermeneutic turn from text to life (as should surprise nobody) is really a turn from text to text – or, perhaps, a turn from text to biocritical meta-text. The latter, generated by the biocritical turn itself, quickly generates (I have argued) its own interpretative difficulties. So we have gotten nowhere. Setting out to account for something – *Lycidas* – we have arrived at something that needs to be accounted for: namely, the relation between *Lycidas* and its perplexing biographical context.

Moreover, even if we were able to describe this relation satisfactorily, we would still have gotten nowhere. We would simply have upgraded from critical difficulties to theoretical ones. Our question would then become: in mastering the biocritical meta-text, what have we mastered? Presumably, we are interested in Milton, as an historical individual, only as the author of certain texts. We are not interested in the texts insofar as they are authored by a certain historical individual. Thinking otherwise would mean accepting without question the logic of authorial biography. But the logic of authorial biography is exactly what gives biocriticism its claim on our interest. We are going around in circles, which is usually the way to miss the point.

---

[54]   A.M. Cinquemani, *Glad to Go for a Feast: Milton, Buonmattei, and the Florentine Accademia* (New York, 1998), p. 2.
[55]   *The Works of John Milton*, eds Frank Allen Patterson et al. (18 vols, New York, 1931–38), vol.12, p. 40. Hereafter cited as Milton, *Works*.

Repetition, Repetition

And what is the point of *Lycidas*? For most critics it is the emergence, at several levels, of radical and disorienting difference. At the end of the poem, "I" is distinguished from "he," and both from an omniscient narrator. Narrative is distinguished from "monody," and both from their pastoral inmixing. And performance-text, arguably, is distinguished from performative text. The first-person opening of *Lycidas* is elegiacally effective: it says "I lament," and therefore commences a lament. In other words, the poem opens as an Austinian performative, doing what it says. Its concluding shift to third-person, however, would seem to displace and diminish that performative. It turns out that we have been reading, not a lament for Edward King, but only a story about such a lament. Such a poem appears to track massively toward the fictive, in ironic disjunction with its active opening. In Austin's terms, the text describes an unfortunate illocutionary slippage from the right to the wrong kind of performative, from effective to parasitic utterance. In Derrida's terms, the text describes that same Austinian slippage, deconstructively reconceived as an hierarchical reversal.

This revelation is perhaps particularly jarring in *Justa Eduardo King* (1638), where Milton's elegy appears as the final English poem. In that position, Milton's "yet once more" references the preceding elegies, in the kind of pastoral gesture that Paul Alpers calls "convening." The other poets, although none of them pastoralists, are enrolled as the pastoral interlocutors of Milton's swain, and his elegy becomes the summation and the fulfillment of all theirs.[56] Yet when Milton's elegy turns out not to have been a "real" elegy – when it reveals its performative lament to have been a parasitic performance – it may suggest a displacement and subversion of the entire elegiac "convention." Generic analysis, then, appears to confirm the critical consensus about the poem's concluding disjunction.

Yet the rejection-of-pastoral trope is the quintessential pastoral trope. Spenser's Colin rejects pastoral at both the beginning and the end of the *Shepeardes Calendar.* Virgil looks to epic (in his fourth eclogue), and to urban pressures on Arcadia (in his first and ninth). And Sidney constructs *otium* as a turning-away from political responsibilities that always involves the consciousness of eventual turning-back. Alpers reads a quasi-pastoral episode in Primo Levi's *If This Is a Man* to show how modal self-cancelling gives pastoral its force. It is precisely the "painfully unlikely circumstances" of a noonday break in Auschwitz that allow Levi's narrative to acquire bucolic overtones. Levi looks back to Virgil's ninth Eclogue, which looks back in turn to Theocritus. The relevant literary topos is the walk taken by two shepherds. But even in Virgil, the walk is taken from the country to the brutal town, and the songs that the sheperds swap are fragmentary or inappropriate. "In the very act of re-singing their predecessors," Alpers writes, "Virgil's shepherds and the poet himself question the extent to which such revoicing is possible."[57] That

---

56   See Paul Alpers, *What is Pastoral?* (Chicago and London, 1996), pp. 79–136.
57   Alpers, *What is Pastoral?* pp. 5–6.

questioning is not a sophisticated gloss on or subversion of pastoral; it is absolutely typical of pastoral.

Lycidas, in this respect, proves genuinely surprising. During his song, Milton's swain certainly sounds like an alienated pastoral poet: he looks to the "higher mood" of epic (87), catachretically associating Arethusa (Theocritus' fountain) with Mincius (Virgil's river) (85–86); he makes a long and ostentatious detour into ecclesiastical polemic (108–131); and he fusses over over the "inefficacy" (as Victoria Silver puts it) that Lycidas' death "portends for pastoral conventions of meaning."[58] Yet in the end – after rehearsing the ways and means by which pastoral singers can abandon pastoral – Milton's swain turns around and runs right back into pastoral. He does not break his pipe, or lie down to die, or seek *Londinium, urbem huic nostrae non similem.*[59] Instead, after "warbling" an entire day, from morning to sunset, he goes off to "fresh Woods, and Pastures new" (193). Fresh and new, to be sure – but all the more recognizable as pastures and woods. Moreover, we are given no reason to expect that the anonymous speaker of the poem's conclusion will *not* be observing the swain in his further warblings. The poem's opening presents it as a member of a pastoral series, a coming "yet once more" to emblematic literary leaves. Its conclusion points toward a continuation of the series, to more pastoral, yet once more, in a landscape of yet more of the same. The "new" landscape is projected as formally separate, but substantively identical. We can expect the swain, apparently, to crush berries there "tomorrow" (193).

And tomorrow, and tomorrow: the series in question has been intertextually overdetermined. "Yet once more...and once more" quotes (as is well-known) Hebrews 12, which itself quotes and glosses the Old Testament prophecy of Haggai. Haggai, urging the post-Babylonian rebuilding of the temple, foresees a singular iteration of divine favor within the Mosaic covenant: "Thus saith the LORD of hosts; Yet once, it *is* a little while, and I will shake the heavens, and the earth, and the sea, and the dry *land*; / ... and I will fill this house with glory" (2:6–7). Hebrews, by contrast, reads the Christian covenant out of Haggai by glossing the latter's prophecy as apocalyptically re-iterative. "Yet once more, I shake not the earth only, but also heaven. / And this *word*, Yet once more, signifieth the removing of those things that are shaken.....that those things which cannot be shaken may remain" (12:26–27). The author of Hebrews (in both the Geneva and the King James versions) moves from Haggai's "yet once" to his own "yet once more," which he then identifies as the significant content of the divine promise. It is "this *word*, Yet once more," that allows us to distinguish between mount Sinai and mount Sion – between things that

---

[58]   Victoria Silver, "'Lycidas' and the Grammar of Revelation," *ELH* 58 (1991): 779–808; 795.

[59]   I allude to Spenser, *Shepeardes Calendar*, "January" and "December"; and paraphrase Virgil, *Eclogue* 1, Tityrus to Meliboeus: "*Urbem quam dicunt Romam, Meliboee, putaui / stultus ego huic nostrae similem* (The city they call Rome, Meliboeus, / I foolishly thought similar to our own"), 19–20.

can, and cannot be shaken on the last day. The author of Hebrews teaches his fellow ex-Jews the repetition of a repetition – itself irresistibly repeated in his own text.

For much modern thinking, reiteration of this kind takes the royal road to meaninglessness. It is the pattern of infinite series, which is the logical consequence of deficiency or circularity, which is what Derrida calls the logic of the supplement and uses to prove the operation of the differentiating "trace."[60] Yet it seems that for the author of Hebrews (1) reiteration does not indicate deficiency, but typological expansion pointing toward termination, and (2) the termination is to be welcomed even more than the expansion. Reiteration, the meaning of meaning, is the sign of the apocalypse. This, of course, is a good thing (in period terms). The figure of repeated repetition functions as a figure of antirepetition: of the singular type in which an infinite number of tokens will be summed and destroyed.[61]

All of which is to say that the ruling motif of Milton's pastoral ending is not one of emergent difference at all. It is, rather, the short-circuiting of difference in sameness. *Lycidas* presents itself as a member of an infinite series, eschatologically conceived as a function of identity. And indeed, as Gadamer points out (in contradistinction to Derrida), only identity allows reiteration at all.[62] If repetition entails alteration, then there is no repetition. But if there is no repetition, there is nothing to entail alteration. To be sure, reiteration on the typological model involves transformation – but the nature of the transformation is precisely to reveal the reiterated more perfectly. This is certainly the attitude of Hebrews 12 to Haggai: the New Testament scripture says clearly (so the author of Hebrews claims) what the Old Testament scripture said obscurely. The same goes generally for the attitude of the Christian church to the Jewish covenant: they are apocalyptically identical, which is why the church can retrace the covenant with louder and surer steps. The church makes available for full recognition what the covenant should have known, and in a sense did, all along.

Thus *Lycidas,* as a typological text, entails explicit and self-conscious reiteration. We have seen this insight manifested with regard to the pastoral landscape of *Lycidas*, and its scriptural quotations. It remains to consider the problem of its speaker. The narrator of the poem's conclusion indicates (as I have argued) no post-pastoral transcendence. He simply converts the poem's pastoral speaker from an "I" to a "he." About the poem's "I," we know quite a lot: friend of Lycidas, pupil of Damoetas, avoider of Amaryllis, etc. About the "he" we know nothing, except that he is the same as the "I." So why introduce him? The only point seems to be the identity that is thereby introduced, the re-presentation of the poem's first person as the conclusion's third. The only point of this representation, in turn, seems to be its projection of another, larger person: the overseeing narrator, who has no role or narrative content apart from his overseeing function. I is distinct from he, formally, but substantively the same. I and he are overseen by the narrator, who creates them as I and he solely

60   See Culler, *On Deconstruction*, pp. 89–155.
61   See Matthew Prineas, "'Yet once, it is a little while': Recovering the Book of Haggai in "Lycidas," *MQ* 33.4 (1999): 114–123.
62   *TM*, pp. 121–169.

by his intervention. And the narrator himself is the primary upshot of this intervention – the Big He who distinguishes and equates the poem's tautological pronouns.

In short: the vocative structure of *Lycidas* is the structure of the conscience. The poem's expressive intelligence has two and/or three iterations: I is represented as he (one and two), while that representation represents the omniscient narrator (three). The mind is represented as conscience (one and two), while that representation represents the divine *conscientia* (three). *Lycidas* is a psychological emblem. That is precisely not to say that it is a work in biocritical (or any other) code. It is, rather, to say that *Lycidas* allows a unique and immediate recognition of something otherwise abstract and unrecognizable: the structure of the seventeenth-century English Protestant conscience. The poem is a representation in Gadamer's sense: an image of something that is thereby imaged in the heightened truth of its being.[63]

There is one more point. The voicing of *Lycidas* compels us to work out the poem's interrelated subjectivities. We have to wonder, albeit momentarily, how the "I" of lines 1 to 185 becomes the "he" of 186–193. We have to wonder, in turn, how "I" and "he" relate to the unnamed narrator. Wondering means considering; considering means checking. But to check on the poem's subjectivities is to act like a conscience toward those subjectivities. We are forced to mimic the function of the omniscient narrator – or, perhaps, to assume that function. Either way, the chain of casuistical iterations leads out of the poem, and into our own reiterations. The final effect of Milton's elegy is to involve us in its psychological dynamism, making us members of its casuistical performance.

Prophylaxis, *pro se*

Now it may be a slight flaw in my reading of *Lycidas* that the word "conscience," or an explicit casuistical gesture, appears nowhere in the poem. The same cannot be said for Milton's major polemics, essential texts for the disciplinary tendency I have called Milton biocriticism. The Miltonic *rhetor* is a private man with public behavioral standards. His inner life reflects his outer life, while both reflect the image of God. In short, the polemical Milton constructs himself as a perfect man of conscience. He gains authority, in both senses of that word, through self-representation as casuistical reiteration.

Milton's polemical life-writing describes a virtuous circle. He presents himself, in other words, as compelled to present himself, and thereby as guaranteeing his polemical integrity. In the *Second Defense of the English People* (1654), sketching himself as Englishman abroad, Milton explains that among Roman Catholics he was "unwilling to be circumspect in matters of religion." He would "hide nothing" about his faith or origins, "whatever the consequences." Milton even claims that his openness placed him in mortal danger, despite which he continued speaking, "openly," "in the very stronghold of the Pope." (*CP* 4.619). This irrepressible Puritan, this lighthouse of the faith, is an autobiographical development from Milton's *Reason of Church-*

---

63   Warnke, *Gadamer*, p. 179.

Government (1642). There, the poet emulates the prophet Jeremiah, forced to speak the burning word that he carries in his bones. The word is what Milton simply had to speak in Italy; now he has to speak, autobiographically, of that speaking. Self-exposure acquires an almost prophetic urgency, and provides the credibility that Milton defines by self-exposure.

In the *Apology* for Smectymnuus (1642), troping himself as a divinely-donated garment, Milton declares that he is (so to speak) fully reversible: if externally stained by libels, "what help but to turn the inside outward – especially if the lining be of the same, or as it is sometimes, much better." He goes on to a lengthy "discovery" of his "inmost thoughts" (*CP* 1.889). The discovery of the inmost thoughts proves, in essence, that Milton has nothing to discover; both because the thoughts are edifying, and because Milton is prepared to discover them. And the readiness to expose, rhetorically characterized as moral compulsion, means that Milton publicly abjures the privacy or secrecy that could ever contain the unexposable.

Milton's favorite proof-text, for all his political self-presentations, might be called the divine subpoena: the calling of God to witness. Associated, ultimately, with St. Paul (2.Cor.1:23), the gesture is quite common in seventeenth-century casuistical talk. Milton performs it frequently, as do his opponents, but they only blaspheme (he says), because they do it wrong. At the end of his *Public Faith*, Milton's nemesis Alexander More calls God to witness that men have judged him falsely. He has many "true things to confess," he confesses, but he will not confess them, except to God.[64] More's is an esotericist appeal to the incommunicability of the conscience, and to God as sole "searcher of hearts." It all seems quite reasonable, pious and humble; yet Milton, in the *Defense of Himself*, castigates More for this peroration. The appeal to the heart, he complains, demands "a Delian diver." It appears to be "ingenuous," but is actually "after the fashion of a lawyer." For More is attempting "to destroy what is known with what is unknown and to wash away what is manifest with what is hidden." Almost hysterically, Milton calls More's confession "an infamous libel." "Confession" turns into "libel," it seems, because More calls God to witness secretly; he calls for authentication of a different More from the one that men see. What is wrong with this procedure, according to Milton, is that More's sins thereby "lie utterly hidden and unconfessed to us," the readers (*CP* 4.824).

Milton's divine subpoenas are the opposite of More's. Milton calls God to witness that he sees *the same* Milton that men see: the Milton that Milton has already revealed, or is in the process of revealing, autobiographically. In the *Second Defense*, concluding an account of his blindness, Milton calls "upon thee, my God, who knowest my inmost mind and all my thoughts, to witness that (although I have repeatedly examined myself on this point as earnestly as I could, and have searched all the corners of my life) I am conscious of nothing, or of no deed, either recent or remote, whose wickedness could justly occasion or invite upon me this supreme misfortune" (*CP* 4.587). Since Milton is on the way to revealing his mind and his

---

64   Milton, *Works*, vol. 9, p. 293.

thoughts and his deeds in this very text, the divine subpoena, at the simplest level, authenticates his autobiography. But the autobiography, in turn, tends to authenticate the divine subpoena; because (unlike More's Delian diving) it makes Milton's readers – "us" – "conscious" of the very thoughts and deeds that he is now submitting to God. In calling on the witness, therefore, Milton is simultaneously calling on those readers who are already sworn within his text. That More does not do this, but calls on a divine witness distinct from the readers ("us"), is exactly what Milton says is wrong with More. Milton enacts his own polemic as a self-presentational tautology. He calls on his confessional text to certify itself.

This kind of circular procedure is quite typical of English Protestant casuistry. William Perkins, for example, writes that "all such persons as are troubled with doubtings, distrustings, unbeleefe, [and] despaire of Gods mercie" should understand that they are bound in conscience to believe and not to doubt their own salvation."[65] This is as much as to say that the doubting conscience should doubt itself for doubting – and should, therefore, stop doubting. Perkins is like the therapist who tells his patient he is sick, and should therefore feel better. Jeremy Taylor, even more bewilderingly, writes that we call God to witness to show that "our conscience is right, and that God and God's Vicar, our conscience, knows it."[66] The divine subpoena proves our conscience to our conscience, a circle that Taylor placidly recommends as a test of right conscience. Meanwhile, "right" conscience is itself technical talk for the kind of conscience that can effectively call on the divine witness; and the divine witness, the eye of God, is (effectively) little more than a reflection of right conscience. So we are calling on our conscience to prove our conscience to our conscience, and the subpoena thus inscribed must be endlessly delivered.

The way our conscience becomes right in the first place is similarly numbing. We are made right, in the Calvinist tradition, by God's unmerited grace, in a soteriological operation that leaves us definitively transformed. Yet Perkins, following Calvin quite closely, nominates the whole process "the first grace." If it is the "first" grace, it cannot be a definitive or final grace after all. There must be a second grace, lest we "fall away" from the first. And the second grace, Perkins explains, "is nothing else but the continuance of the first grace," maintaining our singular and final transformation by "new and daily supplies."[67] The gift of grace produces the need for another gift; which produces the need for another gift; which produces, and so on, and so on. Infinite series of this kind is frankly congenial to Reformed thinking. It is a profound sign that the ineffable has been contacted. As I have already suggested re: *Lycidas*, infinite series functions in this tradition as a guarantee of eschatological singularity. "The yet once more" of earthly reiteration signifies the heavenly un-iterable – the engine that smites once, and smites no more.

---

65   Perkins, *Discourse*, p. 22.
66   Taylor, *Ductor*, book 1, p. 2.
67   Perkins, *Discourse*, p. 103; Calvin, *Institutes*, pp. 304–305.

Reiteration is also a leitmotif of Milton's divine subpoenas. Coming to Geneva after his Italian travelogue, Milton writes that "the mention of this city brings to mind the slanderer More," and "impels me once again to call God to witness" that "in all those places where so much licence is allowed I lived upright and undefiled by any flagitious or immodest conduct, ever aware that if I could conceal aught from the eyes of men, I certainly could conceal nothing from the eyes of God" (*CP* 4.772).[68] Milton's "once again" refers to his earlier subpoena, which asked the witness to review and approve the poet's entire life. Now, the witness is being asked to review a part of that life, the Italian journey; which is certainly more specific, but is nonetheless redundant. Meanwhile, Milton summarizes the relevant autobiographic segment as nothing other than a story of witnessing. He was unable to misbehave in Italy because he was constantly calling God to witness – "ever aware" (as he puts it) of that judicial eye. This is of course a repetition of Milton's basic autobiographical claim, the claim that his life consists in theocentric exposure. With formal elegance, the repetition itself repeats the exposure – and repeats it, like *Lycidas* repeating Hebrews repeating Haggai, as a repetition of an earlier repetition. These multivalent accords between autobiography and autobiographical frame begin to give a strong formal suggestion of casuistical proof. Exposure must be enacted even in the telling of Milton's exposure, while his repetitive subpoenas mimic the repetition that he claims for the subpoenas – that he has called God to witness previously, and can therefore call him once more.

And yet once more. In the *Defense of Himself* (1655), Milton recalls that second calling to witness in the *Second Defense*. He totally divests his new account of anything beyond its reiterative form. "Perhaps you would have it," he tells More, "that I am criminal because I have called God as my witness;"

> "Hence," you say, "that really too anxious protestation." And what was that, More? You shall hear, however unwillingly; nor do I now merely recite it, but *in the very same words which I first composed* ... I again call God as my witness that in all those places where so much licence is allowed I lived upright and undefiled by any flagitious or immodest conduct, ever aware that if I could conceal aught from the eyes of men, I certainly could conceal nothing from the eyes of God. (*CP* 4.772) (my italics)

Milton is complaining, it is important to note, that More *might as well* have attacked his earlier divine subpoena. More has not done so; Milton forcibly creates the opening, into which he rams this almost talismanic repetition. He even dares More to repeat the repetition, word for word, as though founding a new Lord's Prayer. More,

---

68   Here I have actually quoted the *CP* text of the *Defense of Himself*. I am about to make the point that in that tract Milton repeats his earlier statement from the *Second Defense*, "*ubi tam multa licent, ab omni flagitio ac probro integrum atque intactum vixisse, illud perpetuò cogitantem, si hominum latere oculos possem, Dei certè non posse*," word for word. Unfortunately, the *CP* translators of the two tracts are different, and translate the passage differently. I have therefore taken the rhetorical liberty of citing just one of their versions here. For the Latin, see Milton, *Works*, 8.126, and 9.178.

of course, can't (in good conscience). He has not avoided licence where licence was allowed, has not always remembered that he could conceal nothing from the eyes of God. Like all Milton's opponents (all to some extent straw men), More is a creature of disgusting and shameful secrecy. Because More has violated and contaminated his secrecy, he can no more retreat to it than he can display it. In his mouth, Milton's mantra would be as bad as the "vain repetitions" of the heathen, who "think that they shall be heard for their much speaking" (Matt. 6:7). Or rather, it would be worse, because More's "Father which seeth in secret" (Matt. 6:6) already knows that the disgraced minister has done a lot more in secret than just pray. His, therefore, becomes the terrible situation of being unable to pray at all. From his mouth, even the purest performatives would emerge as corrupt parasitisms.

Confronted by the exhibitionist Milton, then, so perfect that all he can do is repeat the spell of his perfection, More can only be imagined in howling retreat. This is of course what Milton recommends, to all his unfortunate opponents. He fills his polemics with figures of warding-off, directed at his enemies and based in his own pious exposure. More, the anti-Milton, is most aggressively targetted. "I have given an account of myself in order to stop your mouth, More," Milton says, "and refute your lies, chiefly for the sake of those good men who otherwise would know me not." He goes on imperiously: "Do you then, I bid you, unclean More, be silent. Hold your tongue, I say! For the more you abuse me, the more copiously will you compel me to account for my conduct" (*CP* 4.628–629). At one point, Milton tropes himself as an avenging Medusa, and More as a hapless Perseus, unprotected by his "helmet of Pluto." "You will swear," Milton growls, "as long as you live, either that I am not blind, or that at least I do not shut my eyes to you" (*CP* 4.564). The petrifying eye of the gorgon looks out of Milton's mini-autobiographies. Those foolish enough to prompt his self-portraits are supposed to be driven off by them.

Called to Witness

In that sense, a biocritical cue seems quite the wrong one to take from Milton's polemical self-presentations. The point of these presentations, worked out through their casuistical gestures, is that Milton has nothing to present. His conscience is just the conscience of his polemical work. Secretly open and public, it is fascinatingly uninteresting. Travelling through many times and places, it iterates and re-iterates its origins. In the same way, the point of Milton's divine subpoenas is that God, the casuistical witness, has nothing much to witness when he enters the box against Milton. And this because Milton (the latter states) resolutely avoids doing or thinking anything that he would not want the witness to witness. And this because his conscience is so tautologically perfect that his thoughts and actions, even in the deepest secrecy, have always-already been witnessed as witnessable by the divine witness that he then calls to witness.

This is an extraordinary, spinning casuistical mechanism. I have argued that it is powered by the rhetorical device of reiteration, the repetition of a repetition.

Contra Derrida, reiteration does not necessarily mean hermeneutic enervation or logical attenuation. Rather, in the tradition of "yet once more," reiteration means singularity, authority, and a mimesis of finality. In this, paradoxically, reiteration is both preferable and prior to mere iteration; just as Hebrews' re-reading of Haggai, typologically, is both preferable and prior to Haggai.

That much goes for the general significance of the figure. Its casuistical significance is narrower but greater. For conscience itself works through reiteration. The seventeenth-century mind, repeating itself as the conscience, does so only in order to repeat the conscience as the witnessing of the divine mind. That necessary repetition of a mental repetition is the way the mind understands its relationship to the divine – a relationship that underwrites, not only the mind's moral function, but also its function and existence as a mind at all.

What this means for Milton is that his self-presentational reiterations provide a formal mimesis (as I have suggested) of the conscience he is presenting. Just as Milton's conscience must call on the divine witness to witness that his conscience has always-already called on the divine witness; so his casuistical text, in the *Defense of Himself*, calls on the divine witness in the presence of the reader to witness that the divine witness has already been called in the presence of the reader (in the *Second Defense*), to witness that the divine witness has already been called, in the presence of the reader (earlier in the *Second Defense*), to witness that the divine witness has always-already been called. The reader, if he is to read Milton's account, cannot but participate in this somewhat maniacal scheme.

It may be possible to push "participate" a little farther. I have said that Milton's text is mimetic of his conscience, but that may be too much of an immanentist concession. After all, conscience is text, too. Think of the scribal and readerly metaphors through which English casuists constantly work: *synteresis* as book, or the tables of the law; *conscientia* as secretary, or notary, or judge. It may be that Milton's casuistical text, rather than representing his conscience, simply *is* his conscience. "I call God to witness," says the man in his heart. "I call God to witness," says the man in the marketplace. "I call God to witness," says the man in the book. In all three cases, performance of the divine subpoena – its expression of the conscience as always-already expressed – is nothing other than the self-performance of the conscience. But if so, it is hard to see any difference between the performance of the heart, and the performance of the book.

It follows that Milton's self-presentations are not merely rhetorical. They are genuinely casuistical. His is a textualization of something that is, in the first place, a textualization. Therefore, in reading Milton's casuistical text, we are actually reading his conscience. What is more, reading of the conscience is itself a function of the conscience – the very highest function, performed by the divine secretary. And so the conclusion seems to be that Milton's casuistical text makes us members of his conscience, in the place of the divine eye.

Obviously, like the conclusion of my discussion of *Lycidas*, this conclusion accords with the Gadamerian aesthetics of non-differentiation (see pp. 25–9). The reader is not allowed, if he attends, to read Milton's casuistical self-presentations as meaningful objects from which he is alienated. Instead, he must read them as meaningful sites of which he is part. Equally obviously, the contribution takes the form of hermeneutic recognition, rather than discovery. The reader is supposed to know again, in reading Milton's reiterations, what he was told before. In knowing again, moreover, he is supposed to know. In being invited to recognize, he is empowered to understand.

Finally, and troublingly, this whole conclusion seems to violate an opposition without which it is hard to make sense of thinking, writing, or reading. I am not talking about the opposition between reader and text – that is old news, at least according to the well-established discipline known as reader-response theory. Neither am I talking about the opposition between a performance and what is performed – the token/type opposition, which simply invites deconstruction. I am talking, rather, about the opposition between intention and expression. I have been led to conclude, in effect, that Milton's casuistical expressions make us members of his intentions. But it is hard to see, at least initially, the validity of such a claim.

Making out its validity will occupy me for the next two chapters. I need to follow up the suggestion I made some time ago, that Calvinist casuistry tends to identify expressions with intentions. Since the key casuistical concept seems to be performance, I will mount an extended consideration of Miltonic drama. Since intention is, if you like, the *prima facie* hermeneutic concept, my discussion will become quite theoretical. And since this is all too much to pose on a narrow theological basis, I will branch out to Renaissance Neoplatonism, and Stuart ideology.

It is on the latter note that I would like to conclude this chapter. In the *Basilikon Doron*, James I warns his heir about the surprising dangers of armor. "Banish not only from your court all traitorous offensive weapons forbidden by the laws," he writes, "but also all traitorous defensive arms, as secrets [coat of mail under clothes], plate-sleeves [armored sleeves], and suchlike unseen armour."

> For besides that the wearers thereof may be presupposed to have a secret evil intention, they [the varieties of concealed armor] want both the uses that defensive armour is ordained for: which is to be able to hold out violence and by their outward glancing in their enemies' eyes to strike a terror in their hearts; where, by the contrary, they can serve for neither, being not only unable to resist but dangerous for shots, and giving no outward show against the enemy, being only ordained for betraying under trust, whereof honest men should be ashamed to bear the outward badge, not resembling the thing they are not.[69]

For James, armor is supposed to be offensively defensive. It should preclude battle, apotropaically, by its "outward glancing." The king's comment indicates and

---

[69]   James I, *The True Law of Free Monarchies* and *Basilikon Doron,* eds Daniel Fischlin and Mark Fortier (Toronto, 1996), pp. 161–163. See also McCrea, *Constant Minds,* pp.186–187, for this sort of advice backed up by Henry's tutor Joseph Hall, *contra* Bacon; and pp. 56–57 for the alternative, neo-Stoic attitude in Prince Henry's circle, associated via Robert Dallington with the work of Lipsius.

projects a broader assumption that men should – and, for the most part, do – make their intentions known outwardly. Indeed, "traitorous defensive arms" demonstrate, willy-nilly, the "secret evil intention" of their wearers. I have argued that Milton's conscience becomes exoteric to the extent that he is able to textualize its processes. As More finds out, the effect is apotropaic: Milton's conscience becomes a magnificent armor of intention. I have been focussing on the mechanisms of the armor as an expression, while largely neglecting the obverse question of its relation to intention. To this important topic, both psychological and semantic, I now will turn.

Chapter 2

The Armor of Intention

Students open *Samson Agonistes* (*SA*), Milton's closet drama of 1671, expecting dusty and untopical stuff. Instead, they get an Aristotelian tragedy about pre-Davidic Israel. The play is a retelling of Judges 16:23–31, in which the defeated and blinded Samson takes revenge on his Philistine captors. He does so spectacularly (in both senses of that word), pulling down the building in which he has been performing feats of strength. "So the dead which he slew at his death were more than *they* which he slew in his life," says Judges (16:30); "O dearly-bought revenge, yet glorious!" comments Milton's Chorus.[1] Because he acted on a Philistine feast-day, Samson killed "Lords, Ladies, Captains, Councellors, or Priests ... not only / Of this but each *Philistian* City round" (1654–1656). All died "while thir hearts were jocund and sublime, / Drunk with Idolatry, drunk with Wine" (1670–1671). Only the "vulgar" survived – and those only because they "stood without," too poor to enter the theatre (1660). The Chorus apostrophizes: "Living or dying thou hast fulfill'd / The work for which thou wast foretold / To *Israel*" (1662–1664). Samson's father Manoa concurs, saying of his son's death that "nothing is here for tears, nothing to wail ... Nothing but well and fair, / And what may quiet us in a death so noble."

> Let us go find the body where it lies
> Sok't in his enemies blood, and from the stream
> With lavers pure and cleansing herbs wash off
> The clotted gore. I with what speed the while
> (*Gaza* is not in plight to say us nay)
> Will send for all my kindred, all my friends
> To fetch him hence and solemnly attend
> With silent obsequie and funeral train
> Home to his Fathers house: there will I build him
> A Monument, and plant it round with shade
> Of Laurel ever green, and branching Palm,
> With all his Trophies hung, and Acts enroll'd
> In copious Legend, or sweet Lyric Song.
> Thither shall all the valiant youth resort,
> And from his memory inflame thir breasts
> To matchless valour, and adventures high. (1722, 1724–1725; 1726–1741)

---

[1]   Milton, *Paradise Regaind. A poem. In IV books. To which is added Samson Agonistes* (London, 1671), line 1661. All further citations to this edition, abbreviated to *PR*, parenthesized by line number in body of my text.

Samson's "nuptial choice" of the Philistine Dalila will always be regretted (1744), but apart from that he will be remembered as the Danites' greatest champion.

It is not hard to see why this text has become a discussion-starter. In his final action, especially as construed by his compatriots, Samson resembles a terrorist. Specifically, he resembles the suicide attackers who have confronted modern Israel and the West, for a generation now, in the name of national liberation and fundamentalist Islam. His culture roundly approves his action (for all the world, Manoa is like the sad-but-proud father of a Palestinian *shaheed*) and the play ends by projecting a cult of the champion's martyrdom. Since September 11, 2001, this reading of *SA* has come to seem extremely urgent, rendering the play an academic site of the so-called "war on terrorism." The latter boils down, apparently, to a hostile separation between war and terrorism – between the military and non-military spheres. Samson violates the separation both subjectively and objectively. He is a non-military fighter, claiming divine appointment, who single-handedly annihilates regular Philistine armies. When he is forced to discontinue those activities, he seizes his first opportunity to kill large numbers of enemy civilians. He is, in short, an insult to the principles (so it might be argued) that memorialize the casualties of terrorism.

One distinguished Miltonist, theorizing *SA* along these lines, has gone so far as to wonder in print whether the tragedy should be banned. But the same critic, John Carey, gave the tactical answer to his rhetorical question. *SA* is not really an "incitement to terrorism," he wrote, because Milton does not direct us to approve Samson's action. On the contrary, Milton hints that we should not approve it – and 9/11 helps us to see why we must take the hint.[2] As my summary indicates, Carey's argument was formed long before the destruction of the World Trade Center. Indeed, arguments like Carey's are characteristic of a modern interpretative tradition, which is usually called "revisionist" but which I will call "anti-Samsonite."[3] Anti-Samsonites support their position through a variety of close readings and source studies, but centrally claim that Milton purposefully obscures his protagonist's catastrophic motivation and authorization. In Judges, Samson prays for violent revenge immediately before his final act (16:28–30). Since the act is successful, the implication is overwhelming that God has answered, and approved, Samson's prayer. So much for the war on terrorism. Milton, however, departs from his source in exactly this respect, cloaking Samson's prayer in a series of indeterminacies. One of these is provided by his text's dramatic form, which replaces inward speech with outward – therefore (we assume) questionable – performance. Another is provided by Greek tragic form,

---

[2]   John Carey, "A work in praise of terrorism?" *Times Literary Supplement*, September 6th, 2002.

[3]   See John Carey, *Milton* (London, 1969); Irene Samuel, "*Samson Agonistes* as Tragedy," in Joseph Anthony Wittreich (ed.), *Calm of Mind: Tercentenary Essays on* Paradise Regained *and* Samson Agonistes*, in honor of John S. Diekhoff* (Cleveland, 1971); Joseph Wittreich, *Interpreting* Samson Agonistes (Princeton, 1986), and *Shifting Contexts*; and Derek N.C. Wood, *"Exiled from Light": Divine Law, Morality, and Violence in Milton's* Samson Agonistes (Toronto, 2001).

which removes the catastrophe off-stage and relates it to us only indirectly. A third indeterminacy is provided by the indirect account we actually get of Samson's prayer, which does not make absolutely clear that Samson prayed at all. Milton's Messenger tells us only that Samson stood "with head a while enclin'd, / And eyes fast fixt ... *as* one who pray'd, / *Or* some great matter in his mind revolv'd" (1637–1639, my emphasis). The possibility that Samson might have been doing something other than praying – meditating on his own suffering, perhaps, or even putting on an artificial performance of prayer – opens the text to a range of anti-Samsonite possibilities, and allows its alignment with irenic ideology.

Pro-Samsonites respond that we know Samson prayed because we know that Milton is scripting Judges 16. And in Judges 16, Samson prays.[4] Moreover, before going to the theatre Samson expresses, on-stage, the "rouzing motions" he newly feels within (1393). Has Milton not taken care, here, to suggest the hero's reinvigoration by the holy spirit? The alleged indeterminacies of the play's off-stage catastrophe are merely dramaturgic epiphenomena – and anti-Samsonites remove their own arguments from the uncertainty they adduce. How are we supposed to know, for example, that the Messenger reports the crucial scene correctly? Doesn't he admit that he was not standing very close to Samson, but had to hear the champion's earlier comments "from such as nearer stood" (1632)? On the Messenger's own account, no fully reliable eye-witness could even have escaped the theatre. Anti-Samsonites might well retort, on this point, that we are in the same boat as the Messenger – that Milton is telling us how hard it is to perceive divine commission. But pro-Samsonites can turn that point, too, to their advantage. As Stanley Fish puts it (in the comments that excited Carey), "Samson's act is praiseworthy because he *intends* it to be answerable to the divine will; whether it is or not, especially in the terms in which he conceives it, he cannot know, nor can we; and in relation to the problem of judging him as a moral being, whether it is or not does not matter" (my italics).[5] Fish leaves open the possibility that Samson's judgment may err. He simply denies that such a possibility is interpretatively relevant. Samson's action is justified, as much as any action can be, just as long as Samson is sincere in performing it.

---

[4]   See David Norbrook, "Republican Occasions in *Paradise Regained* and *Samson Agonistes*," *MS* 42 (2002): 122–148; Angelica Duran, "The Last Stages of Education: *Paradise Regained* and *Samson Agonistes*," *MQ* 34.4 (2000): 103–117; Carol Barton, "'In This Dark World and Wide': *Samson Agonistes* and the Meaning of Christian Heroism," *Early Modern Literary Studies: A Journal of Sixteenth- and Seventeenth-Century English Literature* 5.2 (1999); Alan Rudrum, "Discerning the Spirit in *Samson Agonistes*: The Dalila Episode," in Charles W. Durham and Kristin A. Pruitt (eds), *All in All: Unity, Diversity, and the Miltonic Perspective* (London, 1999), pp. 245–258; Tayler, *Milton's Poetry*, pp. 105–122; Michael F. Krouse, *Milton's Samson and the Christian Tradition* (Princeton, 1949); *Milton Studies* 33 (1997); and Alan Rudrum, "Milton Scholarship and the Agon over *Samson Agonistes*," *Huntington Library Quarterly: Studies in English and American History and Literature* 65 (2002): 465–488.

[5]   Fish, *How Milton Works*, p. 428.

Carey objects, correctly, that terrorists are always sincere. One Danite's freedom fighter is another Philistine's jihadist. Pro- and anti-Samsonite debates often degenerate into this sort of definitional tussle, reproducing the tautologies of post-9/11 discourse. A better way forward has been suggested by Alan Rudrum, on the authority of the conservative literary theorist E.D. Hirsch. Rudrum claims, in Hirschean terms, that the Samson-as-terrorist debate confuses textual "meaning" with textual "significance." "Meaning" is what the author meant in his work; "significance" is the work's possible and multiple historical resonances. Significance is sexy, but it is interpretatively dubious, because it bears no direct relation to authorial intention. And for Hirsch, authorial intention is the *sine qua non* of textual meaning. Thus Carey is wrong to claim that "9/11 has changed *SA*, because it has changed the readings we can derive from it." An event subsequent to a text, on the Hirschean view, cannot change "the readings we can derive from it," because our readings are – or should be – only a function of what the author meant. Since Milton knew nothing about 9/11, 9/11 is *a priori* irrelevant to what *SA* means.[6]

True, Milton might have meant us to see something in *SA* that would support an analogy with modern terrorism. If so, critics might be able to recover something of Milton's meaning by meditating on Samson's post-9/11 significance. They are much more likely, however, to fall into anachronism: the back-propagation of postmodern concerns into an early-modern text. The pro-Samsonites, on this view, have the better position, precisely because they would really rather not think about Samson and terrorism at all. Indeed, Rudrum presents his argument as recuperating a traditional pro-Samsonite account, according to which Milton's drama simply and wholly presents the story of its hero's soteriological regeneration. Thus the whole Samson–terrorist connection is a non-interpretative caprice – an attempt at relevance, as Fish might say, by literary critics who wish they were something else.[7]

Rudrum's theoretical intervention, his chastising of *SA*-scholars for their hermeneutic imprecision, nonetheless works by according with their deeper hermeneutic assumptions. Implicitly or explicitly, most Milton scholarship is strongly intentionalist.[8] This is a natural corollary of the author-centeredness I discussed in the opening of my last chapter. When they debate *SA*, moreover, scholars reproduce author-intentionalism at the characterological level. That is, they move from Samson's action to his pre-active motivation, just as they move from Milton's

---

    [6]   See Rudrum, "Discerning the Spirit," and "Milton Scholarship"; Hirsch, *Validity in Interpretation* (New Haven, 1967); Gary Iseminger (ed.), *Intention and Interpretation* (Philadelphia, 1992); and Annabel Patterson, "Intention," in Frank Lentricchia and Thomas McLaughlin (eds), *Critical Terms for Literary Study* (Chicago, 1995), pp. 136–146.

    [7]   See Fish, *Professional Correctness: Literary Studies and Political Change* (New York, 1995).

    [8]   See the Introduction to Diana Treviño Benet and Michael Lieb (eds), *Literary Milton: Text, Pretext, Context* (Pittsburgh, 1994); and John T. Shawcross, *Intentionality and the New Traditionalism: Some Liminal Means to Literary Revisionism* (University Park, PA, 1991).

text to his pre-textual intention. In both cases, Miltonists consider an intentionalist reduction both necessary and sufficient for interpretation. Intentionalist reduction is the hermeneutic move that unifies critics of *SA*.

Thus anti-Samsonites read the play's catastrophe as the sign of Samson's desire for revenge, or of his theological misprision. Pro-Samsonites read it as the sign of divine commission, or of the champion's attempt to perceive such a commission. A third group of scholars, whom we might call the *incerti* (or uncertain ones), assigns multiple significations to Samson's action – but only, and precisely, in the absence of knowing what it signifies to Samson. Only God and the champion himself (they allege) can know that; and since we are neither God nor the champion, our attitude to the catastrophe must be, as it were, definitely uncertain.[9] (Here one sees, with a glance back at Carey, how the *incerti* can be grouped with the anti-Samsonites.) In short, all commentators on Samson's action, the pro, the con, and even the undecided, interpret it as a function of Samson's intentions. It is always what the champion *means to do* that gives the meaning of what he does.

The interpretative principle here is, in effect, Hirschean, with considerable support from common sense. The principle, which I will designate "strong intentionalism," might be formalized as follows: actions and/or expressions – speech-acts – are determined and caused by mental intentions which are prior to, discrete from, yet utterly probative for the speech-acts in question. Expressions are not intentions, but are hermeneutically reducible to intentions. Mental intention is to speech-act as signified is to signifier.

"Mental intention," by the way, is not a redundant phrase. Things other than minds – utterances, most importantly – are also sometimes said to have intentions (or "intensions-with-an-s," as John Searle likes to say). This is a technical semantic usage that will be relevant to my next chapter. Here, I am solely concerned with what Searle calls "intrinsic intentionality": the mental property of being "directed at or about states of affairs in the world."[10] (Having explained that, I will just say "intentionality.") Intentionality, so defined, departs somewhat from the common-sense notion of intending or planning to do something. Believing something, feeling something, and many other mental states are also intentional. But not all mental states: feeling unhappy about nothing in particular, for example, is (arguably) non-intentional; while feeling unhappy for some reason (e.g., because one cannot understand intentionality) is intentional. Intentionality is thought informed by

9   See Wittreich, *Shifting Contexts*; John Shawcross, *The Uncertain World of* Samson Agonistes; and the Introduction to Mark R. Kelley and Joseph Wittreich, (eds), *Altering Eyes: New Perspectives on* Samson Agonistes (London, 2002), pp.12–13.
10   John Searle, *Consciousness and Language* (New York, 2002), p. 12; and Searle, *Intentionality: An Essay in the Philosophy of Mind* (Cambridge, 1983), pp. vii and 1–3. For a similar definition, see Edward N. Zalta, *Intensional Logic and the Metaphysics of Intentionality* (Cambridge, MA, 1988), pp. 10–11. See also William Lyons, *Approaches to Intentionality* (Oxford, 1995).

reference, and causally related to its own "conditions of satisfaction."[11] That is to say, an intentional state – for example, desire for a cup of coffee – is an inward mental proposition that reflects certain aspects of the external world (cups of coffee, drinking them, etc.). Behaviorally, it may also produce the attempt to make the world match the inward proposition: viz., by the procuring and drinking of a cup of coffee. In a word, intentionality is representational. It represents the world, and tries to make the world represent its representation.[12] Since representation would seem to be the framework of all meaning – and is without question the framework of linguistic and literary meaning – it follows that intentionality is intrinsically productive of meaning. But is it uniquely so? And does meaning therefore remain, ultimately, immanent (existing in a mental source)? To understand a speech-act, must we always appeal to its prior, separable, yet probative intention?

Affirmative answers to these questions are not limited to Hirschean literary criticism. Strong intentionalism has a persistent force in all interpretative disciplines. Perhaps most immediately relevant is speech-act theory *per se*, but in the version worked out by H.P. Grice.[13] For Grice, communication of "non-natural" (conventional or symbolic) meaning is a function of speaker intention, eked out by conversational implicature. Truth is "(primarily) a property of utterances," rather than of social convention or linguistic structure; and "utterer's occasion-meaning" forms the basis of overall or "timeless" meaning.[14] In short, "what words mean is a matter of what people mean by them," even as – or, perhaps, because – everything people *say* they can first of all silently *think*.[15] Grice's version of language philosophy (like most) denies a cognitive role to language, but not by way of logical-positivist formalization. On the contrary, Grice is attempting, like a number of his post-war Oxfordian colleagues, to retrieve "ordinary language" from the logical-positivist junkheap. He wishes to show, as though in re-appropriation of Bertrand Russell's contemptuous formulation, that "common speech is good enough, not only for daily life, but also for philosophy."[16] Gricean common speech is "good enough," however, only if it can be made to manifest the consistency and coherence of the positivistic meta-speech that it manifestly is not. Intention is the tool by which Grice tries to erase the difference between ordinary language and logical notation. By anchoring

---

[11]   See Searle, *Consciousness and Language*, pp. 87 and 130–141, and *Intentionality*, pp. 41–49 and 82–107.

[12]   Searle, *Intentionality*, pp. 19–26; Lyons, *Approaches*, pp. 40–74.

[13]   See H. Paul Grice, *Studies in the Way of Words* (Cambridge, MA, 1989). Compare Searle, *Consciousness and Language*, p. 5, and *Speech Acts: An Essay in the Philosophy of Language* (London, 1969).

[14]   Grice, *Studies*, pp. 56, 90–91, and 117–137.

[15]   Grice, *Studies*, pp. 340 and 357.

[16]   See Bertrand Russell, "Mr. Strawson on Referring," in Jay L. Garfield and Murray Kiteley (eds), *Meaning and Truth: Essential Readings in Modern Semantics* (New York, 1991), pp. 130–35: 132.

meaning to a fully-knowable intention, while separating it from social and semiotic arbitrariness, he sets out to prove that ordinary language is scientific.[17]

Against this enterprise stands Wittgenstein's assertion that one cannot mean "I am going out for a walk" just by saying "bu bu bu."[18] Intention cannot be the sole quantity to which the immensely complex phenomenon of language is reduced. To be sure, strong intentionalists might insist (and have) that one *can* mean "I am going out for a walk" just by saying "bu bu bu," in circumstances that allow "bu bu bu" to mean "I am going out for a walk." To work out that scenario, however, the strong intentionalist would either have to (1) posit the predetermination of an appropriately-organized language, thus discarding the strong-intentionalist premise of intention and intention alone, or (2) propose "bu bu bu" as privately-encoded, thus departing from any account of normal communication. The latter course is the one commonly taken in strong-intentionalist theories, leading to top-heavy claims about secret language, words not being the words they are, etc.[19] It is in part to avoid results like these that Searle articulates his own moderate and flexible theory.

Meanwhile, Grice's quasi-Augustinian hierarchy of locution – speaking as the key to all meaning, and thinking as the perfect form of speaking – opens up a general semantic contradiction. For the semanticist, seeking intentional meaning, goes from the sign to the mind. But in the mind, he finds only a pre-representation of the sign. But the mind is supposed to be prior to, and removed from, all representation; which means that a further mind must be posited, beyond the one that merely thinks what is said. Grice recognizes this regress, but is not particularly troubled by it. He simply observes, somewhat playfully, that we may have to be content with the "sublunary performance" of non-representational intentions that are "only celestially realized."[20] The rhetoric is, again, Augustinian (or perhaps Platonic), and nothing wrong with that. But the semantics of intentional presence has proved to be a semantics of intentional absence, and there does seem to be something wrong with that.

A similar breakdown – part absurd result, part interpretative regress – occurs in legal and constitutional hermeneutics. Here, strong intentionalists, or "strict constructionists," or "originalists," hold (1) that a statute must be understood today as it would have been understood at the time it was written, and (2) that effecting this kind of understanding entails recovering (*inter alia*) the intentions of the

---

[17]   See Grice, *Studies*, pp. 22–85.

[18]   See Culler, *On Deconstruction*, p.124.

[19]   Thus Grice, *Studies*, p. 102, claims that the phrase "you English pig" means "come into my shop" if uttered in Arabic by a smiling souvenir salesman. But clearly "you English pig" means nothing other than "you English pig." Grice is ignoring the basic distinction between sentence-meaning and utterance-meaning; on which, see P.F. Strawson, "On Referring," in Garfield and Kiteley (eds), *Meaning and Truth*, pp. 108–129; and Searle, "Literary Theory and Its Discontents."

[20]   Grice, *Studies*, pp. 301, 303.

original legislators.[21] (1) would seem to suggest the following. Imagine that a certain society's basic law held that "all men are created equal." At the same time, imagine that the same society practiced and defended, through innumerable judgments under the basic law, *de iure* race-based slavery. Clearly, the originalist must conclude, "all men" in the basic law was not supposed to mean "all men," nor "equal" "equal." Equally clearly, the basic law or constitution could never be used to invalidate the society's race-based slavery, because applying the law in such a way would always be inconsistent with the way it was "understood at the time" it was written. Should the society ever wish to escape its legal racism, and to do so by constitutional means, it would have to redraft the basic law. But the redrafted version could hardly do better than the statement that "all men are created equal." Originalism would dictate *re-incantation* of the same old words, before it would ever allow society to ask what those same old words mean *now*. ("Women," meanwhile, would have to wait until the fire next time.)

That is the absurd result. (2) produces the interpretative regress. Since most statutes emerge from multiple or collective authorship, they confront the diehard originalist with heterogenous historical intentions. More often than not, the intentions are conflicting and even hostile, the starting-point of a conversational process that found quietus only in the statute. A constitutional convention, for example, may consist of delegates sharing only the broadest of principles. All the delegates eventually (and painfully) agree on is the text they eventually agree on. Inquiring into their pre-textual disagreements is precisely not the same as inquiring into their textual agreement. Looking from statute to intentions does not clarify, but undoes the statute.[22]

Moreover, the intentions themselves are unlikely to be self-justifying. This point holds even in cases of single legal authorship. The originalist looks from text to intention; but to be sure of that intention, he must (surely) look in turn to the earlier texts that informed that intention – especially given the precedent-based methodology of Anglo-American legal thinking. And what about the intentions behind that earlier text, and the texts behind *those* intentions? It is hard to see where

---

[21]   See Natalie Stoljar, "Postulated Authors and Hyopthetical Intentions," in Ngaire Naffine, Rosemary Owens and John Williams (eds), *Intention in Law and Philosophy* (Aldershot, 2001), pp. 271–290; John Williams, "Constitutional Intention: The Limits of Originalism," in Naffine, Owens and Williams (eds), *Intention in Law and Philosophy*, pp. 321–344; and Terence Ball, "Constitutional Interpretation and Conceptual Change," in Gregory Leyh (ed.), *Legal Hermeneutics: History, Theory, and Practice* (Berkeley, 1992), pp. 129–146. For an explicitly Gadamerian account, see David C. Hoy, "Legal Hermeneutics: Recent Debates, " in Kathleen Wright (ed.), *Festivals of Interpretation: Essays on Hans-Georg Gadamer's Work* (Albany, 1990), pp. 111–135. Andrei Marmor, in his *Interpretation and Legal Theory* (Oxford, 1992), pp. 156–184, defends a moderate intentionalist stance. High originalism is set out by Robert Bork in his *The Tempting of America: The Political Seduction of the Law* (London, 1990).

[22]   See Ball, "Constitutional Interpretation," p. 138.

the originalist will stop. Richard Posner (sometimes pragmatist, but here originalist), in construing the eighth U.S. constitutional amendment (1787), stops just where he likes: the amendment's prohibition against "cruel and unusual punishment," Posner claims, does not mean what we think it means. This we can tell because the amendment's phrasing was borrowed from the English Declaration of Rights (1689). The intention of the framers was, therefore, to accord with the broad political aims of the English Declaration, not (as we might think today) to impugn punishments like the death penalty.[23] It may be so; but the only way to know, on the originalist theory, would be to inquire into the intentions of the writers of the English Declaration. For Posner is claiming that the writers of the eighth amendment wished to agree with their predecessors. How can we know if they succeeded, other than by determining what their predecessors thought? And how can we determine *that*, on the originalist theory, other than by inquiring into their predecessors' intentions, and the earlier texts informing those intentions, and so on? Posner does not make this move, and is wise not to. For it is plain that the chain of texts and intentions will stretch all the way back to Hammurabi. Posner arbitrarily terminates the regress, but only by contradicting the hermeneutics on which he is operating.

No doubt the survey I am providing is absurdly over-simplified. Over-simplified, and incomplete: I have said nothing about Quentin Skinner's historiographic originalism, though this is a model of great influence on Milton studies. Neither have I commented on abstract psychological theorizations of intentionalism.[24]

Nonetheless, I hope I have said enough to indicate that intentionalism, especially in its strong form, operates as a widely available and extremely insidious weapon of mass deconstruction. It attracts conservative exegetes who wish to stabilize their discipline; but proceeds, once acquired, to explode the desired stability from within. It is not surprising, therefore, to find strong intentionalism at the center of deconstruction itself. We are accustomed to thinking of post-structuralism as an anti-intentionalism, like its structuralist parent, and the latter's New Critical forbear.[25] Yet where New Criticism dispensed with authorial intentions, and structuralism went so far as to dispense with authors, post-structuralism dispenses with meaning – but precisely insofar as meaning depends on authors and their intentions. Stanley Fish famously describes receiving by mail a copy of Derrida's *Grammatology* "with the compliments of the author," and finding himself "a very emblem of the difficulties or infelicities that attend distanced or etiolated communication: unable to proceed because the words were cut off from their source in a unique and clearly present

---

[23]   Richard A. Posner, *Law and Literature: A Misunderstood Relation* (Cambridge, MA, 1988), pp. 226–227.

[24]   See Tully and Skinner (eds), *Meaning and Context*; and Charles Taylor, *Sources of the Self: The Making of the Modern Identity* (Cambridge, MA, 1989).

[25]   See Catherine Belsey, *John Milton: Language, Gender, Power* (Oxford and New York, 1988), pp. 1–15.

intention."[26] Fish's point is that, for Derrida, all communication is "etiolated" in this way. My point is that, for Derrida, Fish, and other post-structuralists, the text's etiolation from "unique and clearly present intention" clearly, presently, and uniquely *matters*. This is the whole premise of Derrida's semiotic mysteries, his Daliesque eyebrow-raisings over the impossibility of *s'entendre parler*. Deconstruction understands meaning as a function of semiotic displacement, a lapse or exile of texts from the text-making mind. That makes the theory a strong intentionalism, for which secure interpretation would entail re-establishing an originary text–mind relation. Deconstruction claims, of course, that no such relation can ever be established; but this claim gains its force only against the persistent idea of the relation. As always-already text, as the proof and engine of *différance*, mental intention is maintained by Derrideans like a deposed and mummified priest-king. This is not just strong intentionalism; it is neurotic, arch-ultra intentionalism. It is unutterable commitment to immanent meaning, coupled with an uncompromising insistence that such meaning can never be. The result is hermeneutics as a "taste for the secret": a strange notion of interpretation as all seek and no find.

And the alternative is – what? Not, I think, strong anti-intentionalism, which usually circles back to the intentionality it abjures. New Criticism (as Gerald Graff has shown) had frequent recourse to the "fallacy" of authorial immanence. Structuralism simply deferred the phenomenon, from individual to collective minds.[27] Philosophical anti-intentionalism, meanwhile, is usually either implausible or insignificant: implausible when it claims that intentional phenomena are not facts of nature; insignificant when it claims that intentionality is not what it seems. In the first case, the anti-intentionalist philosopher contradicts (as Searle has argued) vast empirical evidence.[28] In the second case, he invites the traditional realist rejoinder that even if things are *not* what they seem – indeed, precisely to the extent that they may not be – it is a matter of considerable importance to describe just how they do seem.[29]

Finally, as is made particularly clear in legal and constitutional hermeneutics, the exclusion of intentionality makes even less sense than its fetishization. And that – let me loudly admit – is because of the *prima facie* plausibility of the intentionalist impulse. A law banning vehicles from the park, for example, is probably not meant to prevent (per Steven Knapp and Walter Michaels' whimsical suggestion) the uttering of metaphors there. But the only way to figure that out is to ask, however provisionally, what sorts of "vehicles" the legislator probably had in mind; whether

---

[26]   Stanley Fish, "With the Compliments of the Author: Reflections on Austin and Derrida," in Fish's *Doing What Comes Naturally: Change, Rhetoric, and the Practice of Theory in Literary and Legal Studies* (Durham and London,1989), 37–67: 37.

[27]   See Gerald Graff, *Professing Literature: An Institutional History* (Chicago, 1987), pp. 183–192.

[28]   Searle, *Consciousness and Language*, pp. 9–12 and 61–89, and *Intentionality*, pp. 197–230.

[29]   See Searle, *Intentionality*, pp. 70–79.

he had been reading I.A. Richards, and, if so, whether that matters.[30] Moreover, even not asking such questions, but interpreting the law at one's own ludic will, can only proceed by a mental imposition of meaning on the text – that is, intentionalistically. Yet thinking from these insights all the way back to strong intentionalism means falling down one or more of the rabbit-holes that I have already described.

I cannot solve this problem in the current preamble. I do think that the problem of intentionalism has a compelling solution, or perhaps a Searle-like dissolution. This is indicated, to some extent, by Steven Knapp and Walter Benn Michaels in their faux-naïve deconstruction of Hirsch. It is also suggested by Fish, in his aggressive critique of Posner.[31] Yet all of these theorists fail (in my opinion) to draw the conclusions of their own arguments. As a result, they struggle in the hermeneutic mire. Only Gadamer can help us to firmer ground. I will attempt to explain how at the end of this discussion; which, however, must be deferred to the theoretical sections of subsequent chapters.

For now, I must turn from the theoretical to the critical. Here, too, I am on firmer, or at least more familiar, territory. I began this chapter with the *SA*-debate because that debate devolves very clearly on Samson's intention, understood as the real or probative form of his speech-act. I will continue by arguing, via Milton's *Mask at Ludlow Castle*, that such strong intentionalism (because that is what it is) is inimical to Milton's depictions of the ideal exoteric conscience. Strong intentionalism consists in an interpretative penetration from outward appearance to an underlying or inward reality, which wholly determines the appearance while remaining wholly discrete from it. In other words, strong intentionalism is esoteric, and potentially Satanic. It is the interpretative theory of the mind as its own place. That is the deductive premise of my argument, which I will pursue through inductive readings of Miltonic drama. Drama is most relevant because it is by definition a performance of minds, and because both of Milton's major (quasi) dramatic works explicitly thematize this performance. I will argue that the dramatic Milton constructs an ideal of exoteric behavior, according to which intentional secrets must be displayed for all to see. The one thing that Milton's dramatic heroes must never attempt is the one thing that most critics assume to be normative: namely, a retreat from outward expression to inward and secret experience. This argument constitutes a characterological and narratological analogue to the authorial model I constructed in my last chapter. Bringing the argument to a conclusion will take up both this and the next chapter, where I will move from *A Mask* back to *Samson*, and from intention (with-a-t) to intension (with-an-s): from Milton's exoteric conception of minds to his exoteric conception of words.

---

[30]   The example is traditional. Knapp and Michaels suggest the absurd version in "Against Theory 2: Hermeneutics and Deconstruction," *Critical Inquiry* 14 (Autumn 1987): 49–68.

[31]   See Fish, "Working on the Chain Gang: Interpretation in Law and Literature," and "Don't Know Much About the Middle Ages: Posner on Law and Literature," both in Fish's *Doing What Comes Naturally*, pp. 87-102 and 294314, respectively.

A Mask at Ludlow Castle: **Walls of Glass**

I begin with Milton's first major performance-work, his aristocratic commission of 1634.[32] The rhetoric of virtue in *A Mask at Ludlow Castle [Comus]* has been very widely interpreted as "reformist" or "Puritan."[33] I propose a less political view, less dependent on esoteric decoding. The masque's fundamental concern (it seems to me) is not cultural revolution, but casuistical performance. Its overriding rubrics are not, or not only, "chastity" and "temperance," but critically include "conscience" and "virtuous mind." With that suggestion I am of course touching on the vexed topic of early-modern inwardness, which has been treated by sophisticated readers of *Comus*.[34] As far as I can tell, however, the masque's specific rhetoric of inwardness has not been understood; and this because its casuistical profile has not been understood.

Inwardness is mooted from the beginning of the Ludlow piece. The Lady, lost in a wood, enters looking for "late Wassailers" – whom she is "loath / To meet," but thinks may be able to "inform [her] feet" (179, 177–178, 180). Contradictory impulses project characterological perspective, and thus the Lady starts to talk about her mind. "Why they came not back," she says of her foraging brothers, "is now the labour of my thoughts" (191–192). "A thousand fantasies," she later complains, "begin to throng into my memory" (205–206). Mental gesticulating, however, is quickly terminated in the young woman's monologue; an inward retreat is offered only in order to be renounced. "These thoughts may startle well," she observes, "but not astound / The vertuous mind, that ever walks attended / By a strong siding champion Conscience" (210–212).

Conscience, it is important to note, walks beside the mind. There it is, evidently, able to protect the mind. From her unseen companion, the Lady immediately derives her prophylactic solecism of faith, hope and Chastity (213–215). She gets a vision of the masque's Attendant Spirit, a "glistring Guardian" that God would send to protect her "if need were" (219). She even secures meteorological confirmation for her suddenly confident talk. "Was I deceiv'd," she asks, looking skyward, "or did a sable cloud / Turn forth her silver lining on the night? / I did not err," she

---

[32]   Citations from John Milton, *Poems, etc. upon Several Occasions* (London, 1673), parenthesized by line number in the body of my text.

[33]   See Leah S. Marcus, "The Earl of Bridgewater's Legal Life: Notes toward a Political Reading of *Comus*," in J. Martin Evans (ed.), *John Milton: Twentieth-Century Perspectives, Volume 2: The Early Poems* (New York, 2003), pp. 297–307, and *The Politics of Mirth: Jonson, Herrick, Milton, Marvell, and the Defense of Old Holiday Pastimes* (Chicago, 1989); Barbara Lewalski, "Milton's *Comus* and the Politics of Masquing," in David Bevington et al. (eds), *The Politics of the Stuart Court Masque* (Cambridge, 1998), pp. 296–320; Michael Wilding, "Milton's 'A Masque Presented at Ludlow Castle, 1634': Theatre and Politics on the Border," *MQ* 21 (1987): 35–51; Norbrook, "The Reformation of the Masque"; and Maryann McGuire, *Milton's Puritan Masque* (Athens, GA, 1983).

[34]   See Debora Shuger, "'Gums of Glutinous Heat' and the Stream of Consciousness: The Theology of Milton's *Maske*," *Representations* 60 (1997): 1–21; and Katharine Eisaman Maus, *Inwardness and Theater in the English Renaissance* (Chicago, 1995), pp. 198–209.

answers herself, "there does a sable cloud / Turn forth her silver lining on the night" (221–225). The reiterative structure of those lines is not merely a Baroque affectation, any more than is Milton's choice of Echo as addressee for the Lady's subsequent song (276). For the Lady has just outlined a psychology of echoing, doubling, between her "conscience" and her "virtuous mind."

That psychology, as I discussed in my last chapter, is the standard one for seventeenth-century English Protestants. The trope of companionate conscience allows Protestant casuists to explain the mind's judicial intimacy – its excellent compulsion (in their view) to reflexive moral discipline. God is like "the master of a prison," writes William Perkins, sending conscience as a man's keeper, "to follow him alwaies at his heels, and dogge him," and bring him home again "in time convenient."[35] For Jeremy Taylor, conscience must be "guard and guide" not only through morally complex experience, but also through the supercomplex mazes of casuistical theory. These put, Taylor writes, "a wood before your doores, and a labyrinth within the wood, and locks and barrs to every door within that labyrinth."[36] The seventeenth-century conscience is capable of guiding people through their moral pilgrimages and labyrinths and woods because it is (as I have already described) the syllogistic application of *synteresis*. And the conscience that applies *synteresis* can and must be considered distinct from the wandering mind, because it is conceived – through a range of pithy metaphors – as the representative and agent of God himself.

Of course, the conscience is also identical with the inmost mind. In that sense, it is the pilot of our ship; it is "the wagginer in the waggin."[37] Camille Wells Slights and Katharine Eisaman Maus have both cited this aspect of the theory as evidence for the intentionalism of early-modern English psychology. They are correct to note that the theory of conscience protects, in some ways, individual interiority. Slights and Maus are sensitive, however, to the possibility of contradiction between the inward and the outward conceptions of conscience: between the idea that it can be "in the midst of our hearts" and yet "a certain mean between God and man."[38]

Early-modern English Protestants, it seems, perceive no such contradiction. They simply and simultaneously assume that their mind is inside, and that it is outside. Indeed, the inwardness of the mind seems to generate or require external figuration, and then to be explained and protected by that figuration. "Cleare" conscience, writes Geoffrey Whitney, "is like a wall of brasse" (a vitreous catachresis that will be relevant to my discussion below): "Eauen so there by, our liues wee quiet passe."[39] It is only because the conscience generates an external force-field that the mind, internally, can go safely about its business. And it is only because the Lady places

---

[35]   Perkins, *Discourse*, p. 9.

[36]   Taylor, *Ductor*, book 1, pp. viii–ix.

[37]   Perkins, *Discourse*, p. 5.

[38]   See Slights, *Casuistical*, and "Notaries, Sponges, and Looking-glasses: Conscience in Early Modern England," *ELR* 28.2 (1998): 231–246; and Maus, *Inwardness*, pp. 9–22.

[39]   Quoted in Simmonds, "The Conscience in Emblem Literature," p. 318.

her inmost mind beside herself that she can take cover from her fears, as though behind a holographic projection.

One sees how the Lady's trope could be used to support the New Historicist scepticism that Maus and Slights are trying to refute. Since the 1980s, a number of scholars have claimed that early-modern people simply did not have our (alleged) experience of subjective interiority. Either our forbears lacked, *tout court*, an hierarchical discourse of inward and outward experience; or their inward experience was always-already conditioned by outward forces and structures.[40] The first of these claims, as Maus has convincingly demonstrated, is false. The second claim is more interesting, but needs careful articulation. After all, the inwardness of modern people, too, could be explained as a function of their social experiences. The Foucauldian goal of the New Historicist project is, for that matter, to denature bourgeois interiority for all periods.

In this connection, the most important recent work is undoubtedly Ramie Targoff's.[41] Targoff's contribution has been to weigh (carefully), and (convincingly) find wanting, the basic assumption that the Reformation entailed or produced a new social psychology of inwardness and individualism.[42] Even the New Historicist claim of a conditioned or structuralistic inwardness does not dispute that inwardness is newly prominent in the period. Targoff, however, at least for the English context, demonstrates that the Reformation entailed (if anything) a diminution and suppression of individual inwardness. Whereas the Catholic liturgy had allowed and encouraged private and personal devotion – *precisely because* the majority of congregants could not understand the Latin service – mainstream English Protestantism demanded a "collective model of public prayer."[43] And whereas auricular confession had always provided a model for secret communication between the sinner and his Lord, the English church so abhorred secrecy that it sometimes made public confession a prerequisite for communion.[44] The devotional gaze, formerly directed down to the congregant's soul, was now redirected outward and upward, to the communal and intelligible word. Meanwhile, the homely primers and silent prayers that had

---

[40]   For a summary of these views, see Maus, *Inwardness*, pp. 2-3 and 26–34; for a perpetuation of the second of them, see Elizabeth Hanson, *Discovering the Subject in Renaissance England* (Cambridge, 1998).

[41]   See Ramie Targoff, *Common Prayer: Models of Public Devotion in Early Modern England* (Chicago, 2001); and "The Performance of Prayer: Sincerity and Theatricality in Early Modern England," *Representations* 60 (1997): 49–69.

[42]   See Thomas Luxon, *Literal Figures: Puritan Allegory and the Reformation Crisis in Representation* (Chicago, 1995), p. 6. See also David Gay, *The Endless Kingdom: Milton's Scriptural Society* (London, 2002); and Timothy Rosendale, "Milton, Hobbes and the Liturgical Subject," *SEL* 44.1 (2004): 149–172. Compare Beverly Sherry, "A 'Paradise Within' Can Never Be 'Happier Far': Reconsidering the Archangel Michael's Consolation in *PL*," *MQ* 37.2 (2003): 77–91.

[43]   Targoff, *Common*, p. 28.

[44]   Targoff, *Common*, pp. 32–33.

been exemplary for Catholics were denounced and destroyed, even criminalized, by the Protestant regime.[45] The result is an ideal of Christian subjectivity in which individual interiority "is less a benefit ... than a fault."[46] The early English Protestant heart, in Targoff's account, is not just a secret member. It is also a member's secret, in a club that places a high priority on psychic nakedness.

At the same time, Tudor-Stuart culture seems to have believed that whatever is worn on the outside may end up being secretly or inwardly manifested. For Puritan polemicists, and establishment divines, outward postures matter because they can produce their inward correspondences.[47] That is why, for all sides in the period's liturgical controversies, indifferences like kneeling are anything but indifferent. That is why, for neo-patristic fulminators like Stubbes and Prynne, there is something uniquely horrible about the theatre. The problem with dramatic impersonation is not just that it is hypocritical; inward/outward disjunction is found outside the theatre, too. The problem, rather, is that spectacular hypocrisy, through its mimetic power, tends to produce a foul and post-representational sincerity. Actors become their roles, and the audience becomes the play. *Imitatio*, for this culture, is ethical and behavioral metamorphosis.

Targoff notes that Hamlet, encouraging his repentant mother, addresses her not in the language of the heart, but in the Aristotelian terms of habit: "Refrain tonight," he tells her, "and that shall lend a kind of easiness / To the next abstinence, the next more easy —/ For use almost can change the stamp of nature."[48] Hamlet's "almost" (like the one that trails the dyer's hand [sonnet 111]) may indicate ambivalence about the imitative theory. But Shakespeare's church and culture are "firmly aligned behind it."[49] As James I tells his sons in the *Basilikon Doron*: "press then to shine as far before your people in all virtue and honesty as in greatness of rank *that the use thereof in all your actions may turn with time to a natural habitude in you*."[50] Hypocrisy and sincerity, inwardness and outwardness, change places neatly in such a public and serious statement.

Targoff says relatively little about the origins of her English model. Locating its major confound in the Augustinian psychological tradition, she traces the English renegotiation of that tradition to Tyndale's *Exposition of Matthew*.[51] In my opinion, going back to Calvin would be more effective (and would draw out the contrast Targoff finds between Tyndale and Luther). I say this not only because Calvin underwrites English Reformation theology, but also because the Gospel emphasis on

---

[45]   Targoff, *Common*, p. 26.

[46]   Targoff, *Common*, p. 11.

[47]   Targoff, *Common*, pp. 10–13.

[48]   *Hamlet, Prince of Denmark*, in *The Complete Works of Shakespeare*, ed. David Bevington (New York, 1997), 3.4.172–175. All further citations of Shakespeare will be from this edition and will be parenthesized, as appropriate, in the body of my text.

[49]   Targoff, *Common*, p. 4.

[50]   James I, *True Law*, p. 154. My italics.

[51]   Targoff, *Common*, pp. 7–9.

secret prayer (as I discussed in my last chapter) is treated by Calvin precisely as an imperative to public and exoteric devotion. This point seems to be generally missed, so may be worth restating: Calvin does not propose mental secrecy as the measure of correct theism. On the contrary, he proposes that secret prayer be measured by its public and outward iterations, because only those iterations provide the Christian with a test of his own sincerity. The good church-goer (to put this one more way) will not necessarily be the one who prays in private. But the prayer-in-private will always be good if he is already the good church-goer, who cannot help but speak the word of God wherever he goes. This is the model of Milton's Jeremiah, who must get out the fire that is burning in his bones (*CP* 1.801–804). It is the model of Milton's Abdiel, who must denounce Satan, though an army sit ready to silence him (*PL* 5.803–907). And it is the model (as I will argue in my next chapter) of Samson, who only recovers his dignity when he moves toward expression. The logic involves performance as the *a fortiori* proof of an intentional state, in which one was "*weary of forbearing, and could not stay*" (*CP* 1.803).

A similar logic, re: the problem of election, was canonized by Beza as the "practical syllogism." According to this familiar argument, sanctification (pious behavior) is not sufficient evidence for justification (the effect of election); but since the justified are invariably sanctified, sanctification seems a pretty good bet. The Bezan view was adopted (though rarely explicitly) by the English in what is sometimes called practical Calvinism. In this form, it ran to – but not over – the radical margins of English Protestantism. (Anne Hutchinson's refusal of the "good bet" argument, and her insistence that election was a totally inaccessible intentional mystery, were what led Puritan Plymouth to try and exile her as Antinomian.[52]) Indeed, while Targoff focuses on mainstream sixteenth-century Protestantism, much of her model holds for seventeenth-century groups that we call Puritan (but not sectarian). Public confession, for example, more-or-less defines Congregationalism.[53] And all such Targoffian shibboleths can be traced to Genevan soteriology, and to the outwardly-tested inwardness that tends to emerge from that soteriology.

Casuistry provides the technical discourse of this psychic heritage. In part, I think, the English version of the theory confirms Targoff's work; in part, qualifies it. As I have discussed, not even the most tutioristic casuistry denies individual inwardness. On the contrary, it guarantees such inwardness, precisely by way of exposing the mind to divine surveillance. Conscience is exactly and only what renders the created mind secret from all other created minds. Yet God's indwelling eye, and only God's indwelling eye, is what makes mind mind, and conscience conscience. The theory of conscience, in other words, predicates social secrecy (which it provides) on spiritual exposure (which it demands). As Protestant casuists are very aware, dissonance is immanent within this somewhat paradoxical structure. Rebellion against casuistical

52   See David H. Hall (ed.), *The Antinomian Controversy, 1636–1638* (Durham and London, 1990).
53   See Edmund S. Morgan, *Visible Saints: The History of a Puritan Idea* (Ithaca and London, 1963).

surveillance – making, or trying to make, the mind its own place – is an available and appalling Satanic reaction.

Available and admirable, however, is the opposite response: submitting to the surveillance, above and beyond its spiritual requirements, by socially opening the secret mind – making it everybody else's place. After all, it is really no big deal to offer God the access to one's inwardness that He already has. What is a big deal is to offer other human beings the access to one's inwardness that they do not have. One turns the private into the public, the mental into the social, and claims the moral credit that is appropriate to the trick. Maneuvers of this kind do not consist (*pace* New Historicist subjectivity-sceptics) in a simple absence of inwardness. Neither do they consist (*pace* post-New Historicist subjectivity-realists) in a simple reliance on inwardness. They consist, rather, in an abjuration of inwardness: a rhetorical turning of the psyche, not without discomfort, inside out. The abjuration is predicated on a normative assumption of inwardness, but precisely as a moral redoubt that can be supra-normatively renounced.

I argued in my last chapter for Milton's self-presentational employment of this move. His polemical autobiographies articulate Bacon's trope of the naked mind, "the companion of innocence and simplicity, as once upon a time the naked body was."[54] At the same time – and this is where the trope is highlighted as supra-normative – Milton loves to apologize for his mental exhibitionism. In the *Apology* for Smectymnuus, the *Reason of Church-Government*, and the *Second Defense of the English People*, authorial memoirs appear within elaborate exculpatory frameworks. By the *Defense of Himself against Alexander More*, apology for autobiography has outcrowded autobiography: the hottest parts of the text answer More's preceding charge that Milton has talked too much, and too intimately, about himself. Yet in defending his exhibitionism, Milton explicitly repeats his exhibitionism. Sometimes (as we have seen) he repeats it in exactly the terms of its prior iterations. This is not to say that Milton is hypocritical or incoherent, but that he charts his rhetorical course through a secrecy that demands exposure, while retaining its moral and rhetorical value as secrecy.

Milton is always careful to fortify the privacy that he is renouncing, the intimacy of the apparel that he treats as outerwear. In the *Second Defense*, he describes "blissfully" re-entering obscurity after his travels, "willingly" leaving the Caroline crisis to the proper authorities (*CP* 4.621). The move is reasonable enough, for a poet who (in the narrative) is not yet a civil servant – but it is quite inconsistent with Milton's previous autobiographical claim, that he came home from Italy specifically for the crisis. "I thought it base to travel abroad," he has just told us, "while my fellow-citizens at home were fighting for liberty" (*CP* 4.620). The incongruity of Milton's long march into seclusion, his struggle in "tumultuous times" to find a house for himself and his books, is the sign (I suggest) of an overriding rhetorical imperative: the imperative of the poet's privacy, from which he will produce publicity. "This

54 Bacon, *The New Organon*, p. 14.

service of mine, between private walls, I freely gave," Milton goes on to write of his post-Italian tracts (*CP* 4.627). It is the walls that turn the tracts into gestures of authorial exposure, even as authorial exposure provides the tracts with their claim of credibility.

A similar juxtaposition of secrecy and openness can be traced in Milton's non-reflexive polemics. In *A Treatise of Civil Power* (1659), for example, Milton deconstructs Pauline subordination of the conscience to the magistrate (Romans 13:11). He does so, however, by theorizing the conscience as always-already the sternest possible magistrate. Precisely because he is "all spiritual and to outward force not lyable," "the inward man" finds in himself the highest possible civility (*CP* 7.257). In *The Reason of Church-Government* (1642), similarly, "inward reverence" is a "radical moisture" which "hath in it a most restraining and powerful abstinence, to start back, and glob itself upward from the mixture of any ungenerous and unbeseeming motion" (*CP* 1.842). Hermetic separation of the inward man from his outward form is exactly what prevents him, even when "feare of infamy" is absent, "from doing or imagining that which is sinful though in deepest secrecy" (ibid). The very property that would seem to guarantee Derrida's "right to the secret" becomes the property that mandates renunciation of that right.

In short, the Miltonic abjuration of inwardness is dialectic and contrapuntal. It is a play of opposing forces, eventuating in a Baroque swirl of movement. Readers (including, regrettably, Targoff) who notice *only* Milton's emphasis on inwardness miss this point.[55] For Milton seems to reckon, as a matter of rhetorical strategy, that his readers (1) assume the normativity of individual intentionality, and (2) recognize the exemplarity of individual extensionality. That is to say, Milton counts on both the legacy of outwardness described by Targoff, and on an ongoing cultural resistance to that legacy. Per his sartorial metaphor in the *Apology* for Smectymnuus, he turns himself inside out, passing from (1) to (2). His is by no means a unique strategy for the period, but has affinities with the books of secrets and other exotericisms reviewed in my Introduction. As I will now discuss, the strategy also hews close to the social-psychological heart of early seventeenth-century English culture.

Windows on the Soul

In the *Anatomy of Melancholy*, Robert Burton laments: "I have layd my selfe open (I know it) in this Treatise, turned mine inside outward, I shall be censured, I doubt not."[56] Burton's image is so close to Milton's "turn the inside outward" as to look like its original. Yet Burton anticipates punishment where Milton hopes for credit.

---

[55]   Targoff, *Common*, pp. 36–37 and 48–49.

[56]   Robert Burton, *The Anatomy of Melancholy*, eds Thomas C. Faulkner, Nicolas K. Kiessling and Rhonda L. Blair (Oxford, 1989), p. 13. See Jean-Marie Goulemot, "Literary Practices: Publicizing the Private," in Chartier (ed.) and Goldhammer (trans.), *Passions of the Renaissance*, pp. 362–396.

The credit, meanwhile, is to be paid in the same currency as the fine: it is because Burton's sense of the proprieties remains valid throughout the period that Milton can offer his own performance as daringly virtuosic. Again: Alexander More thinks it quite proper to close the door of the confessional in his readers' faces. Milton excoriates that move as an echo of the old religion. But those turgid echoes, lingering through the century, are the necessary background to his own clear Protestant tones. If seventeenth-century English Protestants could respond to the demand for "common prayer," they could also recall the Elizabethan caution – directed, there can be no doubt after Targoff, to followers of the old dispensation – against making a window into men's souls. Elizabeth herself may or may not have expressed such a sentiment. But Tudor-Stuart culture believed that she had.[57] And if Milton's rhetorical strategy makes any sense at all, there can be little doubt that many of his compatriots accepted the Calvinist demand only along with the Elizabethan assurance. It is by flouting the Elizabethan qualification, showing that he doesn't need it, that Milton seeks the wonder and praise appropriate to a moral contortionism. He demonstrates both his commonality with his fellow English Protestants, and his exceptionality among them in their terms.

Peculiarly relevant here is a "proverbial hyperbole" that Erasmus codified with reference to Lucian and Plato. Glossing the adage *Momo satisfacere, et similia* (to satisfy Momus, and the like), Erasmus relates the following tale about Momus, the Olympian god of fault-finding:

> Minerva, Neptune and Vulcan were competing with each other for the prize of the best craftsmanship. Each produced an outstanding specimen of his art: Neptune created a bull, Minerva planned a horse, Vulcan put together a man. Momus was chosen a judge of the contest and assessor of the workmanship. He inspected the work of each one; apart from the deficiencies he had noticed in the works of the others, he particularly complained that in the making of the man the craftsman had not added some windows or openings in the breast, to allow an insight into what was hidden in the heart, which he had made full of caverns and winding sinuosities.[58]

To "satisfy Momus," then, is to face the severest possible judgment without misgivings, on the grounds that one has nothing untoward to be judged. For Erasmus, *Momo satisfacere* is important primarily as an example of hyperbole, which fascinates him; he ends his gloss by referring the reader to the theoretical introduction of the *Adages*. For the early-modern English, however, the story of Momus' window had moral and political charges. To this standard (in qualification of Targoff) England's Elizabeth had said that she would *not* hold her subjects.

Burton mentions Momus no less than three times in the introduction to his *Anatomy*. The first is a passing reference in the poem *ad librum suum* (25), but

---

[57]   Francis Bacon, "Certain Observations Made Upon a Libel Published this Present Year 1592," cited in Maus, *Inwardness*, p. 83.

[58]   See *Collected Works of Erasmus*, eds Sir R.A.B. Mynors et al., trans. Margaret Mann Phillips et al. (43 vols, Toronto, 1982), vol. 31, p. 449.

the second immediately precedes the lament for exhibitionism that I quoted above. "Wer'st thou all scoffes and flouts, a very *Momus*," Democritus jr. tells an imaginary critic, "Then we our selves, thou canst not say worse of us."[59] (Burton then indicates the Erasmian heritage of his figure by citing the arch-humanist on the peevishness of men's judgments.[60]) The association of the original Democritus with Momus had already been made by Leon Battista Alberti, in his comic neo-Latin romp *Momus* (1520).[61] As Burton goes on to show (though without reference to his Italian predecessor), the relationship between the dissector and the would-be glazier is by no means antagonistic. In the last, longest, and most significant of his references, Burton wonders aloud how the Abderan scientist might have used the critical god's imaginary window. The notion brings to crescendo a ludic jeremiad:

> To see horses ride in a Coach, men draw it; Dogges devoure their Masters; Towers build Masons; Children rule; Old men goe to Schoole; Women weare the Breeches; Sheepe demolish Townes, devoure men, &c. And in a word, the world turned upside downward ... But these are obvious to sense, triviall and well knowne, easie to be discerned. How would *Democritus* have beene moved, had he seene the secrets of their hearts? If every man had a window in his brest, which *Momus* would have had in *Vulcans* man ... what a deale of laughter would it have afforded? He should have seen Windmills in one mans head, an Hornets nest in another.[62]

Momus' window would be like "*Gyges* invisible ring, or some rare perspective glasse." It would allow Democritus to observe "foolish vowes, hopes, fears, and wishes"; "*cubiculorum obductas fores recludere, et secreta cordium penetrare* [to open the locked doors of bed-chambers, and penetrate the secrets of the heart]." The last fantasy reinscribes, with a significance that will shortly become clear, Cyprian's *Ad Donatum*. The original speaks of conscience, but Burton speaks of the heart.[63] Overall, while Burton's other references to Momus are uncomfortable and defensive, here he cries out in favor of the ultra-Democritean exoteric scheme. As in Milton's self-eviscerations, the window in the torso becomes a renovative moral ideal. It is ideal precisely to the extent that it is difficult to, well, stomach.

That brings me to the period's most important proponent of transparent innards. As Kevin Sharpe has shown, James I valorized a quasi-naïve openness.[64] Without exactly cancelling the Elizabethans' anti-panoptic homily, James loudly disapproved of intentional secrecy – and presented himself as living proof that one could and should do without it. In part, the king was moved by strong-intentionalist trends

---

59   Burton, *Anatomy*, p. 12.

60   Burton, *Anatomy*, p. 13.

61   See Leon Battista Alberti, *Momus*, trans. Sarah Knight, eds Virginia Brown and Sarah Knight (Cambridge, MA, 2003), pp. 213, 227–229, 245–253, and 261.

62   Burton, *Anatomy*, pp. 54–55.

63   Burton, *Anatomy*, p. 55.

64   Sharpe, "Private Conscience ... James VI and I," in his *Remapping Early Modern England*.

that seemed to be threatening the stability of his reign and the unity of his church. Modern political theorists were offering principled accounts of dissembling; James denounced them, both cynical Machiavelli and "proud inconstant Lipsius."[65] Meanwhile, the "precisian" forcers of ecclesiastic controversy were undermining the church from one side, just as Jesuits and recusants were undermining it from the other.[66] Typically, and importantly, James associates Puritans with Catholics on the basis of a mutual commitment to mental reservation. Whether or not Puritans (however defined) actually had that commitment is a matter for debate; but that it served James politically to claim that they did is proved *ipso facto*. Like Burton, and like Milton, James perceives his culture's moral high road, both difficult and excellent, to lie through an uncompromising exotericism.

"A king will have need to use secrecy in many things," he tells Prince Henry in the *Basilikon Doron*, "but yet behave yourself so in your greatest secrets as ye need not be ashamed suppose they were all proclaimed at the Mercat Cross."[67] The king's secrecy, though a necessary expedient, should be no secrecy at all. Instead it should be a gloriously empty category, always-already made public. Rather than oppressing his people or seeking stratagems to control them, the Stuart ruler should draw them after him with his excellence and honesty. He should take care "so to rule as may justly stop their mouths from all such idle and unreverent speeches, and so to prop the weal of your people with provident care for their good government, that justly Momus himself may have no ground to grudge at."[68]

Momus, via Elizabeth, provides James with his favorite symbol for perfect royal probity. The king offers his speeches and writings as a "fair and chrystal mirror" of his soul; "a chrystal window in my breast wherein all my people might see the secretest thoughts of my heart."[69] That the king's imaginary implant is a mirror *or* a window accords with the phenomenology of glass in early-modern English literature. "Tis much that glass should be," writes Donne, "As all-confessing, and through-shine as I; / Tis more, that it shows thee to thee, / And clear reflects thee to thine eye."[70] The surface that reflects also refracts, making the spectator's image a function of her lover's transparency. In James' case, the people are to look through his clear breast and see that his heart is good. They are to see, moreover, that its goodness basically consists in its transparency. How else would it be possible for James to offer the view? Finally, the king's subjects are to recognize their own image, their own transformative social and cultural ideal, in the king's window/mirror and their own looking in/at it.

65 See McCrea, *Constant Minds*, pp. 24 and 174–175.
66 See Burton, *Anatomy*, pp. 40–41.
67 James I, *True Law*, p. 158.
68 James I, *True Law*, p. 127.
69 Sharpe, "Private Conscience ... James VI and I," p. 161.
70 Donne, "A Valediction: Upon My Name in the Window," in *John Donne's Poetry: Authoritative Texts, Criticisms*, ed. Arthur L. Clements (New York and London, 1992), lines 7–10.

Thus James does not propose to implant windows in his subjects, but he does propose to render them transparent by the light of his own transparency. Indeed – *contra* M.H. Abrams' canonical distinction between classical and Romantic aesthetics – the mirror of transparency is supposed to be radiant as well as reflective.[71] Abrams opposes mirror (classical) to lamp (Romantic); but James tells his sons that the king's glass should be both "a lamp and mirror to your company, giving light to your servants to walk in the path of virtue."[72] It must be so, because only the radiant heart of virtue could make the Momus-scope commodious in the first place. Conversely, willingness for the scope is exoteric proof of one's esoteric luminosity. It testifies "inward uprightness" "by the outward using." It sets forth the "vive image" of the king's "virtuous disposition."[73]

Of course, James was much too sensible to practice what he preached. He drank his kingdom dry while sternly recommending temperance; he was almost certainly a sodomite (whatever exactly that meant in the period) who called sodomy an unforgivable sin. (Happily, there is no evidence that he kept a pack of cigarettes in the garage.) His son and heir, however, seems to have lacked his father's rather remarkable capacity for irony. For Charles, satisfying Momus was a real and achievable goal – in his personal life, if not in his management of policy. That, at least, was the overwhelming ideology of Caroline culture. Thus in Carew's *Coelum Brittanicum* (1633), the married chastity of king and queen is so mimetically efficacious that it has transformed the Olympian gods themselves. "Your exemplar life," the royal couple is told,

Hath not alone transfus'd a zealous heat
Of imitation through your virtuous Court ...
But the aspiring flame hath kindled heaven;
Th'immortall bosomes burne with emulous fires,
Iove rivalls your great vertues, Royall Sir,
And *Iuno*, Madam, your attractive graces;
He his wild lusts, her raging jealousies
She lays aside, and through th'Olympique hall,
As yours doth here, their great Example spreads. (212)

Ethical imitation, we are told, has already worked in the Caroline court. Indeed, it is enacted in the plan of Carew's *Poems* itself, which moves from pornographic lyrics to the hushed *renovatio* of the masque. Now, in a Neoplatonic reversal of classically Platonic mimesis, the earthly representation of a transformed Olympus transforms its original. The imitative mechanism of this achievement is, by now, utterly familiar: it was in the "chrystall mirrour of your reigne," Charles is told, that Jove "view'd himselfe," and "found his loathsome staines" (212).

---

[71]   See M.H. Abrams, *The Mirror and the Lamp: Romantic Theory and the Critical Tradition* (New York, 1953), pp. 32–33.
[72]   James I, *True Law*, p. 143.
[73]   James I, *True Law*, p. 174.

The speaker here is Mercury, but he is soon partnered on stage by none other than Momus. Initially, the fault-finding god functions as a kind of anti-Hermes, considerably more scurrilous than he is in Carew's source, Giordano Bruno's *Spaccio de la Bestia Trionfante*. However – like Carew's lubricious visions, like the Olympian lusts – Momus' causticness exists here only to be laid aside. As the masque proceeds, it is Momus who takes moral command, directing Mercury's purge of the "adulterate" zodiac (221). And it is Momus who relates Jove's inscription, on his bed-chamber door, of "CARLOMARIA," "to eternize the memory of that great example of Matrimoniall union which he derives from hence" (220).

In short, the Caroline version of exotericist ideology differs from its Jacobean antecedent only by forgetting its own ideologicality. Momus can be satisfied, and has been. Erasmus' hyperbole, James' conceit, becomes Charles' absolutely naturalized and anti-ironic claim. There is one technical alteration of the discourse, however. James' pectoral window is a symbol of his conscience, which St. Bernard called the "spotless mirror of the divine majesty," and Jeremy Taylor will call "the looking-glass of the soul."[74] Charles, to be sure, relies a great deal on claims of conscience, but Caroline exotericism is also expressed (as in Burton's revision of Cyprian) through the language of the heart. Relevant here is the Petrarchan imagery mocked by Donne, and recuperated, in their different ways, by both Crashaw and Herbert. But perhaps more relevant is the work of William Harvey, whose association with the Caroline court was both public and intimate.

"The heart of animals is the foundation of their life," Harvey tells his "Most Illustrious and Indomitable Prince" in the *de motu cordis* (1628), "the sovereign of everything within them, the sun of their microcosm ...The King, in like manner, is the foundation of his kingdom, the sun of the world around him, the heart of the republic, the fountain whence all power, all grace doth flow." The "prime mover in the body of man," therefore, also serves as an "emblem" of the king's "sovereign power," and as a "Divine example of his functions."[75] In the *Anatomical Exercitations Concerning the Generation of Living Creatures* (1653), where the good doctor is compared to Momus' old friend Democritus, Harvey describes examining, at Charles' behest and in his company, a young nobleman whose heart had been rendered externally visible by a poorly-healed chest wound. This person, surely, is a prodigy of *Momo satisfacere* (even though, in the spirit of the new science, Charles and Harvey find the heart "deprived of the *Sense* of *Feeling*").[76] The old anti-Machiavellian ideal

---

74 Taylor, *Ductor*, 1.1–2.
75 William Harvey, "To the Most Illustrious and Indomitable Prince Charles," in *Exercitatio Anatomica de Motu Cordis*, trans. Chauncey D. Leake (Springfield, IL, 1958), p. 3. See also Robert A. Erickson, "The Phallic Heart: William Harvey's *The Motion of the Heart* and 'The Republick of Literature'," in Erickson's *The Language of the Heart, 1600–1750* (Philadelphia, 1997), pp. 61–88.
76 See Jonathan Sawday, "The Transparent Man and the King's Heart," in Claire Jowitt and Diane Watt (eds), *The Arts of 17th-Century Science: Representations of the Natural World in European and North American Culture* (Aldershot, Hants, 2002), pp. 12–24.

of a heart that "stands o'th'outside" can finally appear in the flesh (so to speak) through the new anatomy.[77] Moreover, as Harvey offers his book to a "Commonwealth surrounded with intestine troubles," the royal sharer in that anatomy recalls the whole ideology of Stuart exotericism.[78]

Porno-Platonic

Milton's Comus offers a "cordial" julep when he seeks to transform the Lady (672). With this observation I do not mean to suggest that Comus is a subversive Charles, but that Comus' elixir is a subverted Caroline metaphor. It is a draught of alienated inwardness, a portable and potable heart. Meanwhile, the vessel in which Comus carries his beverage recalls the period's orthodox fascination with visible inwardness. Critics typically talk about the enchanter's "cup," but that is not quite right. Comus' mother Circe, the Attendant Spirit tells us, carried a "charmed Cup" (51). Her son's vessel, however, is usually described in the masque as a "Crystal Glass" (65). He enters for the first time "with a Charming Rod in one hand, his Glass in the other" (92–93). At the beginning of the temptation scene he offers the Lady "his Glass" (658–659). The brothers are urged to "break his glass" (651), and at the end of the temptation scene they "wrest his Glass out of his hand" (813–814). The enchanter's first imperative to the Lady is not "drink" but "see" that "here be all the pleasures / That fancy can beget on youthfull thoughts" (668–669). He further instructs her to "behold" his julep, "that flames, and dances in his crystal bounds" (672–673). In short, the compound object that Comus urges on the Lady is a synthesis of two great Tudor-Stuart imageries of the exoteric. It is the enchanter's heart in a glass, and the mirror of his soul.

Can a drinking-glass be a looking-glass? Comus' intensely Shakespearean phrasing – alluding (for the most part) to the first dozen or so sonnets – suggests that it can. Conflating window with mirror, as Donne and James do, is child's play in the period. The real trick is the third conflation: mirror + window + vessel. With the conceptual binary of looking in a mirror at oneself / looking through a window at another, Shakespeare combines the notion of one person as the "vial" of another (6.3). "Thou art thy mother's glass," he tells the dubious young man,

> and she in thee
> Calls back the lovely April of her prime;
> So thou through windows of thine age shalt see,
> Despite of wrinkles, this thy golden time. (3.9–12)

The mother's glass is a window, through which she sees herself playing in eternal spring. It is a mirror, in which she sees her own wrinkled face superimposed on her

---

[77]   Cyril Tourneur, *The Revenger's Tragedy*, ed. R.A. Foakes (Manchester and New York, 1996), 3.5.11.

[78]   William Harvey, *Anatomical Exercitations Concerning the Generation of Living Creatures* (London, 1653), Epistle Dedicatory.

son's young and lovely one. And, finally, it is a vessel, in which she finds a summer's distillation, a "liquid pris'ner pent in walls of glass" (5.10). In the glass, she enjoys the prisoner and calls back lovely April. Idiomatically, she is in her cups. The nymph Sabrina will enter *Comus* through similarly polysemous imagery: called from under a *"glassy"* wave (861), she offers "vial'd liquors" from a broken-bottle chariot (847), *"thick set"* with agate and emerald (893–894). And indeed the apparition of Sabrina – a virgin turned into the river of her highly-favored virginity – is a liquid mirror-image of the Lady's "vertuous mind."

The semantic fuzziness of glass *qua* mirror is such that James, in asking his subjects to look through his pectoral window, is also asking them to see their reflections in their king's conscience. The implications of Harveian heart-talk are similarly communal: the king is the heart that should beat throughout the commonwealth, and his subjects should remain in unity with him through a kind of symbolic transplant. The operation that Comus wishes to perform on the Lady is thus morally perverse, but formally orthodox. He is asking the Lady to "see" the glass he holds as her own image, and the "cordial" that flames and dances therein as the life-blood of her master-spirit. He is inviting her to "be wise, and taste" (813), to accept psychological identification with him through gustatory participation in him. The artifactuality of Comus' vessel/window/mirror invokes the full power of Tudor-Stuart mimesis, its placing of esoteric efficacy under the exoteric sign. The Lady is in exactly the position feared by Stubbes and Prynne, subjected to the evil models that are the nightmare of *imitatio*. Finally, the command to drink is put through an epanaleptic mirroring that inscribes both a paranoid mimesis, and the synaesthesia of seeing and drinking, mind and mouth. For "be wise" and "taste" both translate the imperative of *sapere*, such that "be wise and taste" translates *"sape et sape."* This is in fact the quintessential Miltonic Anglo-Latin pun: "taste," the fallen Adam tells the fallen Eve in *Paradise Lost*, is "of Sapience no small part" (9.1017, 1018).

The Lady is not moved – figuratively, or literally. Her physical immobility confronts all commentators on the temptation scene. Yet if most critics find themselves asking why the young paragon can't get up, I am compelled to wonder why she doesn't lie right down. After all, she has no haemony to protect her, and Comus' multivalent magic is, evidently, powerful. Indeed, if I am right about the overdetermination of the glass, it would seem that the Lady ought to be transformed just by her reflection in the enchanter's desires. Drinking the julep would be a welcome but unnecessary variation. Perhaps, by that very argument, I am wrong about the glass: drinking is what matters, and the Lady does not drink. But in that case, I have to ask why Comus doesn't simply force her. Drinking is a bodily function. Comus has asserted and demonstrated control over his victim's body – and she has explicitly and contemptuously surrendered it. The freedom of her "minde" is predicated, she claims, on the discarding of her "rinde" (663–664). The latter Comus has imprisoned, and threatens to petrify. Since he has performed the first, we tend to believe that he can follow through, if he wishes, and perform the second. Now, he has also subjected his "corporal" victim to the carnal temptation of the glass.

This he offers, by the end of the scene, very urgently. Why can't he follow through in this case, too, pressing the magic object to his victim's objectified lips? They are "vermeil-tinctur'd" (752), in the best tradition of Petrarchan emblazoning; the enchanter is carnally-obsessed, and the Lady can therefore defeat him by giving him what he wants. So why can't he take possession? Why can't he pour a wanton heart into that unwilling body?

The answer, of course, is that he seeks his victim's consent. He wants her to want him. In more formal language, he desires a transformation in her intentional state. That the transformation does not occur – that the Lady's mind does not change – provides my argument in this chapter with its problematic crux. For Comus is trying to seduce the Lady through strictly extensional or exoteric means, waving a mimetic template in his victim's face. The failure of this technique suggests its functional limit: an object, a signifier, has no necessary effect in and of itself, no matter how culturally-(over)determined it may be. Absent an intentional and subjective validation of the sign, the latter remains arbitrary, a cigar just a cigar. Obviously the alternative view would be for some kind of magical or emanationist semiotics, which, in period terms, we tend to call "idolatrous." Equally obviously, everything I have been saying about early-modern English mimesis – everything about the transformative power of the "outward using" – conflicts with the view, both venerable and current, that early-modern English Protestant culture obsessively opposed idolatry, at a theoretical or semiotic level.[79] Accordingly, the Lady's impassivity before Comus' mimesis may well count as iconoclastic resistance. Such a reading would accord with the standard view of the temptation scene, making it a prime site of religious reform.

Meanwhile, the Lady's immanent retreat suggests nothing less than an early-modern version of strong intentionalism. If not a genuine Cartesian dualism, the Lady certainly invokes the Augustinian tradition of inwardness, which Targoff found English Protestantism renegotiating. Her whole move thus contradicts, arguably, the Targoffian exotericism that I have traced to Calvin, and have constructed as basic to early-seventeenth-century English Protestant culture. Similarly, it contradicts the exoteric casuistry that I have called the moral high-road of that culture, and have mapped onto Milton's rhetorical self-presentations. The conscience that the Lady adduced, earlier, as without her because it was within her – Whitney's clear wall of brasse – is not mentioned at all in the temptation scene. It has reverted to its simple identity with the virtuous mind, which the Lady is forced to claim as the inward and singular crucible of her being. Under pressure, under threat, she gets no help at all from her "glistring Guardian." She does not call on her tableau of virtues, or defend herself by the "strong siding champion." All she does is speak – and that reluctantly, and artificially. "Fain would I somthing say," she says, "yet to what end?

Thou hast nor Ear, nor Soul to apprehend
The sublime notion, and high mystery

---

[79]   See David Hawkes, *Idols of the Marketplace: Idolatry and Commodity Fetishism in English Literature, 1580–1680* (New York, 2001).

That must be utter'd to unfold the sage
And serious doctrine of Virginity,
And thou art worthy that thou shouldst not know
More happiness then this thy present lot.
Enjoy your dear Wit, and gay Rhetorick
That hath so well been taught her dazling fence,
Thou art not fit to hear thyself convinc't;
Yet should I try, the uncontrouled worth
Of this pure cause would kindle my rap't spirits
To such a flame of sacred vehemence,
That dumb things would be mov'd to sympathize,
And the brute Earth would lend her nerves, and shake,
Till all thy magick structures rear'd so high,
Were shatter'd into heaps o're thy false head. (783–799)

This speech articulates a traditional Christian rhetoric of plainness. It does so forcefully enough, however, to sound like special pleading. The Orphic threat, in particular, of rhyming Comus' palace to the ground is the kind of claim that must be tested to be true. It is as if Samson, while still at the mill, said that he could kill many Philistines if he wanted to. As a matter of fact, Samson does say things like that – but he proves as good as his word. The Lady says only that she will not speak hers. Even her virginity is immanent here, a *doctrine* that Comus is not fit to embrace. Samson's speech-act at least gives us something to work with, but the Lady expresses only her abjuration of expression. She rests in the secret interiority that no expressive glass can reach.

This attitude does not only contradict the Lady's earlier exotericism. It also, and more seriously, contradicts her Elder Brother. The latter sets out the exoteric position in his famous lecture to Second Brother, who has spoken of his sister's excellence as requiring esoteric concealment. An unprotected maiden, the Spenserian lad has asserted, is like a miser's treasure spread out "by an out-laws den" (399). The "Hesperian Tree" of beauty, "laden with blooming gold," is safe only under "dragon watch with uninchanted eye" (393–394, 395). Elder Brother, however, replaces outward terms with inward ones, while explaining that excellent inwardness is really the ultimate outwardness. To his brother's wild imagining of "Savage hunger, or of Savage heat" (358), he opposes the "constant mood" of the Lady's "calm thoughts" (371). To an image of the Lady hopelessly wandering in darkness (350–355), Elder Brother offers a counter-image of her as her own lantern. "Vertue could see to do what vertue would," he says, "by her own radiant light, though Sun and Moon / Were in the flat Sea sunk" (373–375). That watery apocalypse leads into an image of virtuous radiance as a contrast (classically Miltonic) between regenerate and reprobate mind:

He that has light within his own cleer brest
May sit i'th center, and enjoy bright day,
But he that hides a dark soul, and foul thoughts
Benighted walks under the mid-day Sun;
Himself is his own dungeon. (381–85)

The gist here is not simply that good inwardness is good and bad inwardness is bad. The gist is, rather, that bad inwardness is terminally inward, while good inwardness is paradoxically, or outwardly, so. The crucial phrase, familiar by this point in my discussion, is "clear brest": an anatomical dispensation of moral transparency. There can be no clear breast over a "dark soul, and foul thoughts," because these require darkness and concealment by definition. But a clear breast *is* the definition of the virtuous light within, which creates the propriety and the necessity of its own glorious external manifestation.

Thus chastity, in Elder Brother's formulation, is an inward quality so pure that it becomes radically and aggressively outward: it is a suit of armor, a bow and arrow, a military passport (420–445). The chaste soul is attended by "a thousand liveried Angels," who "cast a beam on th'outward shape," turning it "by degrees to the souls essence" (455, 460, 462). Body as soul's essence does not hierarchize soul over body, or render them as a "contrast" in which we are "the same as the soul and other than the body."[80] Rather, the process envisioned by Elder Brother makes the soul visible in the body, as a Neoplatonic continuum. Meanwhile, the expression of inwardness *leaves inwardness on the outside*, such that external behaviors – "unchaste looks, loose gestures, and foul talk" – redound immediately and destructively to the "inward parts" (464, 466). Paradoxically enough, the soul that properly despises the body must take very good care of the body, lest it (the soul) find itself "link't.. by carnal sensuality / To a degenerate and degraded state" (474–475). The "*Gorgon* sheild," finally, is Elder Brother's symbol for his sister's prophylactic chastity (447). With a glance at psychoanalytic interpretations, we can see that the gorgoneion protects the chaste vagina by representing the chaste vagina. The hidden strength of chastity is displayed – but displayed in all its hiddenness. The symbol goes beyond moral nudism, into a kind of reverse pornography.

Many critics have found this ecstatic vision more than a bit excessive. Indeed, ironizing it has been a traditional recommendation.[81] Yet such a response grossly underestimates the orthodox Neoplatonism of Elder Brother's speech – and may involve a misunderstanding of just what the "Neo" in Renaissance Neoplatonism means. As numerous scholars have shown (and as I have already had occasion to suggest), the Renaissance teaching of Ficino *et al.* is, in some ways, an inversion of Plato's own thought. The Academic emphasis on soul–body dualism is a particular object of theoretical revision: the body that was, for Plato's Socrates, an insignificant shell for the soul becomes, for Ficino's Plato, the sign and image of the soul. This transformation, or even deconstruction, occurs through a logical reduction of classically-Platonic intentionalism. Platonism places the soul beyond all corporeality, while also placing that "beyond" deep within corporeality. Like the meaning in a

---

[80]   Krier, *Secret Sights*, p.127, quoting Kerrigan.

[81]   See Victoria Kahn, *Machiavellian Rhetoric from the Counter-Reformation to Milton* (Princeton, 1994), p. 201; Cedric C. Brown, *John Milton's Aristocratic Entertainments* (Cambridge and New York, 1985), pp. 92–93, giving the critical heritage of the reading; and Tayler, *Milton's Poetry*, p. 137.

word, like intention in an action, the soul provides the body with all the being that it will ever have. By that very token, however, the soul must provide the body with being; it must "cling to things divine," as Ficino says, *and fill things mortal*."[82] If the only point of the body is to provide a house for the soul, then the soul is certainly valorized and dominant within the binary. But if the task and achievement of the body is to provide a home for the soul, then the body tends to be valorized as a consequence of the binary. This is the move that the Renaissance consistently makes: the soul's earthy residence is renovated, becoming a house of glass.

It may be worth illustrating this familiar shift by a few prominent texts. In Petrarch's *Secretum* (c.1374) St. Augustine teaches a classical (but largely unread) Plato to the pre-Ficinian Francesco.[83] The saint finds, disapprovingly, that the poet of the *Rime Sparse* would not have "taken equal delight" in his Laura's soul, had it been "lodged in a body ill-formed and poor to look upon." This is to Francesco's grave discredit: for "the beauty of the body should be reckoned last of all."[84] One hundred and fifty years later, however, we find Pietro Bembo, in Castiglione's *Cortegiano* (1528), assuring the company that "only rarely does an evil soul dwell in a beautiful body, and so outward beauty is a true sign of inner goodness ... for the most part the ugly are also evil, and the beautiful good." For proof, Bembo turns to physiognomy and anthropomorphism. [85] The Platonic idea, in the wake of Ficino, has reverted to the ancient somatic prejudices that Plato was trying to refute (via the body of shallow Charmides, the soul of ugly Socrates, etc.). It has aligned itself with the doctrine of outward signatures that persisted in even the most advanced pre-Enlightenment science (as David Freedberg has recently shown).[86] Seventy years after Castiglione, Spenser paraphrased Bembo in the *Fowre Hymnes* (1596): "Beautie is not, as fond men misdeeme, / An outward shew of things, that only seeme ... For of the soule the bodie forme doth take: / For soule is forme, and doth the bodie make" (91–91; 131–132). While placing greater emphasis than does Castiglione on exceptions to the rule (141–154), Spenser completely agrees with his predecessor's articulation of that rule. "Where ever that thou doest behold

---

[82]   Marsilio Ficino, *Platonic Theology: Volume I, Books I–IV*, ed. James Hankins w. William Bowen, trans. Michael J.B. Allen w. John Warden (Cambridge, MA, and London, 2001), p. 237.

[83]   See William H. Draper (trans.), *Petrarch's Secret: Or, The Soul's Conflict with Passion, Three Dialogues between Himself and S. Augustine* (Westport, CT, 1978). "You have learned this truth," says Augustine of classical dualism, "in Plato's writings, to the study of which you said not long ago you had given yourself up with ardour" (p. 77). Francesco, living too soon for Ficino's translations of (most of) the dialogues, squirms: "Yes, I own I had given myself to studying him with great hopefulness and desire, but the novelty of a strange language and the sudden departure of my teacher cut short my purpose" (pp. 77–78). Petrarch goes on to synthesize his metaphysics from Augustine himself, Cicero, Virgil, and others.

[84]   Draper, *Petrarch's Secret*, p. 125.

[85]   Baldesar Castiglione, *The Book of the Courtier*, trans. and introd. George Bull (Harmondsworth, 1976), p. 330.

[86]   See Freedberg, *The Eye of the Lynx*, pp. 176–177, 178, 181, 184–185, 194, 201–202, 233–234, 236–237, 304, 325, 330, and 349–366.

/ A comely corpse," he writes, *"know this for certaine*, that the same doth hold / A beauteous soule" (134–137, my emphasis).[87]

Fifty years after Spenser, Henry More gave the Ficinian position its most elaborate statement in English poetry. In his *Platonick Song* (1647), More argues for the in-animation of the inanimate substratum. "Each outward form's a shrine of its magnetick spright," he writes:

> The ripen'd child breaks through its mother's womb,
> The raving billows closely undermine
> The ragged rocks, and then the seas entomb
> Their heavy corse, and they their heads recline
> On working sand: The Sunne and Moon combine,
> Then they're at ods in site Diametrall:
> The former age to th'present place resigne:
> And what's all this but wafts of wind centrall
> That ruffle, touze, and tosse Dame *Psyche*'s wrimpled veil?[88]

The world-soul fills, and makes, the world. Psyche's "wind centrall," constantly blowing, moves and manifests the physical reality which is nothing other than Psyche's metaphysical "veil." That "veil," however, does not commit More to esotericism. It is not something that one can or should remove in order to observe what lies beneath. Quite the contrary: according to More's late and sophisticated Neoplatonism, veiling, not unveiling, is the mode of knowledge. More contends that our understanding can only become "more obscure" if "the crusty fence / Of constipated matter" is "laid aside." "Therefore those sonnes of Love," the angels, "when they them dresse / For sight, they thick the vest of *Uranure*, / And from their centre overflow't with beauty pure" (*Psychozoia* 1.28). "Uranure" or "Uranore" is More's synonym for Psyche, coined as a Graeco-Hebraic term meaning "light or beauty of heaven" (624). Because that light is so far beyond human capacities – and because it is, in its beyondness, really all that matters – the highest perception involves creation, not removal, of covering form. It is *because* they chose to clothe themselves in "lilly limbs" that More was able to perceive two angelic "lovely Lads" one day (1.26). ("And as I passed, I worshipped.") He apostrophizes:

> And if you list to mortall eye appear,
> You thick that veil, and so your selves array
> With visibility: O myst'ry rare!
> That thickned veile should maken things appear more bare! (*Psychozoia* 1.27)

---

[87]   For the soul, filled with sunlight, "when she in fleshly seede is eft enraced, / Through every part she doth the same impresse / … And frames her house, in which she will be placed, / Fit for her selfe" (114–115; 117–118).

[88]   Henry More, *Psychozoia*, in A *Platonick song of the soul*, ed. and introd. Alexander Jacob (Lewisburg, PA and London, 1998), 1.46–47. Further references by heading, section and stanza in the body of my text.

A better slogan of exoteric secrecy can scarcely be imagined.

Now, ultimate reality does remain associated with the non-apparent, for More, just as the soul remains conceived as an inward and non-corporeal presence. But two qualifications, of the deconstructive kind that I have already described, place these esoteric commonplaces under exoteric imperatives. First, More considers that it is in the nature of inward being to manifest itself outwardly. This, we might say (recalling Psyche's "wind centrall"), is the mode of being of Neoplatonic being. The "hid soul" "doth her self ... variously bewray / In different motions" (*Psychathanasia* 1.2.12). Her "inward centre hid" is "nought but Nature's fancie ti'd / In closer knot" (*Psychathanasia* 1.2.28). More places great emphasis on the Ficinian definition of soul as "self-moving substance," with the implication that the soul requires a non-self-moving substance to move. To be sure, this implication is logically unsound, and at one point More explicitly concedes that "some souls at least are self-active / Withouten body having *Energie*." Even these souls, however, "put out their force informative / In their ethereall corporeity" (*Psychathanasia* 1.2.24). More glosses his word "*Energie*" as "a peculiar Platonicall term," designating "the rayes of an essence, or the beams of a vitall Centre" (614, 615). The soul is such a vital centre, ineluctably radiant. Like the Calvinist word, and like the Stuart conscience/heart, the Baroque Psyche reveals herself irresistibly and transformatively.

The second qualification of More's residual (paleo-)Platonism is that his psychic exomorphism tends to produce a soul–body continuity. The continuity, moreover, works both ways. The carter's whip, laid across his donkey's back, "revives / That inward life" (*Psychathanasia* 1.2.39). The plants, "fairly invited by Sols piercing ray," are "inward tickled with his chearing spright" (*Psychathanasia* 1.2.31). Horses' hooves, ringing on the ground, make the operation of an inward presence "plain" (*Psychathanasia* 1.2.32). One sees how the logic of exomorphic soul can function as an analogue of the Bezan practical syllogism: just as post-Calvinist sanctification becomes a general guide to justification, so the Neoplatonic body becomes a general proof of the soul. And just as Calvinism argues from the esoteric to the exoteric – from the intentionality of election to the necessity of its expression – so Neoplatonism argues from the incorporeal to the corporeal. That is to say, the Neoplatonic insistence that the soul is not the body is exactly what binds the body to the psychic field of value.

All of which brings me back to More's, and Spenser's, and Castiglione's source. Ficino says that the soul cannot be in the body just as a spark of the divine fire, for then "it would be united with a point not with a body." Neither can the soul fill the body by quantitative extension, for then it would be divisible, just as the body is. Rather, the soul must be "present in its entirety in the individual parts of the body ... Remaining whole and simple ... present as an undivided whole in the individual parts." At every conceivable point of the body, the soul must be encountered, in its entirety, as the soul. This can only be a mimetic plan: the infinite intra-corporeal self-reproduction of the soul by the mechanism of self-representation. Ficino explains via the following analogy:

A point imprinted somewhere in any radius of a circle is not present in the other radii, nor is it spread along the length of the whole radius or throughout the circle. But the point which is the center of the circle and does not belong to any particular radius is found in a way in all the radii that are drawn from the center to the circumference. And although no point imprinted on the circumference regards the whole circle equally, yet the center, which properly is not attached to any circumference, does regard the whole circle equally. [89]

"At the center, the permutation or the transformation of elements ... is forbidden ... the center is, paradoxically, *within* the structure and *outside* it."[90] Derrida finds the relation of structure and center "contradictorily coherent," but Ficino finds the relation of soul and body mutually insistent. Both versions are dialectical; the difference between them basically comes down to the difference between splitters and joiners. For Ficino, a joiner in a joining age, soul and body are each other's condition. Just as the circumference can enclose no field except around a center, so the center cannot be a center except as surrounded by a circumference. The strong implication is that the circle represents and reproduces the center, in much the same way as the center re-presents and reproduces itself throughout the circle. A similar mutuality characterizes Ficino's other metaphor for the soul–body relationship: it is like the way "a spoken word and its meaning are wholly and simultaneously present."[91]

With that suggestion of an extremely unDerridean semantics, the subject of my next chapter has crept up again. It is time for me to conclude this one. Briefly: Elder Brother is right to construct his sister's exteriority as the inevitable, inextricable, and powerful manifestation of her interiority. He is right on the Neoplatonic ontology that is utterly current in the middle seventeenth century; on the Caroline ideology that is utterly relevant to masque; and on the practical-Calvinist soteriology that is utterly orthodox for early-modern English culture. Arguably, the young visionary reaches unusual heights in asserting the revealed soul's apotropaic invincibility. But this, I think, is the challenge of a moral ideal. It is not a challenge, in and of itself, to that ideal. Critics are right to observe an inconsistency between Elder Brother and the Lady, between his theory and her practice. They are wrong, however, to infer or assume that the Lady is therefore in the right, or that practice trumps theory. It is equally possible, as a matter of mere logic, that the Lady is in the wrong, for failing to fulfill theory. I will now lay out the evidence for this second possibility.

Keeping It Together

Debora Shuger has suggested (anticipating Targoff) that the Lady's immanent dualism has recusant overtones. It is the Catholic tradition, after all, that separates rind from mind, flesh from consent. It is Erasmus who articulates the Gregorian view that good minds are not responsible for bad bodily events. The Genevan

---

[89]   Ficino, *Platonic Theology*, pp. 237, 239.
[90]   Derrida, "Structure, Sign and Play," p. 248.
[91]   Ficino, *Platonic Theology*, p. 239.

Protestant teaching is quite different: not only must the doors of the psyche be set open (as I have discussed), but the psyche must also accept responsibility for its bodily misfortunes. These include – crucially – *involuntary* misfortunes. Shuger's focus is natural concupiscence (specifically, wet dreams), but the point holds also for external malfeasance (e.g., rape). The distinction between forced and voluntary sin – however ethically indispensable it may appear to us – is identified by Calvin with the Pelagian heresy. If compulsion, Calvin argues, absolves the sinner of sin, then (1) all human beings are absolved of original sin, which Adam forces upon them, and (2) divine determinism absolves all sinners, including Satan, of all sin. Both results are intolerable; therefore, the distinction between compulsion and volition must go. For Calvin, nobody is truly blameless.[92]

Of course, Milton may be intervening in that position. His Lady may exemplify a strong intentionalism that includes a moral privileging of sincerity and volition. This would be an intelligible position on the contemporary scene – and would support readings of Milton's masque as (very) radically Puritan or reformist. As Targoff shows, the Puritan critique of the established church included, from early on, a partial return to pre-Reformation assertions of interiority.[93] That is why James was able to align (as I have mentioned) the Puritan claim of "tender conscience" with Jesuitical equivocation. I have suggested that James is propagandizing with this parallel, and that the kind of intentional nullification he abhors is found only at the extreme left of pre-revolutionary English Protestantism. But even if I am right in this assessment (and it is far from certain that I am), theorists of the radical *Comus* can only take comfort. For it would then seem that the Lady is taking a strong-intentionalist stand of the kind that the Stuart church associates with radical groups; and that, to the extent that there really were such groups, they were located on the sectarian fringe of the reform movement. Here, arguably, we have an Antinomian Lady, whose mirroring of Catholic solipsism simply helps to identify her.

But if so, it is really too bad for the Antinomians. Because whether the Lady's mental retreat is read as popish or precisian – or even if we shrug it off as a mere literary gesture – it is, in Milton's terms, Satanic. It is a claim of impregnable and secret intentionality, the defiant assertion that "the mind is its own place" (*PL* 1.254). That statement's significance, in *Paradise Lost*, is not that Satan makes it. Satan's significance, rather, is that he makes that statement: the performative and psychological speech-act of rebellion against God. To be sure, the Lady's intentionalism differs from Satan's in its devotional qualification. "While Heav'n sees good," she will have her secret mental redoubt (665). But this qualification does

---

[92] Calvin, *Institutes*, pp. 317–320; Shuger, "Gums." See also Ken Hiltner, *Milton and Ecology* (Cambridge and New York, 2003), pp. 64–65; and Julie Crawford, *Marvelous Protestantism: Monstrous Births in Post-Reformation England* (Baltimore and London, 2005), pp. 16–21 and 62–72. Compare Ishtiyaque Haji, "On Being Morally Responsible in a Dream," in Gareth B. Matthews (ed.), *The Augustinian Tradition* (Berkeley and London, 1999), pp. 166–182.
[93] Targoff, *Common*, pp. 40–41.

not dissolve her Satanism; it simply aligns the Lady with those Miltonic reprobates who attempt to *get away* with Satanism. Alexander More, we recall, calls God to witness that he, More, will only witness to God. Milton excoriates More for that public assertion of secrecy, while demonstrating that the correct procedure is a public extrusion of secrecy. Milton's exotericism, silencing and humiliating More, achieves an apotropaic effect that is much like the one prophesied by Elder Brother. The Lady of Christ's, in short, confronts his enemies correctly. The Lady of *Comus* does not. So much is wrong with "the mind is its own place" that one should not come anywhere near repeating it, prefiguring it, or suggesting it.

That is why Milton, for example in his autobiographical presentations, valorizes the opposite speech-act: the exoteric claim of the clear breast, by which the mind becomes everybody else's place. Not all people are obliged to perform such an uncomfortable maneuver, and indeed its value is partly derived (I have been arguing) from the small number of its adepts. But the Lady of Ludlow, surely, should be among them. She makes a good start with her "strong siding champion." Elder Brother magnificently programs her exoteric triumph. Yet in the end, the Lady gives us an esoteric cop-out – in a form, masque, that would fully support the revelatory alternative.

In this respect, it is both appropriate and disturbing to find the Lady reduced, ultimately, to silence. At the end of the temptation scene, when her long-lost brothers rush in, she says not a word. Perhaps Comus has pressed the glass to her lips before exiting; perhaps the young woman is silent before the Attendant Spirit's lawful authority (though it is hard to credit the latter argument, given that the Spirit is pretending to be a minor household employee).[94] Admittedly, the two brothers are silent too – but they have not just been theorizing the moral significance of speech. While emphasizing her reluctance to debate, the Lady was an extremely successful debater. The enchanter found her words "set off by som superior power," and was desperate to shut her up (800–806). Yet all the while, on her own account, the Lady wanted only to shut up, too. Milton's villains always want to silence his heroes, who respond – like Jeremiah, like Abdiel, like Samson – with the expressive imperatives of Protestant exotericism. In flouting those imperatives, praising and wishing for silence, the Lady neatly aligns herself with her tormentor.

Meanwhile, she demonstrates the error of her psychic esotericism. For the separation of mind from rind, beginning with an appropriate contempt for the carnal, ends in a carnal refrigeration of the spiritual. The body includes the organs and the media of speech; without speech, there is no way for the Lady to make her soul "testifie his hidd'n residence" (248). Her soul becomes as fully imprisoned, life-in-death, as if the Lady had been petrified (per Comus' threat). She thus enters on the process described by Elder Brother, in which the soul, corrupted by "leud and lavish act of sin," "grows clotted by contagion" (465, 467). In period terms, *it simply does*

---

94   See Jean E. Graham, "Virgin Ears: Silence, Deafness, and Chastity in Milton's *Maske*," *MS* 36 (1998): 1–17.

not matter that the Lady resists that "act of sin"; her failure to maintain soul and body in exoteric continuity constitutes, in and of itself, "defilement to the inward parts" (466). For all the period ideologies I have been surveying, expression is the natural and necessary mode of virtuous intentionality. By shutting her lips before the glass, shutting her lips *tout court*, the Lady swaps her clear breast for a dark dissembling shield. She thereby gives Comus exactly the power he desires over her "prison'd soul" (256).[95]

And what should she have done? Perhaps there is no very good answer to this question. But perhaps she should never have gotten herself into such a fix in the first place. She should never have accepted Comus' invitation, but should have trusted in her own vision of the "strong siding champion" to protect her and lead her to her brothers. Once in thrall to the enchanter, she should have dazzled him into submission – as he indicates she could have – or else she should have retreated, not from her body, but from this world. This is the expedient adopted by the masque's other lady, and the Lady's ultimate rescuer, who exemplifies the exotericism that the Lady does not maintain. When her virtue was impugned – though a "Virgin pure," a "guiltless damsel" (827, 829) – Sabrina did not attempt to detach mind from rind. She did not behave like some martyr of the early church, throwing her body to the dogs of her tormentors' carnality. Rather, Sabrina threw her body, and her soul along with it, into the river Severn. There, she was received and transformed by the local nymphs, who infused "Ambrosial Oils" through "the porch and inlet of each sense" (840, 839). In Elder Brother's terms, Sabrina was "liveried" by supernatural beings, who treated her to "quick immortal change" through the medium of her body (841). It is precisely Sabrina's fulfillment of Elder Brother's vision, her maintenance at all costs of the soul–body continuity, that empowers her to release her less rigorous sister. The "drops" from her "fountain pure" (912) – *because* they have been "kept of pretious cure" – can counteract the "gumms of glutenous heat" (913, 917).

The latter items have been extremely controversial, and I do not mean to argue that they have issued from the Lady's body.[96] But "gluten" is a technical term of seventeenth-century physiology, which is to say that the gums have issued from *somebody's* body.[97] To repeat Shuger's point, it really doesn't matter whether the Lady has willed, or participated in, her imprisonment. The birdlime of Protestant concupiscence "at least asperses / The tempted with dishonour foul" (*PL* 9.296–297). Adam, in *PL*, is wrong when he says that – but wrong because he is unfallen. The standard he articulates is the standard on which the fallen Lady fails: the standard of intention maintained in unity with expression, inwardness with outwardness, mind with rind. Sabrina, who succeeds on the same standard, is thereby empowered to help virgins who do not.

---

[95]   See William A. Oram, "The Invocation of Sabrina," *SEL* 24 (1984): 121–139.

[96]   See John Leonard, "Saying 'No' to Freud: Milton's *A Mask* and Sexual Assault," *MQ* 25.4 (1991): 129–140.

[97]   A.B. Chambers, *Andrew Marvell and Edmund Waller: Seventeenth-Century Praise and Restoration Satire* (University Park, PA, 1991), pp. 15–56.

Chapter 3

The Armor of Intension

As everybody knows, Samson made just one big mistake with Dalila. Admittedly, their whole relationship had been something of a misjudgment. He was a champion of the oppressed Hebrews, she a flower of the oppressing Philistines; he a Nazarite (or Yahwist ascetic), she an idolatrous harlot. Worse, their affection had been conspicuously unmutual, with Dalilah attempting, repeatedly and deceitfully, to betray her strongman to her compatriots. Nevertheless, Samson persisted in the affair. Being invincible, he could, presumably, have persisted as long as he liked. All but for one thing, the one thing that brought him down: he told his fatal Philistiness the secret of his strength.

The Samson story, thus summarized, conforms to the hermeneutics of discovery. It predicates an event of esoteric meaning on a strong-intentionalist psychology, and thereby arrives at a neat tragedy of revelation. Samson's secret – divine championhood, guaranteed by his uncut hair – is the engine and fulcrum both of his deeds and of his identity. Narratologically, everything up to his secret's revelation is generated by its non-revelation; everything after is the consequence of that revelation.

Meanwhile, Samson's mental directedness at the world – his intentionality – is defined by and as a radical mental sequestration from the world. There is something that his mind must not disclose; this non-disclosure is what makes his mind his mind. Appropriately, Samson's downfall occurs through the forbidden disclosure of the non-disclosable. It occurs through an essential and thoroughgoing intentional expression. Had Samson kept mum about his secret (one might infer) he need not have fallen at all. He could have maintained his championhood through unexpressive intentionality. His error was, as Milton says elsewhere, to turn himself inside out. His sin was, as Milton's Satan says elsewhere, to forget that the mind is its own place.

Obviously, I am going to argue against such an account. I am going to argue that the discovery-model cannot make sense of Samson – or at least not of *Samson Agonistes* (1671). My alternative reading will align Samson's secret with the exoteric casuistry of Milton's self-presentations. The immanence of Samson's gift (I will contend), donated and overseen by *conscientia*, does not preclude, but dictates, its public exposure. My reasons for this reading will be much the same as those I offered against the discovery-reading of *Comus*, and against the strong-intentionalist view of its Lady – to whom Samson serves as a pendant. A pendant, or a mirror-image; they are identical but opposed. For where the Lady holds to an esoteric stance, expressly refusing to articulate her being, Samson expresses his being repeatedly and exoterically. Incarnated with the meaning of divine selection, he radiates that meaning with the invincibility imagined by Elder Brother. Tempted by his nemesis in a way that the Lady is not by hers, he cannot resist giving out a small taste of his sapience. And when Dalila spits it back at him – when his hair is shorn, and his conquests avenged – Samson recuperates his position by a catastrophic move to expression. Expression, not intention, is what matters about Milton's Samson. He errs not in revealing his secret to Dalila, but in thinking that he has an option, with regard to revelation, in the first place.

Catastrophic Conscience

Many critics of *SA* infer from the play (as I noted in my last chapter) a thematic recommendation of strong intentionalism, both semiotic-semantic and social-psychological. I am unable to make sense of this view. Samson's reduction to a mental redoubt – by his tonsuring, imprisoning, and (above all) blinding – is experienced by him as his most profound punishment. In terms familiar from *Comus*, and much-echoed in *SA*, the champion's inmost mind becomes his "moving Grave" (*SA* 103). "Ease to the body some, none to the mind," Samson comments on his opening coffee-break,

> From restless thoughts, that like a deadly swarm
> Of Hornets arm'd, no sooner found alone,
> But rush upon me thronging, and present
> Times past, what once I was, and what am now. (18–22)

Samson's bad conscience, rushing upon him precisely in his moment of rest, lines him up neatly with Milton's epic Satan, whose "conscience wakes despair / That slumberd, wakes the bitter memorie / Of what he was, what is, and what must be" (*PL* 4.23–25). Like the fallen archangel, the disgraced champion is a Miltonic meditation on the fundamental agony of a "minde" alienated from its "rinde" (*Comus* 663, 664). Later in his tragedy, Samson gives a much-extended figuration of his psyche:

> O that torment should not be confin'd
> To the bodies wounds and sores
> With maladies innumerable
> In heart, head, brest, and reins;
> But must secret passage find
> To th'inmost mind,
> There exercise all his fierce accidents,
> And on her purest spirits prey,
> As on entrails, joints, and limbs,
> With answerable pains, but more intense,
> Though void of corporal sense.
>
> My griefs not only pain me
> As a lingring disease,
> But finding no redress, ferment and rage,

Nor less than wounds immedicable
Ranckle, and fester, and gangrene,
To black mortification.
Thoughts my Tormenters arm'd with deadly stings
Mangle my apprehensive tenderest parts,
Exasperate, exulcerate, and raise
Dire inflammation which no cooling herb
Or medcinal liquor can asswage,
Nor breath of Vernal Air from snowy *Alp*. (607–629)

The redundancy of this passage – saying the same thing (which has in any case been said before) multiple times in multiple ways – is typical of *SA*. The play is dominated by a reiterative poetics that conforms to the Gadamerian hermeneutics of recognition (see pp. 25–9). More to the present point, Samson's redundancy in describing his sufferings is absolutely appropriate to his sufferings. For redundancy, in his mind-body relation, is what he suffers from. The champion's problem is not only, or even fundamentally, that he has both an unhappy body and an unhappy mind. His problem is also, and even primarily, that he has both a body and a mind *tout court* – radically separate, but liminally joined by a "secret passage." The latter ensures both that physical torments will be echoed mentally, and that in mental form they will be both amplified and undefined, "more intense," yet "void" of "sense." Suffering becomes a nauseating shadow-show of suffering. It is this mirror-effect, this unwanted but inevitable reiteration, that Samson finds the significant content of his intolerable lot.

Stephen Fallon would say that Samson suffers from mind/body dualism.[1] My own preference is to say that Samson suffers from strong intentionalism – which explains, it seems to me, what is wrong (for Milton) with dualism. After all, the dualist model can quite happily accommodate instances of radical mental sequestration. One can be, as the Stoics recommended, a virtuous mind stuck within a vicious body; or one can be, as postmodern popular culture has loved to suppose, a mind floating without a body, in a computerized Matrix. Milton's view, however, is that one can be neither of these things. For him, the separation of mind from rind, in and of itself, leads to degraded, repugnant, and intolerable mental states. This happens because the dualist separation devolves upon a mental autarky that proves, on Milton's examination, to have caused the separation in the first place. In *PL*, Satan is not mentally-secret because he is Satan. Rather, he is Satan because he is mentally-secret, because he has said in his mind that his mind can be its own place. In *Comus*, similarly, the man of "dark soul and foul thoughts" does not have to sequester his intentionality, becoming "his own dungeon," because his intentionality is foul (*Comus* 382, 384). On the contrary, his intentionality is foul because he sequesters it. He has not understood, as Elder Brother understands, that the only way to "enjoy bright day" is always-already to have a "clear brest" (381, 380).

---

[1]   See Fallon, *Milton among the Philosophers*.

Relating this pattern to *SA*, and to casuistry, one sees that Samson's conscience is bad, in the first place, because it has ceased to be a conscience altogether. It has ceased to be a knowledge joined to a knowledge: a mental secret constituted, paradoxically, by its divine sharing. Instead, the secret has been torn from the divine, and has therefore been committed to incoherent reflexivity. Samson has fallen down his "secret passage," not so much by cutting Dalila into his vocational loop (and this is a point I will develop later) as by cutting God out of it. Intentionality remains both the problem, and the solution – but the solution needs to be an exoteric revision of esoteric impulses.

Samson practiced this kind of revision, on Milton's account, from the very beginning of his career. When the holy spirit first began to "move him" (Judges 13:25), his initial response was to make a marriage choice (of the woman of Timnath) that his parents found disturbing and cryptic (14:2–3). Then, he performed a random act of violence (killing the "young lion" of Timnath) about which he told nobody; then derived some honey and a riddle from the lion's putrefying corpse, setting the honey before his parents, and the riddle before his wife's brethren (14:5–14). All this, however, was to provide "occasion" against the Philistines (14:4). All Samson's early harboring of intention served a pre-existing goal of massive and interminable expression. For the Philistine marriage gave him a moral claim on his wife's compatriots; and the riddle, which they answered by compromising his wife, allowed him to commence a moral campaign against them (14:18–19). That things would fall out this way, Milton's Samson explains, "I knew / From intimate impulse,"

> and therefore urg'd
> The Marriage on; that by occasion hence
> I might begin *Israel's* Deliverance. (223–226)

The events of Timnath, note, were not Samson's reason for seeking occasion. They were, rather, the occasion that he had already been seeking. Samson does not predicate public action on private motivation – the esoteric model of political intentionality. Instead, Samson makes private motivation a function of a pre-existing and God-given plan for public action.

Milton's "Governours, and Heads of Tribes" (*SA* 243) committed the error, and offered the insult, of interpreting Samson's intentional actions esoterically. In other words, looking at the public champion, they perceived only "a private person" (1219), a mere "league-breaker" who "presum'd / Single Rebellion and did Hostile Acts" (1220–1221). The pejorativity of this designation is made clear by (of all people) Dalila, when she is accounting for her own civically-minded (mis)deeds. "To the public good / Private respects must yield," the Philistiness intones: "that grounded maxim / So rife and celebrated in the mouths / Of wisest men" (869–870; 866–868). Dalila is, of course, spouting a cliché, and the mouth that spouts it may make us suspect it. But the leaders of Israel themselves spouted exactly the same cliché, when they denigrated Samson for "private respects." The point here is that even Samson's traitress, the moral bankrupt of *SA*, understands that this is how one is supposed to do one's moral and rhetorical reckoning (in early-modern English culture).[2] Recognizing a civic binary of private and public, one constructs the private as the passive substratum of the active and constructive public. The justification of actions, accordingly, follows from a rejection of the private in favor of the public. Such a rejection (as I have argued) is morally orthodox in period terms. Its corollary is that moral heterodoxy is to be associated with a rejection of the public in favor of the private. This is the grave crime, the selfish and secretive breaking of the moral pale, that Samson's compatriots erroneously ascribe to him.

The rhetoric of the public good constitutes (if you like) a weak exotericism. It is public action as non-private action, and the exoteric citizen as the non-esoteric citizen. To put this another way, the public good arises within, and remains within, a binary opposition of public and private. The public, to be sure, is hierarchized over the private – but it retains, through that very binarization, a dialectic and constitutive relation with the private. The strength of this system is that it allows a clear identification of moral turpitude with private respects, and an equally clear identification of moral excellence with public action. The weakness of the system, however, is that it allows no clear distinction, vis-à-vis moral excellence, between public actions. All one can say about Samson's and Dalila's actions, for example, is that both are consistent with public claims. She is acting for her country; he is acting for his. She will have her patriotic tomb (981–991); he will have his (1734–1745). Beyond that point, all one can hope to do is adjudicate the political and territorial claims of their respective peoples – and that is an enterprise (as we find out every day, these days) so bound up with communal and other relativistic considerations as to be interminable, if not impossible.

"If aught against my life / Thy countrey sought of thee," Samson splutters to his nemesis,

> it sought unjustly,
> Against the law of nature, law of nations,
> No more thy countrey, but an impious crew
> Of men conspiring to uphold thir state
> By worse then hostile deeds, violating the ends
> For which our countrey is a name so dear;
> Not therefore to be obey'd. (889–896)

The logic is desperate (is Samson associating, or contrasting, the laws of nations and of nature?), the rhetoric trite ("a name so dear," indeed). Above all, though, the passage is completely hypocritical. Samson himself sits in prison for committing "worse than hostile deeds," *pro patria*, against the Philistines. To some extent, he can justify himself by denying that he acted privately – denying, in short, that he

---

2   Compare Jürgen Habermas, *The Structural Transformation of the Public Sphere*, trans. Thomas Bürger (Cambridge, MA, 1989).

is a criminal. A danger remains, however, in affirming that he acted publicly. This would not be to affirm that he is a terrorist, but to affirm – what is worse – that one will never be able to decide whether or not he is a terrorist. For the question will always come down to the respective claims of the competing national groups. Constantly reviewed in the post-9/11 debate over *SA*, this is the potential stalemate of weak exotericism.

Happily, Samson does not stop with weak exotericism. Instead he articulates a strong exotericism: not just the exoteric citizen as non-esoteric, but the exoteric citizen as anti-esoteric. According to what he remembers, and articulates in *SA*, Samson's heroic action was not just a movement from private to public within a binary. Rather, it was a rejection and dissolution of the private/public binary. "I was no private," Samson says, responding to his leaders' esotericist calumnies. From that point one expects him to say, like Dalila, "I was public." Instead he explains himself to have been "a person rais'd / With strength sufficient and command from Heav'n / To free my Countrey" (1222–1224). Samson counters "private person" – the agent or unit of an esoteric politics – with "a person raised" – an undifferentiated characterization that precedes and avoids engagement with any such politics. The "person raised," charged and defined through and through by an exoteric mission, opposes esoteric imperatives by opposing the whole way of thinking that provides a space for such imperatives. Thus if Dalila (by her own account) acted with public orthodoxy, Samson (by his account) acted with super-public super-orthodoxy. Like Milton in his self-presentational polemics, the Nazarite champion recognized a moral norm – in this case the weak exotericism of the public good – only to raise it to a new magnitude. He seized upon the exoteric spirit of the public/private binary, and made of that spirit a new letter beyond binarization.

Samson's fall, the beginning of his end, consisted in a failure to maintain this difficult stance. The end of his end, and the end of *SA*, consists in his recuperating it – painfully, but explicitly. Like the message that mandated Samson's life (and of this more below), the message that ends it comes twice; but in this case, reiteration is necessitated by the failure of iteration. The Philistine Officer who comes to demand Samson's services at the feast of Dagon is turned down the first time. He warns the champion against angering his masters: "Regard thyself" (1344). Samson retorts: "My self? my conscience and internal peace" (1345). Samson's strong-intentionalist casuistry, in this initial exchange with the Officer, is echoed by the Chorus. They demonstrate, however, that the logic of strong intentionalism would precisely and unproblematically allow Samson to do the Philistines' bidding. "Where the heart joins not, outward acts defile not," they say (1379) – citing exactly the Augustinian-Gregorian line that Ramie Targoff and Debora Shuger have distinguished from English Protestant thought (see Chapter 2). Of course, the Chorus is neither English nor Protestant, and neither is Samson. But of course that is the point. Samson's is the champion-thought that must go beyond his compatriots', overpowering their complaceny with prophecy and cogency.

And it does. Even while he is deliberating whether to accompany the Philistine officer – even while his own strong-intentionalist cliché hangs in the air – Samson strikes down the Chorus' version of it:

> Where outward force constrains, the sentence holds
> But who constrains me to the Temple of *Dagon*,
> Not dragging? the *Philistian* Lords command.
> Commands are no constraints. If I obey them,
> I do it freely; venturing to displease
> God for the fear of Man, and Man prefer,
> Set God behind: which in his jealousie
> Shall never, unrepented, find forgiveness. (1380–1387)

On this rejection of the Chorus' view, Samson decides to go with the officer. He decides to take the risk of "prostituting holy things to Idols" (1369), committing his "Consecrated Gift / Of strength" to the theatrical amusement of Dagon (1365–1366). The rousing motions that allow him to do so are, plainly, intentional. But they are not strong-intentionalist. They direct Samson not toward the esoteric retreat of "internal peace," but toward the exoteric redemption of "some great act" (1400). Samson rejects non-performance in favor of performance – even a performance that may be "execrably unclean, prophane" (1373). He contradicts his earlier assertion of esoteric intentionality, and makes a concluding commitment to exoteric catastrophe.

Seeing It Is Secret

Helpfully, Samson theorizes his commitment before proceeding with it. "Hitherto, Lords," he cries to the Philistine dignitaries, as he prepares to pull their theatre down on them,

> what your commands impos'd
> I have perform'd, as reason was, obeying,
> Not without wonder or delight beheld.
> Now of my own accord such other tryal
> I mean to shew you of my strength, yet greater;
> As with amaze shall strike all who behold. (1641–1646)

Samson's theorization is all the more critical for the dramatic repetition within which it occurs. Just as at the opening of *SA*, the champion has been doing "laborious works" for the Philistines (14). Now he is allowed "intermission" (1630). Just as at the opening, the intermission is granted in festive honor of the false god Dagon, "thir Superstition" (15). Just as at the opening, Samson is led to his rest by an anonymous "guide" (1631). It is as though we are back at the beginning of the play, and Samson is getting a chance, in a meta-theatrical mode, to take the road not taken then.

The champion's key comment, on this extraordinary opportunity to renovate his own tragedy, is "of my own accord." Arguably, "ac-cord" suggests casuistical rapprochement: the internal agreement of heart with heart, parallelling the agreement of (God's) mind with (Samson's) mind. [3] More importantly, and unarguably, the phrase presents Samson's action as the expression of his core intentional state, in a figure that goes back to Comus' "cordial julep," and to the whole Tudor-Stuart fascination with *momo satisfacere*. "Of my own accord" presents the destruction of the theatre – this intentional expression with which Samson erases his earlier, unexpressive intentionality – in heart-talk. It presents Samson's final speech-act as a vision of the clear breast; an unbosoming of secrets.

And there's the rub. For it is in exactly the terms of unbosoming secrets, and/or of revealing his heart to a hostile audience, that Samson has described, consistently, the great mistake of his life. "I before all the daughters of my Tribe / ... chose thee," he tells Dalila: "lov'd thee, as too well thou knew'st, / Too well, unbosom'd all my secrets to thee" (878–881). With "blandisht parlies, feminine assaults, / Tongue-batteries, she surceas'd not day nor night" to pester Samson for his secret (404–405). Finally, wearily, and – we are led to think – totally regrettably, he "unlock'd" his "heart" to her (408). Heart-talk led to his downfall.

We have, therefore, a contradiction between Samson's (account of his) disaster, and Samson's (account of his) catastrophe. The play places us between these pillars, painfully and crucially. For the Dalila-disaster teaches immanence, reflexive conservation of conscience, and intentional esotericism. The theatrical catastrophe teaches utterance, transitive revelation of conscience, and intentional exotericism. It seems that we must either conclude (1) with common sense, but also with revisionist or anti-Samsonite criticism, that Samson was wrong to share his secret with Dalila – in which case his speech-act in the theatre is just more of the same old mistake; or (2) with exceptional implausibility, but also with traditional or pro-Samsonite criticism, that Samson was right to share his secret with Dalila – and this because his speech-act in the theatre must be seen as a signal of his redemption. It will not do, in my opinion, simply to draw a line between the two cases, saying that Samson was right to reveal God's "holy secret" in him to the Philistine lords, but wrong to reveal God's "holy secret" in him to Dalila (498). For on both sides of any such line, we would find the same crucial activity. This is the correct management and hermeneutic profile of intentionality under the sign of *conscientia*. Is the God-given psyche to be held within, kept back, savored, buried, protected? Or is to be thrust without, indeed conceived as always-already without, manifested, broadcast, extruded? In short, is Samson supposed to have an esoteric, or an exoteric conception of his intentional secrecy?

There can be little serious doubt that he is supposed to have the latter. Samson is destined, from birth, to go through the world as an exoteric secret. In Judges

---

[3]   See Michael Lieb, "'Our Living Dread': The God of *Samson Agonistes*," *MS* 33 (1997): 3–25.

13, Samson's birth, and instructions for his raising, are announced to his mother in terms of great explicitness (Judges 13:3–5). When Samson's father, Manoah, asks for repetition, the messenger angel provides one (13:11–14), while noting that it is a repetition: "Of all that I said unto the woman let her beware," he says, redundantly (13:13); "all that I commanded her let her observe" (13:14). We have here a careful reiteration that conforms to the hermeneutics of recognition – even as the difficulty of shifting with recognition becomes an issue in the story. For Manoah wants more; he assumes discovery as his task. First he asks for the angel's name, but is sternly informed that "it *is* secret" (13:18). This is not an invitation to or indicator of further understanding, but a limit to all possibility of understanding. Nonetheless, having received an imperative text of overdetermined obviousness, Manoah proceeds to interpret it both esoterically and reductively. It all means, he tells his wife, that "we shall surely die," and this because "we have seen God" (13:22). Mrs. Manoah takes issue with her husband's logic, while redirecting him toward an exoteric exegesis. "If the LORD were pleased to kill us," she reasons, "he would not have received a burnt offering and a meat offering at our hands, neither would he have shewed us all these *things*, nor would as at this time have told us *such things* as these" (13:23). The wonder of a divine vision, of an opportunity to apprehend in life the annihilating light of creation, is then (perhaps) reflected in the name Samson, or "sunny." In contrast to the angel's esoterically-prohibited name, the champion bears a glorious name of exoteric manifestation.[4]

Manifestation, then – not secrecy/discovery – is the hermeneutic leitmotif of Samson's career. The champion makes apparent, through his championhood, the divine favor placed in himself and in his people. In Milton's version, Samson is so vocationally and interpretatively overdetermined that he becomes his own symbol. Even in defeat, he is still "that Heroic, that Renown'd, / Irresistable *Samson*" (126–127). His legend is worked out through apotropaic imagery, of the days when he "ran on embattelld Armies clad in Iron," and "spurn'd them to death by Troops" (130, 139). "On hostile ground," he "walk'd about admir'd of all and dreaded / ... none daring [his] affront" (531–532). Obviously, Samson invincible recalls the Lady of *Comus*, as imagined by Elder Brother, able to "pass on with unblench't majesty," untouched by "savage fierce, Bandite, or Mountaneer" (*Comus* 430, 426). Somewhat less obviously, Samson also recalls the Son of *PL*, driving the rebel angels out of heaven with the terror of his gaze (*PL* 6.824–867). "What if his eye-sight," wonders the Chorus of *SA* on hearing the off-stage catastrophe, "by miracle restor'd, / He now be dealing dole among his foes?" (Omissa) Samson would then be acting as the messenger of God, who "swift as the lightning glance... executes / His errand on the wicked" (1295–1296). The synaesthesia of Samson's strength with his sight, and/or with the sight of him, originates in a memory of his tonsorial blinding. The synaesthesia eventuates, however, in a fantasy of the champion's amuletic showing. Samson becomes a Medusa-figure, a

---

4   "Samson," *New Bible Dictionary*, ed. J.D. Douglas et al. (Grand Rapids, 1971).

spectacular icon. His significance, troped as both grip and gaze, is imagined as totally and instantaneously available in his self-presentation.

The Chorus is wrong, of course, to think that Samson's eyesight has been restored. All the more remarkable that they are right to think that he is "dealing dole" among the Philistines – despite his having been summoned only to "sport" before his masters (Judges 16:25). As I have noted, the catastrophe of *SA* is explicitly meta-spectacular, taking place in a "spacious Theatre" (1606) rather than in the vague "house" of Judges (16:26, 27, 29, 30). Samson's performance, moreover, is explicitly self-representational. Here Milton differs from other early-modern dramatists of the Samson story, who usually have the champion, in a kind of heroic drag, unwillingly mocking his earlier self by playing the lyre, singing, and dancing.[5] Milton's Philistines, in sharp contrast, have the ex-champion perform feats of strength. "What was set before him," we are told,

> Which without help of eye might be assay'd,
> To heave, pull, draw, or break, he still perform'd
> All with incredible, stupendious force,
> None daring to appear Antagonist. (1625–1629)

Brought before his conquerors, Milton's Samson is made to play himself. He is like King Kong beating his chest in a Broadway theatre; like Sitting Bull wearing his war-paint at the behest of Buffalo Bill. Like Kong (though not like Sitting Bull), Samson refuses to be constrained by representation – or rather, he insists on a recognitive continuity between representation and presentation. In playing himself, he becomes himself. In pretending to kill Philistines, he indeed kills Philistines. This is dinner theatre that bites back. It accords, radically and overwhelmingly, with the Gadamerian aesthetics of non-differentiation (see pp. 25–9).

Since the whole point of the episode, furthermore, is that it reproduces the result of Samson's non-spectacular episodes (namely, the death and terrorization of Philistines), we may infer a representational understanding of all those episodes. Samson was never just being Samson. He was, rather, always performing Samson. For the importance of being Samson was a divinely-donated template to which the champion had, mimetically, always to conform. The play's judgment on its catastrophe is that "*Samson* hath quit himself / Like *Samson*" (1710–1711), a recognitive circle that inscribes the champion's hermeneutic profile. To be "like *Samson*" is not a proposition requiring explanation, but is the explanation of the proposition "*Samson*." The champion is a semantic tautology, and a mimetic spell. His power cannot be resisted; his meaning cannot be missed.

Unfortunately, Samson is plagued with missers and resisters. He is plagued, that is, with esoteric interpreters, who simply cannot believe that their champion's meaning

5   See Watson Kirconnell (ed.), *That Invincible Samson: The Theme of* Samson Agonistes *in World Literature with Translations of the Major Analogues* (Toronto, 1964), pp. 67, 109–110, 115, 119–120, and 121. Cited hereafter by page numbers in body of my text.

is not something that they have to discover. Samson's texts, divine judgments writ large on the bodies of the Philistines, prompt his compatriots not to read but only to demand what does it / what do you mean? "Knowest thou not," ask the men of Judah in Judges, "that the Philistines are rulers over us? what *is* this *that* thou hast done to us?" (15:11) Milton's Samson recalls that "seeing those great acts which God had done / Singly by me against their Conquerours," the leaders of Israel "Acknowledg'd not, or not at all consider'd / Deliverance offerd" (244–247). The judge's speech-act, crying out for recognition, met only with vain discovery, and an audience that "persisted deaf" (250). Samson even implies that his erstwhile leaders were in the grip of an intentionalist regress, not prepared to count speech-acts "things worth notice" unless the speech-actor would accompany them and explain them noticeably (251). "I on th'other side," he says, "us'd no ambition to commend my deeds, / *The deeds themselves, though mute, spoke loud the dooer*" (247–249, my emphasis). This exoteric insistence, deployed as an explanation of Samson's victories, is a veritable slogan of Austinian speech-act theory. It is a set toward utterance as the proof of understanding, and an *a fortiori* logic of expression subsuming intention.

Now, the angel of Judges 13 articulates himself on a template of Numbers 6, where the rules for Nazirite asceticism are prescribed. Nazirites, or "separate ones" – from Hebrew *nazir*, separate or secret – are Jews who vow, freely and temporarily, to "separate *themselves* unto the LORD" (Numbers 6:2). Below, I will deal with the separation's behavioral content, but for now I would like to consider its signifier. This is, of course, long hair, uncut throughout the vowed period, cut and burned on the altar at the end of it. All Nazirites have long hair, and are identifiable by it. Logically, we cannot infer, despite the simplicity of this semiotic scheme, that the reverse is true – that all people with long hair are identifiable as Nazirites. Nonetheless, let us imagine what we might think if we were Philistines confronted with the phenomenon of Samson. A member of our slave population is single-handedly destroying our armies. His strength is so extraordinary, so absolutely superhuman, that it strongly suggests divine intervention. As it happens, the slaves claim a special covenant with their god, whom they claim to be omnipotent. Some of them sometimes signify this alleged covenant by an ascetic program that involves long hair. The nightmarish Samson has very long hair. Are we not going to conclude that he may be one of the ascetics? Having so concluded, are we not going to infer (logically or not) that a relationship may obtain between his asceticism and his strength? Having so concluded, are we not going to try to terminate his asceticism – which we may be able to do, according to the slaves' sacred book, by cutting off his hair?

The openness of Samson's secret is constantly implied in *SA*. Poetically, the play points and points, with all the subtlety of a gigantic finger at a football game, to the champion's hair. We hear of "redundant locks / Robustious" (569–570), "those thy boyst'rous locks" (1175), "his hair / Garrison'd round about him like a Camp / Of faithful Souldiery" (1507–1509). Of course this is all after the fact, after the secret is out. But of course it is not irrelevant that we are reading a highly-retrospective tragedy about an *outed* secret. Samson has a lovely pun in his account of Dalila's importunities: "Thrice she assay'd," he tells Manoa,

> to win from me
> My capital secret, in what part my strength
> Lay stor'd, in what part summ'd, that she might know. (393–396)

"Capital secret" is Samson's head secret, the topical head at which Dalila aims. But it is also the secret of his head, the secret on his head – and thus the literal head at which Dalila aims. The pun is surrounded by more of Samson's characteristic redundancy: "summ'd" does the work of "stor'd"; "that she might know" is another way of Dalila's wanting to "win" the secret. The redundancy is (again) appropriate, not only because Samson is describing a repetition of experience ("Thrice she assay'd"), but also because the hermeneutic corollary of redundancy is obviousness. And obviousness – absolute, crashing, overdetermined emblematization – is the suggestion of "capital secret." If Dalila was simply trying to find out the head of Samson's secrets, then she was trying to find out something she did not already know. But if she knew that she was trying to "win" from him his head secret – if she says to her husband, honey, please tell me your capital secret – then how much, in fact, was she trying to find out?

I am not claiming that (Milton means us to understand that) Samson's was a non-secret. I am claiming that (Milton means us to understand that) Samson's was an anti-secret: that the hair, whatever exactly it meant to his wives, his compatriots, and his enemies, was experienced by them as obviously and appallingly meaningful. I am further claiming that Milton makes no attempt (which would, in any case, be a failed attempt) to accommodate Samson's exotericism within a narrative of esoteric discovery. Such a narrative, let it be noted, is not readily-available even in Milton's sources. Three times, in Judges, Dalila pesters Samson for his secret. Three times he fobs her off, perhaps buys her favors, with a lie – only to find her trying it out on him the next morning. How much more obvious could it be that he must not tell her the truth? Yet he does. Milton's response to these very irrational and folkloric materials is not to reduce or explain, but to augment and emphasize, the obviousness of Dalila's intentions. "Thrice I deluded her," Milton's Samson recalls,

> and turn'd to sport
> Her importunity, each time perceiving
> How openly, and with what impudence
> She purpos'd to betray me. (397–400)

The interesting question for Milton is not how Dalila tricked Samson, but how Samson could fall without having been tricked. His error is of a piece with Satan's in *PL*; it is of a piece with Adam's, who falls " not deceav'd" (9.998). Dalila sought, Samson says, "to make me Traytor to my self" (402). This enterprise conforms, not to the hermeneutics of discovery, but to the hermeneutics of recognition. Like Comus to the Lady, Dalila wanted Samson to choose, open-eyed, a treacherous self-image.

As Eve chastizes Adam for having let her be independent (*PL* 9.1155–1162), so Dalila chastizes Samson for having given in to her. "Was it not weakness," she demands in their jailhouse interview, "also to make known / For importunity, *that is for naught*, / Wherein consisted all thy strength and safety?" (*SA* 780–782, my emphasis). "For naught" is a galling pun. It reminds Samson that he fell for nothing, for no cause, no reason; but also that he fell for no-thing, the Elizabethans' joke on the female genitals. Samson fell for nothing because of his weakness for no-thing. Meanwhile, Dalila puts her "naught" at the appositive service of "importunity." This word, which rings throughout *SA*, means pestering and imploring. But it also means prophesying. Never one not to kick a man when he is down, Dalila is reminding Samson, the great he-man, that he was undone by petty henpecking – and henpecking with a manifest goal, a familiar and predictable pattern. Samson was peculiarly well-qualified to participate in this augury, since Dalila was the second Philistiness he had taken up with. The first, the woman of Timna, had betrayed him just as Dalila would, by winning a secret from him and then revealing it to his enemies. Dalila claims that she sought to avoid the fate of "her at *Timna*," and saw "no better way ... then by importuning" to learn Samson's secrets (797, 799–800). But the very experience to which she refers makes it all the more remarkable and pathetic that Samson fell, again, for nothing more than naughty importunity.

Milton emphasizes the symmetry between the woman of Timna and Dalila by upgrading the latter from harlot to wife. He also has Samson associate the two women, consistently, in complaining of his lot. "Did not she / Of *Timna* first betray me," Samson says to his father,

> and reveal
> The secret wrested from me in her highth
> Of Nuptial Love profest, carrying it strait
> To them who had corrupted her, my Spies,
> And Rivals?

"In this other" [Dalila] he rhetorically concludes, "was there found / More Faith?" (383–389) Later, to Harapha, Samson cites his first wife as proof of his onetime *bona fides*:

> Among the Daughters of the *Philistines*
> I chose a Wife, which argu'd me no foe;
> And in your City held my Nuptial Feast:
> But your ill-meaning Politician Lords,
> Under pretence of Bridal friends and guests,
> Appointed to await me thirty spies,
> Who threatning cruel death constrain'd the bride
> To wring from me and tell to them my secret,
> That solv'd the riddle which I had propos'd. (1203–1211)

This seems to me a very remarkable passage. For Samson has already stated that in proposing to marry "the daughter of an Infidel,"

> what I mention'd was of God; I knew
> From intimate impulse, and therefore urg'd
> The Marriage on; that by occasion hence
> I might begin *Israel's* Deliverance. (222–226)

The Chorus has agreed that "In seeking just occasion to provoke / The *Philistine*, thy Countries Enemy, / Thou never wast remiss" (238–240). And Manoa has confirmed that "thou didst plead / Divine impulsion prompting how thou might'st / Find some occasion to infest our Foes" (422–424). As we have seen, the occasion that Samson sought was precisely the compromising of his wife by her Philistine brethren. The compromising of his wife, furthermore, consisted precisely in the brethren's finding out, through her, the secret answer to Samson's riddle about the young lion.

But in that case, doesn't it follow that the secret was supposed to be found out? Doesn't it follow that Samson's whole vocation – his whole divinely-appointed mission – turned upon his artificial and trap-like deployment of a secrecy that was, from the perspective of the mission, always-already revealed?[6]

It is notable that when Samson describes the change in his fortunes effected by Dalila, he does not describe a movement from secrecy to openness. He describes, rather, a movement from openness to openness – but in such a way that the second iteration is suddenly and strangely unbearable. "When in strength / All mortals I excell'd," he recalls,

> Full of divine instinct, after some proof
> Of acts indeed heroic, far beyond
> The Sons of *Anac*, famous now and blaz'd,
> Fearless of danger, like a petty God
> I walk'd about admir'd of all and dreaded
> On hostile ground, none daring my affront.
> Then swoll'n with pride into the snare I fell
> Of fair fallacious looks, venereal trains,
> Softn'd with pleasure and voluptuous life;
> At length to lay my head and hallow'd pledge
> Of all my strength in the lascivious lap
> Of a deceitful Concubine who shore me
> Like a tame Weather, all my precious fleece,
> Then turn'd me out ridiculous, despoil'd,
> Shav'n, and disarm'd among my enemies. (523–541)

---

6   For a somewhat similar account, though with an overlay of psychoanalysis, see William Kerrigan, "The Irrational Coherence of *Samson Agonistes*," *MS* 22 (1986): 217–232.

Samson's account is closely analogous to Milton's account of Adam and Eve, whose fall consists in a change in their experience of nakedness. Before the fall, nakedness is just what they do; it is their form of life. It has the complete integrity and experiential perfection that is characterized by total absence of negative awareness. In other words, before the fall, Adam and Eve do not know that they are uncovered. After the fall, they know that they are uncovered; which is to say that they have come to place their nakedness in a binary relation to non-nakedness. This is not a change in their state, but a change in their understanding of the same state.

I would describe the change, for Samson as for Adam and Eve, as a change from an exoteric to an esoteric conception of a normative openness. What was excellent and sought before Dalila is terrible and feared after her. In both cases, *exposure* is what Samson experiences. But before Dalila, he does not experience it as an exposure *per se*. Afterward, he does. He falls into the esoteric binary of secrecy and openness, whereby openness can only be understood as privation of a normative secrecy.

In this respect, it is easy to make sense of Samson's esotericizing comments – all his laments for, and approbations of, an esoteric attitude toward his divine investment. These comments are, quite simply, evidence of the fallen Samson's getting things wrong. "I / Gods counsel have not kept," he tells Manoa, "his holy secret / Presumptuously have publish'd, impiously" (498–499). Since when, in Milton, or in Milton's post-Calvinist culture, is one supposed to *keep* God's counsel? Since when is it *impious* to publish the secrets that God has already made public through his favor? The "Gentiles in thir Parables" may condemn such publishing to Hell (501), but they are not a very good authority for an Hebrew champion. They are certainly no match for Milton's Jeremiah, or his Abdiel – or his Christ, who, Milton notes with satisfaction in *Areopagitica*, always preached in public (*CP* 2.548). Samson's nostalgia for secrecy is no more appropriate than Adam's analogous nostalgia after his own fall. "O might I here / In solitude live savage," the latter cries to Eve,

> in some glade
> Obscur'd, where highest Woods impenetrable
> To Starr or Sun-light, spread thir umbrage broad
> And brown as Evening. (*PL* 9.1084–1088)

The first man becomes the first pastoral poet – or perhaps the first post-pastoral poet. Adam's glimpse of himself as a lost savage is heavily analeptic, and, for that very reason, grossly inauthentic. For as the narrator makes clear when he brings Adam and Eve out of the woods clothed like two little Indians – "Such of late / *Columbus* found th'*American* so girt / With featherd Cincture" (1115–1116) – the savage mind of covering and uncovering is exactly the historical and cultural prolepsis of Adam's fall.

I am not arguing, in this section, that (Milton means that) Samson meant all along for Dalila to find out his secret. I am arguing that (Milton means that) Samson's keeping of his secret does not make much sense in *SA*; in other words, that it does not help us much to make sense of the play. The secret as *kept* is the very last thing Milton is interested in. He is drawn, much more strangely, and (to my mind) much more interestingly, to the secret as *open*. "Be less abstruse," Samson tells the Chorus, "my riddling days are past" (1075). It is when riddles are irrelevant that Samson begins his real work. And this, for Milton, is the semi-miraculous work of meaning in a non-miraculous world.

Intension and Incarnation

At this point I would like to return to the question of Nazaritism. The contents of the vow, as described in Numbers 6, are quite specific, and somewhat idiosyncratic. During the vowed period, a Nazarite is to eschew liquor and wine, the latter prohibition extending even to grapes, fresh or dried, and indeed to anything "made of the vine tree, from the kernels even to the husk." He is also to avoid dead bodies, even to the extent of shunning his religious duties if a member of his family dies; and he shall have to re-start his consecration, through a complex ceremony, if "any man die very suddenly by him" (Num. 6:3–9).

The Chorus (and some prominent critics) of *SA* find the Hebrew champion quite wanting in these terms.[7] In particular, the Chorus is unreconcilable with Samson's fondness for Philistine women (211–219; 316–322). To be sure, Numbers 6 says nothing about abstaining from women (Philistine or otherwise). The Chorus is extrapolating from the Mosaic text, and placing the Nazaritic spirit of "strictest purity" over its arbitrary letter. Yet without such an extrapolation, the vow would be open to extraordinary probabilisms. A Nazarite could live in a brothel, for example, while strictly abstaining from raisins. Moreover, without a fairly flexible hermeneutic standard, Samson *qua* Nazarite would be in even worse trouble than he is. Strictly speaking, the letter of Numbers 6 would condemn Samson for taking honey from his young lion's corpse – was this not a dead body? – and for killing Philistines, "very suddenly" – for the Philistines (terrorist ideology aside) are men. Samson gets full marks for teetotalling, as both he and the Chorus are at pains to point out (542–558). But even here, while the Chorus praises Samson for his ability to "repress" bibulous desires (544), Samson indicates that he simply doesn't like drinking, and therefore has nothing to repress (548–553).

The fact is that hermeneutic flexibility indicates, but does not fully illuminate, Samson's real relationship to his vow. He is a Nazarite, per God's explicit instructions, "from the womb" (Judges 13:5). The vow of separation is not something he imposes on himself, temporarily, willfully, and more-or-less arbitrarily. Rather, the vow is something that God imposes on him, in his very creation, and as his productive condition. Like one of the Calvinist elect, Samson cannot be alienated from his Nazarite status, because his Nazarite status is the pre-condition of all his potential inter-relations, including the relation of alienation. Samson = Nazaritism. More than just a product of the recipe dictated by the angel of Judges, Samson somehow *is* the recipe, walking around in the world. He bears a quasi-Christological relation to the

---

7   Shawcross, *Uncertain*; Wittreich, *Interpreting*.

letter of his own constitutive law. He directly and dreadfully manifests the power of Yahwist devotion, and embodies a comprehensive and continual re-writing of the Nazaritic letter in terms of its spirit. In doing so, he simply fulfills the instructions set down by the angel of Judges. But God sent down the angel; and God wrote the instructions. We therefore can say that Samson is determined as Samson by an aspect of God's intentions.

A classic semantic sequence, accordingly, presents itself. First, the mind of God has an intention: a mental intention, also called a primary intention, also called an "intention-with-a t." God's mental intention, like all such intentions, is that the world should come into a certain state of affairs. This state of affairs can be called the reference of the intention. (Let us suppose that God has a referential semantics). In this case, the reference of God's intention is a state of affairs in which the chosen people have had a champion with the characteristics of Samson. In order to achieve this reference, God needs to express his intention. He needs to impose his intention on a signifying substratum. He therefore turns to a combination of language, time, space, vision, and flesh – in short, to the world. He expresses his intention in the Nazarite instructions given, via the angel, to Samson's parents. Samson is the expression of those instructions.

As God's expression, then – as a signifying phenomenon – Samson bears the imprint or reflection of God's intention. This is Samson's sense, or intension: a semantic intension, also called (as discussed in my last chapter) a secondary intension, also called an "intension-with-an-s." Both "sense" and "intension" are conventional renderings of the Fregean term *Sinn*, opposed to *Bedeutung* or meaning – for Frege, a matter of reference.[8] The idea, which is technical, but quite commonsensical, is that an utterance is invested by its utterer with a certain sense, in order to achieve a certain meaning. This move is held to be necessary (at least by Fregean "intensionalists") to account for the fact that utterances, in and of themselves, can indicate many different meanings (as well as the converse: that the same meaning can be indicated by many different utterances). Semantics agrees with semiotics that utterances are hermeneutically underdetermined. Thus while I may refer to the planet Venus with my phrase "the morning star," I may, instead, refer to the evening star (without knowing that the latter is also Venus); or I may refer to Christ (as Milton does at *PR* 1.296); or I may refer to Satan (since Venus is also called Lucifer); or I may refer to a person who is especially productive and happy before noon; or I may refer to anything, or nothing, at all. What I actually do refer to – what I mean – is exactly and only a function of my phrase's (secondary) intension. That is to say, in non-technical language, it is a function of what I meant my phrase to mean.[9]

---

[8]   See Gottlob Frege, *Ueber Sinn und Bedeutung*; translated as "On Sense and Nominatum," in Garfield and Kiteley (eds), *Essential Readings*, pp. 35–52.

[9]   For a concise introduction to "with-an-s" intensionality, see Searle, *Intentionality*, pp. 22–23 and 180–181. For classic defenses of the intensional concept, against the early Davidson's Tarskian extensionalism, see Michael Dummett, "What Is a Theory of Meaning? (II)," in Gareth Evans and John McDowell (eds), *Truth and Meaning: Essays in Semantics* (Oxford,

Now the intension-concept, as I have indicated, originates in a Fregean semantics that equates meaning with reference. Yet it is quite clear, even from the brief summary I have already given, that (secondary) intension is supposed to work by linking reference to (primary) intention. For reference is determined (this has become a semantic cliché) by an expression's (secondary) intension. But (secondary) intension is determined, in turn, by the (primary) intention that imposes it on an expression. Therefore, (primary) intention determines the reference of an expression. Two consequences follow. One is that accounts of meaning-as-reference typically devolve upon, and end up as, accounts of meaning-as-(primary) intention – what I would call strong-intentionalist accounts. For (primary) intention is exactly and only what allows an hermeneutic securing of expressions in terms of their referents. One finds this identity of reference and (primary) intention – this collapsing into one of the two great hermeneutic pillars – in, for example, E.D. Hirsch. Hirsch aligns his theory of meaning-as-(primary) intention with Frege's term *Sinn* (intension).[10] But by *Sinn*, Frege means the semiotic imprinting of (primary) intention on its way to reference; so that Hirsch is, in effect, aligning (primary) intention with reference. Donald Davidson, working the other way around, is known as an "extensionalist" for denying (secondary) intension and reducing all meaning to reference (via Tarskian truth-theory). Yet Davidson is also, some of the time, a strong-intentionalist.[11] Since (primary) intention produces (secondary) intension, one might accuse Davidson of committing himself, via a slippery slope, to the semantic property he denies. But he would no doubt turn the tables and say there is no such commitment, because the alleged property in question is completely ephemeral once we have committed ourselves to (primary) intention.

That, indeed, is the second consequence of the model we are considering. Secondary intensionality is *epiphenomenal*. It is the iterative property by which utterances indicate meanings; but meanings that are not, ultimately, a function of the utterances themselves. Rather, the meanings indicated by secondary intensions are a function of referents on the one hand, primary intentions on the other. Since the hermeneutics of reference devolves on the hermeneutics of primary intention,

---

1977), pp. 67–137; and Brian Loar, "Two Theories of Meaning," in Evans and Mcdowell (eds), *Truth and Meaning*, pp. 138–161. For Davidson against intensions, see his "Actions, Reasons, and Causes," in *Essays on Actions and Events* (Oxford, 2001), pp. 3–19; his "What Metaphors Mean," *Critical Inquiry* 5 (1978): 29–45; his "Theories of Meaning and Learnable Languages," in *Inquiries into Truth and Interpretation* (Oxford, 2001), pp. 1–16; his "Truth and Meaning," in *Inquiries*, pp. 17–36; and his "On Saying That," in *Inquiries*, pp. 93–108.

10   Hirsch, *Validity*, 211–212.

11   See Michael Dummett, "'A Nice Derangement of Epitaphs': Some Comments on Davidson and Hacking," in Ernest Lepore (ed.), *Truth and Interpretation: Perspectives on the Philosophy of Donald Davidson* (Oxford and New York, 1986), pp. 459–476. For Davidson as strong-intentionalist, see his "Intending," in *Essays on Actions and Events*, pp. 83–102; and his "A Nice Derangement of Epitaphs," in Lepore (ed.), *Truth and Interpretation*, pp. 433–446.

we can simply say that (secondary) intensions indicate meanings that are a function of (primary) intentions. We can also say that (secondary) intensions indicate that meaning *is*, *tout court*, a function of (primary) intention. Indeed, this indicating – making the expressive unit an advertisement of its own insufficiency – would seem to be the whole point of the concept of (secondary) intension.

Thus we have a technical discussion relevant not only to Fregean semantics, but also to all strong-intentionalist interpretation. For all strong-intentionalist interpretation treats expression as the vehicle of an alienated primary intention; an alienated primary intention that points, moreover, always and already back to its unalienated original. This pointing, for strong-intentionalism, is "meaning." Following the pointer back to primary intention is "interpretation." What remains in expression is, well, nothing – an absence that can only be experienced as a yearning for presence. Hirsch speaks of textual "significance," which he denigrates as insignificant. Derrida writes of the "trace," which he celebrates as non-existent. These are but two versions, one conservative, the other radical, of an overarching intentionalist/intensionalist consensus that expressions appear on the hermeneutic scene only to disappear from it. Intension (with-an-s) is the semantic proper name for the strange and imaginary pulse by which they, allegedly, do so.

In Samson's case, (secondary) intension resides in his hair. This is the sign and vessel of his covenant with God; the pledge and guarantee of the vocation that is his meaning. It is easy to see how strong-intentionalists can theorize the hair. While he wears it, the pledge of his unviolated vow, Samson is wearing a sign of extraordinary divine favor. That is to say, he is wearing a sign of God's (primary) intention. The sign has no power or efficacy in and of itself, but simply and marvellously points back to the almighty presence. Loss of the hair, accordingly, is not really loss of the hair. Or rather, losing the hair is not what matters about losing the hair. What matters about a (secondary) intension is always and only its relationship to a (primary) intention. It ought to follow (1) that Samson's hair is epiphenomenal to the last – that even cut off, it signifies not its own termination, but termination of the divine (primary) intention that projected it as intensional; and (2) that recrudescence of the hair cannot entail recrudescence of its (secondary) intensionality. For if God's (primary) intention toward Samson has been terminated – if that is the point of what happens to the hair – then the hair, *ipso facto*, has ceased to be intensional. The hair could only reacquire its secondary intensionality – it could only ever again become the vehicle of Samson's strength – by a resumption of the divine primary intention. But for God to resume the said intention *just because the hair is regrowing* would be for him to stand the whole system of intentions and intensions (as it were) on its head.

This sort of reasoning, as plausible as it is conventional, is standard in contemporary *SA* criticism.[12] It is also standard, interestingly enough, in Renaissance and Baroque analogues of *SA*. As I have noted, the authors of these texts (collected by Watson Kirconnell forty years ago) invariably have Samson perform self-mocking

---

[12] Shawcross, *Uncertain*, pp. 1–13; Fish, *How Milton Works*, pp. 452–453.

feats of weakness, often accompanied by blows and abuse that he is powerless to resist, in the Philistine theatre. They also, invariably, make the pointlessness and uselessness of Samson's regrown hair a subject of comment. Finally, they have the champion regain his strength just in time to destroy the theatre – but only as a direct result of divine propitiation, which treats the hair as a merely arbitrary vehicle. So Hieronymus Zieglerus' Samson cries, while leaning on the pillars: "O Lord, my God, remember me this day, / And give me back the strength that once I had" (9). Marcus Andreas Wunstius, similarly, has his mocked and abused Samson plead: "O God, high ruler of the angel hosts / ... Breathe back my former strength in these my limbs" (46). Both Samsons regain their strength suddenly and dramatically after their prayers, changing from figures of Nazarite fun to figures of Philistine terror.

Theodorius Rhodius uses a Messenger, like Milton's, to report the ex-champion's final moments:

> Thus he softly prayed: "O Lord of Heaven,
> Who seest all things, grant that I may finish
> This final task!...
>
> ... Nor was his prayer unheard, nor vain the plea
> He made to God for help. For heavenly manhood
> Possessed him now; I saw his strength return
> And pour into his body like a tide. (64)

Vincenzo Giatinni's Samson, similarly, tells God after the prayer: "I feel / My vanished valour / Flood into my heart" (74). Joost van den Vondel imagines a scheming Samson, who seems to think that his returning hair means he should "lie in wait" (90). But even this Samson prays long and loud to have his strength restored in the theatre (122, 138); and at that moment, van den Vondel reports (somewhat cornily), "the hair on Samson's head / Seemed suddenly to grow" (138). The intensional sign of God's primary intention toward van den Vondel's Samson has been returning for some time; but it *significantly* returns (one almost wants to say "fully and richly returns") when and only when the primary intention has been directly renewed.

Milton has it the other way around. His Samson's (secondary) intension – his strength, the means by which God meant through him – returns with the return of its expressive vehicle. This is quite apart from any reconnection to God's primary intention. True, before going to the theatre Samson reports those "rouzing motions" which "dispose / To something extraordinary" his thoughts (1393–1394). But Milton (as anti-Samsonites invariably point out) declines to identify the source of these "motions." More importantly, the motions do not restore Samson's strength. We know this because Milton's Samson has regained his strength while he is still wallowing in the bad conscience that consists (as I have argued) in divine alienation. The feats of strength he performs in the theatre, none daring approach, are continuous with his turning of a grindstone in the mill – not exactly work for wimps. True, we are told that Samson is just one of many mill-slaves; but we are also told that his labor has the old superhuman characteristics. "Wilt thou then serve the *Philistines*," Manoa demands of his son, "with that gift / Which was expressly giv'n thee to annoy them?" (578–579) The Chorus concurs (1374–1375) that Samson has been benefitting the Philistines with his "Consecrated gift / Of strength" (1365–1366) – the very strength that the champion refuses, initially, to represent theatrically at the feast of Dagon. Samson explains that he doesn't mind doing "labour / Honest and lawful" (1379–1380). What he can't stand is labor ludic and "abominable" (1370), or, worse, no labor at all, just Philistine clemency "on the houshold hearth" (567). Under the latter conditions, Samson's hair would be a "vain monument of strength" (571), but not in the sense that it would memorialize something sadly absent. Rather, Samson's locks would be "redundant," "robustious to no purpose," in the sense that they would mark something pointlessly present (569–570). For Samson's strength is, as he puts it, "again returning with my hair / After my great transgression" (1366–1367). Its presence in him, its re-presentation *by his hair*, and *despite* his continuing alienation from God, is not even in question.

Dalila does not question it when Samson threatens to tear her limb from limb (953–954). Harapha does not question it when Samson baits and challenges him (1102–1254). Rather, both of Samson's Philistine visitors take refuge behind his blindness, which prevents Samson from finding his wife, and prevents Harapha (so the giant claims) from accepting the champion's challenge. Milton uses Samson's blindness to make narrative sense of the prisoner's power: yes, Samson is strong again, but he cannot recommence his rebellion because he cannot see what he is doing. At the same time, Milton uses the *issue* of Samson's blindness to demonstrate that the champion, along with his compatriots, tends to misunderstand the significance of what is happening in his hair. Samson spends a lot of time wishing that his sight could miraculously be restored, and lamenting, in an extension of the same logic, that sight had to be restricted to his eyes in the first place (67–110). If all that matters is God's will, he wonders, why couldn't a person just see "through every pore?" (98) The Chorus, similarly, assumes that God's favor to Samson, when and if it returns, will entail restoration of the champion's sight along with his strength. Yet by the end of the play, it becomes clear that Samson has regained his strength, and his strength alone. Sight and strength are not, in fact, joined in Samson's destiny. On the contrary, they are separated, along the axis of what made Samson Samson.[13]

And what made Samson Samson? God's will. What was God's will? It was that Samson should have miraculous strength. It was not that Samson should have miraculous sight. In both respects – in respect of what was given, and what was not – God's will proves totally *effective* in *SA*. This is where the play differs from its Renaissance and Baroque analogues; this is the point that is illuminated by the strength/sight distinction. God's will, in *SA*, has had a certain *result*. The latter is both

---

[13]   *contra* Michael Lieb's conflation of hair, sight and sex in "'A Thousand Foreskins': Circumcision, Violence, and Selfhood in Milton," *MS* 38 (2000): 198–219; and John Rogers' reduction of Samson's strength to God's continuing will in "The Secret of *Samson Agonistes*."

determined and discrete. It is discrete in that it includes certain aspects (e.g strength) but not others (e.g. vision). It is determined in that it is not easily deprived of this formal discretion – even after, and indeed precisely insofar as, God's will ceases to enact and project it. Samson's championhood, like an impression in wax, proves the efficacy of God's will precisely by proving itself detachable from God's will. It does not rely on God's continuing will in order to remain an impression. Thus (Milton's) Samson's strength returns with his hair, because a hair-strength connection is what God willed. Conversely, Samson's eyesight will not be restored, not because God could not will it – of course he could – but because God's continuing will is not entailed in Samson's championhood. Samson is a finished product, a done deal. This is both the premise, and the promise of his tragedy.

In a word, Samson is an *incarnation*. That is to say, he is not merely the material embodiment of a principle, namely God's will, that remains essentially or originally apart from its embodiment. Rather, Samson simply is God's will, re: Samson. He is exactly and uniquely the particular willed effect that God willed, in this case, as an effect. As Gadamer notes, incarnation is (at least in the Western context) uniquely Christian, defined by its difference from Platonic and Pythagorean embodiment. The embodied soul, in Greek idealism, "retains its own separate nature throughout all its embodiments." But the incarnate spirit, in Christian Scholasticism, is only fully realized in its incarnation.[14] On this point the Scholastics were assisted by Aristotle's materialism, according to which there is no form apart from its incidence in matter. In the same way, there is no Christ apart from his incidence as Son of man. To be sure, there is always the Son, and the Son is always God's Word. But the whole point of this doctrine is that the word is an expression from which an intention cannot be idealized or abstracted, without losing sight of the expression.

To put the matter in the technical terms that we have been using: Samson is a secondary intension that has been cut off from, and operates beyond, primary intention. Such a phenomenon dictates a rethinking of the very vocabulary in which it is described. Secondary intension, after all, is supposed to be epiphenomenal on primary intention. It is supposed to have no more independent existence or potentiality than the meaning of a word has (on this view) from the intention of its speaker. Therefore, to find secondary intension operating non-epiphenomenally is to find it operating anomalously. It is to find, indeed, that secondary intension is not necessarily any such thing. Samson (in Milton's version) ought to be a secondary phenomenon. Instead, his secondariness becomes primary. Instead of being like a word determined by what is meant, he is like a word as determinant of meaning.

Thus Milton's Samson, as an incarnation of God's intentions, directs us from primary to secondary intensionality – and then directs us to keep going. He shows us the paucity and the erroneousness of our conventional modes of thinking about speaking, acting and meaning. What remains, after this realization, is not an increased sophistication, but a sudden simplification. What remains is the word. The latter

---

14   *TM*, p. 418.

is what Milton's Samson most closely resembles – not just as an item requiring theorization, but also as a theoreme in and of itself. It is no advance, but a retreat, to break down the latter into its supposed theoretical components. The esotericism of primary intention, and even of secondary intension, does not help, but hinders, our attempt to understand Milton's Samson.

Logos / Word

It is important to recognize that the Christian idea of incarnation, though invoked to explain the mystery of the Trinity, is not itself mystical. It is radically pragmatic. The word is precisely *made available* in the incarnation, since the incarnation is the unique and definitive event of the word. One does not go behind Christ to access Christ (this side Gnosticism). One does not allegorize or esotericize a text in which God, uniquely, spoke. This is why the esotericism of the late-antique period, replete in the (justly so designated) Apocrypha, is so disastrous from an exegetic and theological point of view. If the Word is to be treated mystically, as Augustine complained, then there is no difference between scripture and pagan myth.[15]

Mysticism, and esotericism, are entirely on the non-Christian side of this story. They are entirely on the side of the Greek concept of *logos*. This term, with which ancient philosophy "more or less began," does not simply mean (Gadamer contends) "word," or even "spoken word" (*pace* Derrida). It means, rather, deep word, pre-word, un-word. Faced with the radical mercuriality and mediateness of language – while trying to free themselves from the sense, then still living, of language as essentialist naming – pre-Socratic thinkers posited a non-linguistic epistemology. In doing so, they effectively posited a non-linguistic language. For the only way they could find to free themselves from the power of the word was to propose, in effect, that the word was not the word. Behind the *onoma* or name – both too fickle and too fearsome to be the vehicle of truth – had to stand the *logos*, ineffable and serene. The latter (i) retained the capacity of *onoma* for bearing and managing meaning, while (ii) remaining free of onomatic unclarity, ambiguity, formal entrammelment, etc., and (iii) being guaranteed by correspondence with the cosmic order of things. Such a wondrous item, apparently, is an analytical fantasy, as chimerical and untestable as the metaphysical soul-fantasy that it resembles. Yet the idea of the *logos* begins, and perhaps best explains, the general western binarization of thought over its expression.[16]

In the theoretical preamble to my next chapter, I will characterize *logos*-philosophy under the general heading of "objectivism." Here, I would like to conclude my discussion of strong intentionalism in light of the *logos*-concept, with which strong intentionalism is clearly and profoundly compatible. It is not just because *logos*-philosophy is the default western tradition that strong intentionalists,

---

[15]   Allen, *Mysteriously Meant*, pp. 16–17.
[16]   *TM*, pp. 405–437.

working in that tradition, accord with *logos*-epistemology. It is, rather, because they are *doing* logos-*epistemology in the hermeneutic area* that strong intentionalists accord with *logos*-philosophy. Just as the idea of the *logos* is that the word is not the word, but must be deferred to an immanent pre-word (which may or may not exist); so the idea of strong-intention is that the text is not the text, but must be deferred to an immanent pre-text (which may or may not exist). Thus we have *a priori* reasons for doubting strong-intentionalist hermeneutics, insofar as the latter is a function of *logos*-philosophy. For the idea of the *logos* basically consists in contempt for language. This is unlikely to be a productive tradition in which to do literary criticism or theory.[17]

Now, as I have suggested, the notions on which strong intentionalism is based go back to Plato, via Augustine. Expressions are mimetic of intentions, on the strong-intentionalist view. Mimesis, moreover, is conceived as the degradation and deferral of an original, immanent presence. This model is shared (as I have argued) by conservative exegetes – who reconstruct a lost intention in the name of interpretative stability – and by their radical counterparts – who deconstruct interpretative stability in the name of a lost intention. Interminable tugs-o-war result. A total rethinking seems to be in order.

One such rethinking has been attempted by Steven Knapp and Walter Benn Michaels. Taking as their initial target the conservative hermeneutics of E.D. Hirsch (which I associated in my last chapter with the mainstream intentionalism of Milton studies), Knapp and Michaels argue that strong-intentionalists have a correct interpretative theory; but that the main consequence of the theory is that it has no application. Knapp and Michaels agree with Hirsch that textual meaning is entirely and exclusively a function of authorial intention, but criticize their predecessor for thinking this principle methodologically significant. If meaning, they argue, is the textual form of intention – if it is, hermeneutically speaking, *identical* with intention – what can it mean to turn from meaning to intention? Doing so would be like appealing from the Supreme Court to the highest court in the land. Hirsch's hermeneutics, then, inscribes a mere tautology, by describing what interpreters cannot not do. Finding meaning in texts means finding intentions; finding intentions can mean nothing else than finding meaning in texts. Hirsch's theory eats up itself, and eventuates in a mere pragmatism.[18]

The Knapp-Michaels argument is both clever and productive. It offers a continuing commitment to the hermeneutic plausibility of intentionalism, while avoiding both the theory's conservative and its radical dead-ends. Neither is it a turn to formalism – the only escape, traditionally, from the intentionalist *huis clos* – except, perhaps, in a new and synthetic version: an intentionalist formalism, in which texts are the

---

[17]   See Reed Way Dasenbrock's discussion of what he calls the "conventionalist paradigm" in his *Truth and Consequences*, pp. 1–84.

[18]   See Knapp and Michaels, "Against Theory," *Critical Inquiry* 8 (1982): 723–742; "Against Theory 2: Hermeneutics and Deconstruction"; and "The Impossibility of Intentionless Meaning," in Iseminger (ed.), *Intention and Interpretation* , pp. 51–64.

speakings of minds. With that formulation I am not aligning the Knapp-Michaels anti-theory with Platonic-Augustinian tradition, according to which the mind has an intention, then expresses it in iterative form. Such an account would simply be another exposition of *différance*. I am, rather, aligning Knapp and Michaels with a non- or post-post-structuralist model, according to which the mind's intention is only fully *available* in the text that is its expression. I am also indicating the next step, which is to propose that the mind's intention only fully *comes to be formed* in the text that is its expression. Knapp and Michaels never take this step (indeed, they do not even hold the line they have toed[19]), but it seems to me consistent with their radical hermeneutics. If intention is a matter of meaning, and meaning is a matter of expression, then intention is a matter of expression. It is not to be sought in an utterer's head, where it never was. It is, rather, to be sought in his utterance, where it first appears.

It is our normative experience of many thought-expressions that we work out our ideas only in the course of expressing them. Immanently, no doubt, we sense the possibility or the generality of the idea we wish to express. But we only determine its actuality and specificity by attempting to express it. In short, a non-trivial distinction obtains between intending to mean (primary intention), and meaning (secondary intension). Or, in the monomorphic terms suggested by Knapp and Michaels: a non-trivial distinction obtains between (mentally) intending to intend (in an expression), and intending (in an expression). This far, strong intentionalists are right. They are wrong, however, to think that mentally intending to intend is therefore the only kind of intending that matters. Intending in an expression, rather – speech-action – is the only kind of intending that matters to interpretation. It does not follow that the utterer of a text, or the agent of any speech-act, is not prompted by some immanent or pre-iterative motive – some rousing motions. But it does follow that the rousing motions are not the solely determinative or probative original of the speech-act. They may be formally causative; that does not make them hermeneutically determinative.

Furthermore: the limited explanatory power of an intention-expression sequence seems to vary indirectly with the importance and complexity of the expression in question. That is, even if trivial expressions can usefully be reduced to immanent intentions, it does not clearly follow that more momentous expressions can. The more worth saying something is – the more it makes a genuine contribution to our understanding – the less we can plan, form, or intend it before we start to say it. This is (quite obviously) not to say that we *never* understand ourselves in advance, or that expressions never follow and represent, in a simple and satisfying way, causative intentions. It is to say, rather, that we remain within the ambit of predictability and insignificance to the extent that we remain within this strong-intentionalist model.

---

[19]   See George M. Wilson, "Again, Theory: On Speaker's Meaning, Linguistic Meaning, and the Meaning of a Text," *Critical Inquiry* 19 (1992): 164–193; Dasenbrock, *Truth and Consequences*, 156–157; and Searle, "Literary Theory."

On the other hand: consider a good seminar, or a conference session, or a hallway debate – or any situation in which our interests engage with somebody else's. Extend the example to the reading of a text, the subject-matter of which interests us, but the argument of which dissatisfies us in some degree (no doubt I could have just said "the reading of a text"). Under these circumstances – and I submit this as common experience – we may feel intellectually compelled to annotate or otherwise respond to our interlocutor's utterance. No doubt we feel this compulsion, in part, because it seems to us that we wish to express a meaning that we have formed, immanently, while listening to (or reading) our interlocutor (or author). Yet even this account of the matter places a useful emphasis on the intellectual productivity of the exchange, by making our interlocutor the proximate cause of our thought. As I have already suggested, the thought can only be general or vague until we start to express it; and the only way to do better – the only way to deliver a really pre-fabricated commentary – is to talk or scribble to ourselves before talking or scribbling to others. But why is the pencil so urgent? Why must we get our hands up? Are we crazy? Are we vandals? Are we obnoxiously and aggressively trying to broadcast mental content that we might just as well, and would if we were more polite, keep to ourselves? No: the full significance of our interlocutive compulsion does not seem to be, at all, that we wish to express a meaning that we have already and immanently formed. Rather, the full significance of our compulsion seems to be that we wish to *find out what meaning it is that we want to form.* Always, to the extent that we wish to *find out what we mean*, we are compelled to express. And always, the only way to mean anything *worth* expressing – anything that raises the stakes of our understanding – is to grant in advance that it may be necessary to express it in order to mean it.

Expression, then, is not a copy of the understanding. Expression is an event of the understanding. Gadamer points out that the ancient Greek dialectic differed from the ancient Greek rhetoric precisely in the dialecticians' refusal to claim a pre-iterative understanding of their utterances. In Plato, it is always the sophist-rhetorician (or person influenced by sophist-rhetoricians) who claims his words as a copy of the wisdom in his head. The dialectitian-philosopher claims only that he does not carry any wisdom in his head; except the wisdom that he does not carry any wisdom in his head. But if not – if the *docta ignorantia* is not just a cute trick – where is the wisdom of dialectic? Only in the exchange of words, between teacher and student. True, the full Platonic scheme is powerfully logistic, and includes the semi-mystical notion (worked out in the *Meno*) that we always-already know everything sub-consciously, and that the process of discursive "learning" is really a process of immanent "remembering." But this fail-safe of dialectic simply corresponds to the immanence of intellectual potentiality. Potential knowledge is not knowledge; it is potential knowledge. Moreover, the Platonic upshot of learning-as-remembering is nothing other than the dialectic scene, where, uniquely, potentiality is stripped from knowledge through the work of utterance. Per Socrates' favorite metaphor for his own activities, the dialectitian is a midwife, helping her patients get their knowledge by helping them get it *out*.[20]

This, surely, is the way to make sense of Milton's infamously-odd argument, in *Areopagitica*, that pre-publication censorship (licensing) is an horrible idea even though post-publication censorship is a fine one. If Milton is going countenance "the fire and the executioner" for books which "come forth ... mischievous and libellous" (*CP* 2.569), why can't he countenance licensing, just a little non-violent refusal, in order to keep mischievous and libellous books from coming forth in the first place? Why, indeed, is he so passionately, almost hysterically opposed to the latter system? The answer seems to be that Milton cannot countenance the suppression of thinking; and for him, publication – getting one's thoughts out, participation in discourse – is productively and inextricably interinvolved with thinking. This is not only because Milton perceives books to be the language of the societal mind, but also because he perceives authors to think properly only through their books. It is intolerable that a man not be allowed to be "a doctor in his book." It is intolerable that he be prevented, by the finality and rigidity of the licenser's stamp, from continuing the dialogue with his own thoughts, through revision and addition. Above all, it is intolerable that a book, "in worse condition than a peccant soul, should be to stand before a jury *ere* it be born to the world" (*CP* 2.505). Published, made available, the book would be more than the man who made it: he is a "reasonable creature, God's image," but his book is "reason itself ... the image of God, as it were, in the eye" (*CP* 2.492). Prevented from publication, conversely, the book prevents the reason that would make the man reasonable.

Milton's attitude is consistent, it seems to me, with Gadamer's concept of *Gespräch*. This is "dialogue," or "conversation," theorized as the real mode of understanding. *Gespräch* is not a forensic or tactical exchange. Such exchanges certainly occur, in the police station, the courtroom, the madhouse; but (as Gadamer points out), the whole significance of these venues is that they are not normative. Normatively, a conversation is a productive, indeed a transformative exchange, on a basis of mutual ignorance with regard to the developing conversation itself. It is an iterative communion "in which we do not remain what we were." This failure to remain is nothing other than our understanding.[21] Clearly, the alienation of thoughts from the mind, recognized by *logos*-philosophy as the condition of all speech-acts, is also recognized by Gadamer as the condition of *Gespräch*. The difference between *logos* and *Gespräch*, however, is that for Gadamer there is nothing ironic or unfortunate about the necessary alienation of thoughts from the mind. The alienation of thoughts from the mind is the whole possibility of knowledge. It is *because* thoughts are alienated – because they become words – that they can enter *Gespräch*. And it is at the level of *Gespräch* that we are able to understand.

---

20   *TM*, pp. 362–380.
21   *TM*, pp. 383–398.

Gespräch, therefore, reverses the idealization of *logos*. *Gespräch* denies that the understanding avails itself of discourse; but claims that discourse renders understanding available. (The difference with post-structuralism should be clear: post-structuralism claims that discourse renders understanding *un*available.) Even reflexive understanding is discursive, for Gadamer: after all, "a person who thinks must ask himself questions," and to ask oneself a question is to offer oneself an utterance.[22] Utterance, therefore, is the pre-condition of understanding, which consists in the transformative exchange of utterances in *Gespräch*.

But if understanding devolves on *Gespräch*, and *Gespräch* devolves on utterance, then understanding cannot be a matter of (primary) intentionality. For what could be more inimical to utterance (on which understanding devolves) than an un-uttered, indeed un-utterable, immanent state? Understanding must devolve, instead, on (secondary) intensionality. That is, the ground of understanding must be the meaning of words – and/or meaning as modelled, on a primary basis, by what we think of as the meaning of words. The whole *logos* model – word-meaning as epiphenomenal on mind-meaning – has to go.

In its place, we find a massive hermeneutic re-orientation toward language – not as the analytic tool-box that allows understanding, but as the phenomenon we are trying to understand. (Again: the anti-post-structuralist proviso is that understanding is real and, in principle, achievable.) Ultimately, this re-orientation comes down to the recognition that understanding the phenomenon of language simply *is* understanding. "*Sein, das verstanden werden kann, ist Sprache*" [Being that can be understood is language].[23] To work out Gadamer's slogan we need (secondary) intension – now revealed as an appalling logistic misnomer – and utterance.

Our hero, on both counts, must be Milton's Samson. For Samson turns to utterance (speech-action) in destroying the theatre, on a basis of the (secondary) intension that exists and persists, fundamentally and inalienably, in his hair. Admittedly, his action is not a speech, and neither is his hair a word. But that is to say that word-meaning, far from being a restrictive phenomenon that we understand and can define the parameters of, is to be taken as a general and non-restrictive model for the whole phenomenon of meaning that we do not understand. It is *logos*-philosophers, after all, who always insist on a rigorous distinction between words and things. This distinction is what allows them to hold that words don't matter. If we are to hold that words do matter, we are going to have to consider that words are matter. But if words are matter, then matter – some of it, at least – is words.

I began this discussion, a long time ago, by surveying the strong-intentionalist assumptions of so much *SA*-criticism. I am now in a position to disagree with these assumptions. The whole point of Milton's Samson is that he makes the move – which Milton's Lady never makes – to expression. He turns to the meaning,

---

22   *TM*, pp. 375.
23   *WM*, p. 478; *TM*, p. 474.

the intension, that has been made available in his hair; and he makes this available, with devastating results, to the Philistine audience. Milton's God, moreover, has allowed him to do so. Milton's God has not revoked intension in revoking his favor. The reason this non-revocation matters is that it contradicts, as I have been trying to show, an epistemological and hermeneutic tradition of very great breadth and depth. The significance of *SA* is precisely not (per much criticism) that it adheres to this tradition, the tradition of *logos*-philosophy. The significance of *SA*, rather, is that it departs from *logos*-tradition. Most importantly, it departs from the strong-intentionalism that is the hermeneutic version of *logos*-philosophy. The point is not, despite all strong-intentionalist accounts – pro-Samson, anti-Samson, and uncertain – what Samson means to do. The point is that he means by doing. Milton writes *SA* as a venue in which this point comes to matter.

In my next and final chapter, I will elaborate on the hermeneutic consequences of Milton's anti-intentionalism. These, as I have already indicated, are summed up in Gadamer's concept of *Gespräch*, dialogue, and in a view of language as the ground of meaning, on which we pragmatically rely. Making sense of this model will entail a return to *PL*, and an extended consideration of dialogue – not only as theoreme, but as an epic subject-matter in its own right.

Chapter 4

Talking and Learning in Paradise

Philosophical hermeneutics, Gadamer says, is not a method.[1] Yet method, traditionally, has seemed indispensable to hermeneutics. From its origins in biblical exegesis, to its interactions with modern experimental science, the theory of interpretation has consisted in techniques and standards (methods) for gaining valid results. Arguably, in being methodical, hermeneutics has not been philosophical. Yet in being non-methodical, Gadamer's philosophy seems, perhaps, non-hermeneutical.

This definitional paradox is compounded by the hermeneutic plausibility of method. Presumably, hermeneutics is consistent with the view (expressed at the outset of this book) that interpretation is the matrix of understanding. We interpret data, textual or otherwise, in order to understand it. Now, understanding, insofar as it is correct, must be distinguishable from misunderstanding. This distinction must, moreover, have to do with the facts of the data. Agreement between our minds and the facts – in a word, knowledge – is what defines correct understanding. Therefore, interpretation, in order to arrive at (correct) understanding (and not misunderstanding), must be directed toward the facts. "Method" denotes this direction.

Yet it is hard to see how method itself can be achieved. For the only way to achieve it would be by the very practice, namely interpretation, that it is supposed to control. After all, the distinction (on which method rests) between understanding and misunderstanding can itself only occur as an instance of understanding. Any instance of understanding, moreover, occurs only through interpretation. That, at least, is the view expressed above – which is exactly what has led us to the apparent necessity of method. Now, method becomes apparently necessary because interpretation can produce misunderstanding, as well as understanding. Therefore, the distinction between understanding and misunderstanding, because it must be generated by interpretation, is itself, potentially, an instance of misunderstanding. In other words, we do not really know that there is any such distinction (except as achieved through interpretation). But if not, there is no content to the notion of method.

---

[1]   See *TM*, pp. xi–xxxviii, 3–8, 173–197, 254–271, 346–362, and 474–491. See also Gadamer, "From Word to Concept: The Task of Hermeneutics as Philosophy," in Krajewski (ed.), *Gadamer's Repercussions*, pp. 1–12; Weinsheimer, *Philosophical Hermeneutics and Literary Theory*, pp. 24–40; and Gerald Bruns, *Hermeneutics, Ancient and Modern* (New Haven, 1992), pp. 1–14. For critiques of the possibility of a non-methodical hermeneutics, see Hirsch, *Validity*, pp. 245–264; and Stanley Rosen, "*Horizontverschmelzung*," in Hahn (ed.), *The Philosophy of Hans-Georg Gadamer*, pp. 207–222.

Giving the notion content requires going back to the beginning of our thinking about it. If we are to enable method, we must restrict hermeneutics. We must take the position that some things we understand, and thus some facts we know, originate outside the interpretative matrix. In particular, the distinction between understanding and misunderstanding must be reckoned non-interpretative. Ditto the distinctions between non-interpretative and interpretative; between subjective and objective interpretation; between interpretation *tout court* and understanding *tout court*. Ultimately, method demands a limited hermeneutics in which interpretation is preceded, and foundationally justified, by some kind of non-interpretative apprehension. The latter may be, as modern natural scientists often seem to think, a quasi-Platonic mimesis; or it may be, as Kant held, epistemological immanence. Whatever the posit, the non-interpretative object or objects that guarantee the possibility of method must, indeed, be objective to interpretation.

A convenient label for the resulting view is, accordingly, "objectivism."[2] Of this, strong intentionalism, which I critiqued in my second chapter, is one major variant, directed toward intension as the object of (textual) interpretation. Analogous objects, in other disciplines, include (but are not limited to) the facts of natural science, the aetiologies of disease, and the causative events of history. Objectivism underlies the traditional, technical conception of hermeneutics as an attempt to bring the mind, through interpretation, into understanding of a non-interpretative object. It also underlies and guarantees the hermeneutic trope of discovery, as the means by which non-interpretative objects are revealed, through interpretation. Indeed, objectivism would seem to explain what is at stake in the hermeneutics of discovery: nothing other than the epistemological limitation of our interpretative activity, such that the latter becomes a transient and relatively trivial phase of the understanding. Conversely, Gadamer's hermeneutics of recognition, because it consists in an attempt to think about interpretation in a new and serious way, must reject objectivism. Which (to bring us back to the beginning of our discussion) is why Gadamer rejects method.

Now objectivism, as I have already suggested, is *prima facie* plausible. It is vulnerable to critique, however, on two main fronts. First: objectivism is paralogistic. That is to say, it involves logical question-begging, circularity, or regress. For the objectivist denial of interpretative universality follows from, and is dependent on, the possibility of telling the difference between understanding and misunderstanding. Telling this difference successfully is the task of method. Thus the denial of

---

2   See Richard J. Bernstein, *Beyond Objectivism and Relativism: Science, Hermeneutics and Praxis* (Philadelphia, 1983); G.B. Madison, "Getting beyond Objectivism: The Philosophical Hermeneutics of Gadamer and Ricoeur," in Don Lavoie (ed.), *Economics and Hermeneutics* (London and New York, 1991), pp. 34–58; and Kertscher, "'We understand differently'." For the objectivist position articulated against Gadamer, see Hirsch, *Validity*; Hans Albert, "Critical Rationalism and Universal Hermeneutics," in Malpas, Arnswald, and Kertscher (eds), *Gadamer's Century*, pp. 15–24; and Demetrius Teigas, *Knowledge and Hermeneutic Understanding: A Study of the Habermas-Gadamer Debate* (Lewisburg and London, 1995).

interpretative universality depends on method. Yet method itself depends on the denial of interpretative universality – which is the only thing that makes it possible, even in principle, to tell the difference between understanding and misunderstanding. Objectivism, far from being a linear argument, proves tautological. To be sure, this sort of thing has its philosophical defenders. Among them are Heidegger and, to some extent, Gadamer.[3] The phenomenological interest in paralogisms, however, has to do with the commitments they reveal as subsisting beyond our rational efforts. In these terms, paralogism is genuinely embarrassing to objectivism, which is supposed to be a rational account of facts, and nothing more.

That brings us to the second critique: objectivism is an idealism (in the philosophical, rather than the political, sense). It is a theory of knowledge as determined, ultimately, by transcendent entities. For Plato, these are the Ideas, which render reality knowable as a collection of mere objects. For Kant, they are eternity and God, which guarantee objective knowledge *a priori*. The neo-Kantian Frege founded modern semantics (as I discussed in my last chapter) on the idea of an intension (*Sinn*) that is objective, yet non-material. For Frege, the non-materiality of intension guarantees its objectivity – by placing it beyond both the psychological and the physical realms of doubt. Hirsch, Strauss and others parlay Frege's semantic concept into an hermeneutic one, with the same curious fusion of objectivity and transcendence. Intension is "in" nothing other than the text; but it is not really "in" any part or parts of the text at all. Materially speaking, it is nowhere – and that is its advantage. For intension can therefore be theorized as the ideal projection and final determinant of the material text. No doubt, identifying this way of thinking as idealistic does not, in and of itself, constitute a critique. After all, it is possible that idealism could be right. What does seem to constitute a critique, however, is identifying objectivism, *per se*, as an idealism. For objectivism, the theory of non-interpretative facts, turns out to depend on interpretative posits that can hardly be called factual.

As paralogistic and idealistic, objectivism generates deconstruction. I have already made this argument with regard to strong intentionalism, but it is important to recognize that the point holds generally. Whether they address themselves to intention, intension, or other objectivist postulates, deconstructive critics are able to show that objectivity is not objective; that non-interpretativity is interpretative; that the premise of method can never itself be secured or proven by method. Deconstruction is able to base its paradoxical results on the (apparent) hermeneutic necessity of objectivist premises, because these premises are paralogistic and/or idealistic. When the premises fail, as they must, along the lines that I have suggested, the deconstructionist triumphs. But this is simply because his enemy built him a ruin. Deconstruction is perverse objectivism, because objectivism is latent deconstruction.

---

[3] See Heidegger, *Sein und Zeit* (Tuebingen, 1967), pp. 6–8; and Gadamer, *TM*, pp. 265–271.

Ultimately, what fails in the slide from the one to the other is the theoretical demarcation of non-interpretative knowledge. This, we recall, was the fundamental claim of objectivism. When the non-interpretative claim fails, we end back where we started: in the recognition that all our knowledge is interpretative. Yet what was our opening position now looks like our catastrophe. Because objectivism has argued that non-interpretativity is necessary for knowledge, deconstruction is able to argue that there is no knowledge.

The way to avoid this result is to go in the opposite direction from both deconstruction and objectivism. The way to assert knowledge is to affirm interpretativity. This, of course, deconstruction does, in contrast to objectivism. The opposing theories agree, however, that negative (or at least significant) consequences attend such an affirmation. This is where they are both wrong. For if we affirm that all our knowledge is interpretative, *then there are no consequences whatsoever.* There is simply the ongoing attempt to know, in the conditions that obtain. Consequences (negative or positive) could only follow for our knowledge if there were an *alternative* to universal interpretativity. This is the possibility that objectivism and deconstruction seek to project. But it is the possibility that the logic of interpretation renders null in advance. If we accept this logic as our starting-position, then the objectivist posit does not even arise. We recognize that our epistemological conditions could not be other than they are – and, therefore, that the whole issue is nil.

Nothing, however, does not come of nothing. Everything does. Understanding, universality, correctness, principle – all these and more are recovered and revalidated when we recognize the irrelevance of their interpretativity to their potential validity. We are returned to a completely pragmatic and unremarkable forum, in which making sense, if we can do that, is absolutely sensible. The rule of no consequences does not mean that everything is up for grabs. That influential and popular view, if I may say so, is a veritably Satanic missing of the point.[4] The rule of no consequences means, rather, that everything is grabbable. Our task is to grab – what we can. Yet the distinction between what can and cannot be grabbed – between what makes sense, and what does not – is constantly encountered within our pragmatic activity. Indeed, the said distinction is our interpretative ground.

This is by no means an original argument. It is consistent with Donald Davidson's critique of "the very idea of a conceptual scheme."[5] It is also consistent with the

---

4   *Contra* Stanley Fish, *"Is There a Text in this Class?": The Authority of Interpretive Communities* (Cambridge, MA, 1980); *Doing What Comes Naturally*; and *The Trouble with Principle* (Cambridge, MA, 1999).

5   See Davidson, "Thought and Talk," in *Inquiries*, pp. 155–170; "On the Very Idea of a Conceptual Scheme," in *Inquiries*, pp. 183–198; and "A Coherence Theory of Truth and Knowledge," in Lepore (ed.), *Truth and Interpretation,* pp. 307–319. On Gadamer and Davidson, see Davidson, "Gadamer and Plato's *Philebus*," in Hahn (ed.), *The Philosophy of Hans-Georg Gadamer*, pp. 421–432 ; Gadamer, "Reply to Davidson," in Hahn (ed.), *The Philosophy of Hans-Georg Gadamer*, pp. 433–436; David C. Hoy, "Post-Cartesian Interpretation: Hans-Georg Gadamer and Donald Davidson," in Hahn (ed.), *The Philosophy*

strong pragmatism of C.S. Peirce (as opposed to the weak pragmatism of James and Dewey).[6] Above all, though, the non-consequentiality of universal interpretativity is consistent with Gadamer's hermeneutic rejection of method. For method is precisely the idea of controlling interpretativity for its negative consequences – while constructing interpretativity as having such consequences. Gadamer recognizes (1) that the problem of objectivism is hermeneutical, before it is epistemological: in other words, it has to do with our theory of interpretation, before it has to do with our theory of knowledge; and (2) that the way to resolve this problem is to deny its premise. The way to resolve the problem of objectivism is to deny objectivism's problem. This is what Gadamer achieves by proposing a non-methodical hermeneutics.

But what sort of hermeneutics is that? Obviously, Gadamer cannot be teaching how, or how not, to interpret anything. That would simply constitute a return to method. Neither can Gadamer be teaching that all interpretations are valid. That would mean abandoning the connection between interpretation and knowledge – collapsing hermeneutics into deconstruction, and thereby re-introducing method through the back door. Gadamer must be offering a philosophical account of interpretation that accepts both its universality, and its productivity of knowledge. Knowledge, moreover, must still mean knowledge. That is, knowledge, as considered by philosophical hermeneutics, must have to do with facts. (The error of objectivism, as we have seen, is precisely that it cannot ground the category of facts.) Given, however, that we attain knowledge only through understanding – and understanding through interpretation – which may just as well lead us into misunderstanding, or failure to grasp the facts – how can philosophical hermeneutics avoid the pull of method?

Only through dialogue, or conversation (*Gespräch*). This concept is to philosophical hermeneutics as the concept of method is to traditional hermeneutics. Dialogue is not a method, in the sense of a technique for something that we do. It is, rather, something that we do. Dialogue is practice – in the full Gadamerian resonance of that word, originating with the hermeneutic ontology of the game (see pp. 25–9). In dialogue, we put our understanding of a given subject-matter into play, vis-à-vis our interlocutors. Frequently, we find our understanding returned – that is, rejected, by an opposing understanding. At this point, deconstruction and/or objectivism would infer relativism. Even Bakhtin, the postmodern theorist most closely associated with dialogism, distinguishes it from a monologic certainty

of Hans-Georg Gadamer, pp. 111–130; and John McDowell, "Gadamer and Davidson on Understanding and Relativism," in Malpas, Arnswald, and Kertscher (eds), *Gadamer's Century*, pp. 173–194.

  6   For Gadamer and pragmatism, see Thomas M. Alexander, "Eros and Understanding: Gadamer's Aesthetic Ontology of the Community," in Hahn (ed.), *The Philosophy of Hans-Georg Gadamer*, pp. 323–348; Georgia Warnke, "Walzer, Rawls, and Gadamer: Hermeneutics and Political Theory," in Wright (ed.), *Festivals of Interpretation*, pp. 136–160; and Philip Mirowski, "The Philosophical Bases of Institutionalist Economics," in Lavoie (ed.), *Economics and Hermeneutics*, pp. 76–112.

that remains the standard of knowledge.[7] The confrontation of understanding with understanding would seem to leave no means of resolution. But of course, there is exactly one means of resolution (whether or not it is successful): the mutual attempt of interlocutors to understand each others' understandings. This attempt, which Gadamer calls the "fusion of horizons," is the only way for understanding to be controlled for knowledge on a non-objectivist basis. The latter is necessary because, as we have seen, objectivism simply guarantees deconstruction. Dialogue, uniquely, avoids this result, by grounding knowledge as a synthetic function of non-objective understandings.[8]

Thus dialogue emerges as the hermeneutic game. In this game, our understanding is compelled to experience its own limits. We are compelled to acknowledge the possibility that our interlocutor, who contradicts us, may be right. This remarkable possibility opens understanding to knowledge precisely because it originates neither in a hopeless idealism about getting beyond interpretation of the relevant data, nor in a hopeless reduction to our own interpretation of that data. It originates, rather, in somebody else's interpretation of that data. Dialogue is pragmatic, provisional – and utterly necessary. By trying to come to agreement with our interlocutors about how to interpret something – by trying to come to agreement, in other words, about the facts – we set our understanding on the way to knowledge.

Several points follow. One is inclusivity. Because it is in the nature of the case that we must always be *on the way* to knowledge – joining up truth to truth, as Milton says (*CP* 2.551) – we have no immediate basis on which to refuse porters, guides, or companions. Dialogue is infinitely open to interlocutors. In this sense, as in many others, philosophical hermeneutics proves to be the true opposite of objectivism, for which the multiplication of understandings (of a given subject-matter) can only cause embarrassment. But in dialogue, the more who join, the more knowledge will be increased. The more perspectives that are brought to bear on a given subject-matter, the likelier it is that dialogic agreement about that subject-matter, if achieved, will entail knowledge. Against the objectivist complaint that we can't ever *really* know knowledge, in any final or cosmic way, the hermeneuticist can simply agree – and return to the ordinary work of trying to know through dialogic agreement. The more, the merrier, is the festal rule of dialogue.

The only limit to this rule – the limit that makes it a rule – is that all who join join in. Interlocutive openness is the corollary of dialogic inclusivity. Only by expressing our understanding, while attending to others' expressed understandings, can we make

---

See Donald G. Marshall, "Dialogue and Ecriture," in Michelfelder and Palmer (eds), *Dialogue and Deconstruction*, pp. 206–214.

TM, pp. 180, and 362–389; Beiner, "Gadamer's Philosophy of Dialogue"; Ulrich Arnswald, "On the Certainty of Uncertainty: Language-Games and Forms of Life in Gadamer and Wittgenstein," in Malpas, Arnswald, and Kertscher (eds), *Gadamer's Century*, pp. 25–44; Weinsheimer, *Philosophical Hermeneutics and Literary Theory*, pp. 15–17; and Donald G. Marshall, "On Dialogue: To Its Cultured Despisers," in Krajewski (ed.), *Gadamer's Repercussions*, pp. 123–144.

dialogue occur. This bivalent openness, to be sure, is not easy. It remains very much in our power and privilege *not* to make dialogue occur. Silencing, withholding, and mere ludic foolishness are three popular ways to this terminal achievement. All have to do with intentional secrecy, presupposed as hermeneutically normative by both objectivism and deconstruction. Yet what emerges here, precisely because we are free not to engage in dialogue, is the creditable role of our will in so engaging. We have to make an *effort* not to slip from dialogue into monologue. We have to make an *effort* to refuse the temptation of method. Openness and engagement, against secrecy and disengagement, emerge as the non-methodical tasks of dialogic practice. Dialogue calls upon us to play, and play well. Everything depends – knowledge depends – on our willingness to hear this call.

Finally: expressing our understanding means coming to the end of it. We have to say what we (think we) know, in order to reach the *starting*-place of dialogue. Now, saying what we think we know means encountering its limits. It means passing from truth-statements to a lack of truth-statements. What remains for us, at that point, is no longer saying what is and is not true. What remains, rather, is *asking* what may or may not be true, beyond what we (think we) know. Dialogue entails questioning. Our interlocutors, in taking up our questions and attempting to answer them, must draw upon the resources of what they (think they) know, in ways they could not possibly have anticipated. They then can return the favor to us, asking questions that emerge from their own dialectic experience, and causing us to re-examine what we (think we) know by means of that same experience. The skill we gain in this process – the skill of questioning – is inseparable from the knowledge it attempts to secure.

In the remainder of this chapter, I will argue that *Paradise Lost* is, in part, about dialogic questioning. The non-triviality of that proposal, I hope, is established or at least suggested by the theorization above. Milton represents dialogue, constructed hermeneutically, as his over-arching epic subject-matter. This is the final step in an exoteric series that began with Milton's textualized conscience, and continued with the Lady's (erroneously inward) and Samson's (gloriously outward) intentionality. Dialogue, beginning where intentional expression ends, is what intentional expression serves. Meanwhile, the hermeneutic priority or primordiality of dialogue (*die Ursprünglichkeit des Gesprächs*) guarantees the extra-intentional view of language that is suggested by Samson's hair (as treated by Milton in *SA*).[9] On such a view, language is fundamentally not anything that we possess. It is, rather, something that possesses us. Milton's way of putting this idea is to represent language as a divine entailment – in which the divine, freely and remarkably, chooses to constitute itself. Asking questions within dialogue, the game of language, is how Milton's God's creatures come to know His being, and their own.

---

[9]   *WM*, p. 375. My translation. The translation "primacy of dialogue," which seems to me quite weak, is given in *TM*, p. 368.

In Even Scale

Most Miltonists, it has recently been argued, are willing to accept uncertainty only as the obverse of certainty.[10] It is hard to see how they might do anything else. Certainty and uncertainty spring into thinking together. Both are objectivist properties of statements: utterances gauged by their truth-value (their being true or false). Milton, however, is characteristically committed (or so I will argue here) to the hermeneutic representation of questions: utterances gauged by their wanting truth-value. The significance of questioning, as we learn from Gadamer, is not primarily that it indicates any relationship between certainty and uncertainty. Rather, questions betoken a dialectic epistemology that is beyond uncertainty, because it is prior to certainty.

Consider, for example, the conclusion of *PL* book four. Satan and the archangel Gabriel are preparing for single combat, when God intervenes with a gnomic sign:

> now dreadful deeds
> Might have ensu'd, nor onely Paradise
> In this commotion, but the Starrie Cope
> Of Heav'n perhaps, or all the Elements
> At least had gon to rack, disturbd and torne
> With violence of this conflict, had not soon
> Th' Eternal to prevent such horrid fray
> Hung forth in Heav'n his golden Scales, yet seen
> Betwixt *Astrea* and the *Scorpion* signe,
> Wherein all things created first he weighd,
> The pendulous round Earth with ballanc't Aire
> In counterpoise, now ponders all events,
> Battels and Realms: in these he put two weights
> The sequel each of parting and of fight;
> The latter quick up flew, and kickt the beam. (4.990-1004)

Nothing could be clearer, as far as Gabriel is concerned. "*Satan*," he says, "I know thy strength, and thou knowst mine,"

> Neither our own but giv'n; what follie then
> To boast what Arms can doe, since thine no more
> Then Heav'n permits, nor mine, though doubld now
> To trample thee as mire: for proof look up,
> And read thy Lot in yon celestial Sign
> Where thou art weigh'd, and shown how light, how weak,
> If thou resist. (1006–1013)

Satan, apparently, agrees:

---

10   See Herman, *Destabilizing Milton.*

> The Fiend lookt up and knew
> His mounted scale aloft: nor more; but fled
> Murmuring, and with him fled the shades of night. (1013–1015)

A book that began with Satan's tragic soliloquy (4.32–113), and built to an expectation of climactic battle, ends instead in Satan's pathetic and undramatic retreat.

The effect is quintessentially Miltonic. It replicates the travesty of 2.681–816, where Satan climbs down from his confrontation with Death. It is consistent, too, with Satan's failure in battle against the archangel Michael (6.296–343), and (worse) the mere seraph Abdiel (6.171–202). Throughout *PL,* Satan presents himself as the representative, indeed the embodiment, of classical epic heroism. Throughout *PL,* the reader discovers this alleged heroism to be either insufficient or inapposite for the situations in which Satan finds himself. Milton (as is well known) thereby takes epic tradition itself as his epic target, doing violence to that tradition in order to make an ethical point. Basically, the point is that Satan's heroism is not what it seems; that heroism *tout court,* as classically constructed, is a false ideal. Milton's revisionist tactic is highly literary, and brilliantly reflexive. It is also completely intelligible, once mapped out.

Yet a problem arises, in the current instance. Gabriel's reading of God's scales (here associated with the constellation Libra) is itself revisionist. It appears to be indebted to scripture, specifically to Daniel 5:27, where Belshazzar is "weighed in the balances, and found wanting." No scales, however, actually appear in the episode that gives rise to that famous, but metaphorical, judgment. God's "golden scales," by contrast, hanging visibly in the firmament above Milton's Paradise, are explicitly and inescapably classical. With their attendant rhetoric of battles and realms, they are indebted to *Aeneid* 12, where Jupiter weighs the fates of Turnus and Aeneas in "the two pans of a scale" (725–727). Those pans were borrowed, in turn, from *Iliad* 22.209 (where Hector is weighed against Achilles), and 8.69–72 (where Greeks are weighed against Trojans).[11] The problem for Gabriel's reading of God's version of these scales is that when Homer's Zeus and Virgil's Jupiter weigh outcomes, the *lighter* lot is favored. The heavier is defeated, going down to dusky Tartarus. On a classical reading of Milton's God's classical scales, therefore, the rising lot of fight would be a sign of *favor.* God would be giving Satan a sign of assent (through ascent).

To be sure, this would be a very strange gesture for Milton's God to make. We may infer that he cannot possibly be making it. Gabriel is right, on this view, to perceive that God means the (ostensibly) classical scales with a reversal of their classical intension. For confirmation, we may point to Satan's decision to flee (and not to fight), which seems to indicate dialectical agreement with Gabriel's revisionism. Yet our situation becomes worse as this revisionism becomes stronger. For one thing, it is at God's expense. By reading God's speech-act as requiring hermeneutic inversion, we imply (which is not to say we prove) God's illocutionary incoherence. For another thing, such a reading is to Satan's credit – assuming he agrees with Gabriel. Not only

---

11   See Fowler (ed.), *John Milton:* Paradise Lost, pp. 278–279.

does Satan free himself from the classical idioms in which he is usually stuck; he does so by recovering an intension that God, by reliance on the very same classical idioms, has left extraordinarily obscure. In sum, the revisionist reading of the scales, however sensible and necessary it seems, creates more difficulty than it resolves. It makes God and Satan switch places, across some very important divides.

Perhaps we can backtrack. Perhaps Satan does not agree with Gabriel's reading. Promisingly, the scene makes good sense if we suppose that he does not. The narrator tells us only that Satan "knew his mounted scale aloft; nor more; but fled / Murmuring (4.1014–1015)." "Nor more" is interpretative nullification. It distinguishes and conserves Satan's knowing of the scales (whatever that means) from anything that might challenge or exceed his knowing. Presumably, Gabriel's revisionist speech ought to be the kind of "more" that is not Satan's knowing. Meanwhile, "but fled" – as opposed to "and fled" or "thus fled" – makes Satan's flight disjunctive with his knowing of the scales. "But" makes "fled" a logical surprise: something that does not follow. But it would follow, naturally and adjunctively, if Satan knew the scales as a sign meaning "flee." We may infer that Satan knows the scales as a sign meaning "fight." We may infer that the would-be classical hero reads "his mounted scale" classically.

In the opening monologue of book four, Satan has explained his peculiar nightmare as terror of God's grace. "Say I could repent and could obtaine / By Act of Grace my former state," he hypothesizes:

> how soon
> Would highth recal high thoughts, how soon unsay
> What feign'd submission swore: ease would recant
> Vows made in pain, as violent and void.
> ... Which would but lead me to a worse relapse,
> And heavier fall: so should I purchase deare
> Short intermission bought with double smart. (4.94–97, 100–102)

The worst part about being Satan is that there is always a worse part. "In the lowest deep," as he puts it in this same speech, "a lower deep / Still threatning to devour me opens wide"(4.76–77). ("I would be at the worst," he tells Christ in *Paradise Regained*: "worst is my Port" [3.209].) But even within this deconstructive experience of the worst, the worst as always-worse, Satan identifies divine forgiveness as the very worst. A gesture of favor from God would send Satan careening through his entire damned trajectory yet once more. Or so it seems to Satan. His worst fear is not God's wrath, but God's love. Arguably, book four ends with a sign from God that Satan reads as a manifestation of this uniquely terrible possibility. His mounted scale, read as a classical sign of God's favor, is actually more repellent to Satan than it would be if read (with Gabriel) as a non-classical sign of God's disfavor. The book's anticlimax, then, results from Satan's soteriological inversion. His "murmuring," accordingly, resumes and travesties the grandiose soliloquizing with which he opened the book.

Or perhaps not. Perhaps Satan does just agree with Gabriel. Perhaps the non-classical reading of the scales is right; perhaps it is wrong. Perhaps, in a word, perhaps is all we have. Our interpretative dispossession, if such it be, is predicated on the simultaneous projection and sequestration of key intentional states. We need to know, but do not know, how Satan reads the scales. We need to know, but do not know, how God means the scales. Ultimately, we need to know, but do not know, how Milton means the episode. The same state of unknowing, according to many prominent critics, emerges in episode after episode of *PL* (and Milton's other work – *SA*, for example).[12] The effect is, perhaps, analogous to (and represented by) the one that God achieves with the scales – this emblem of ambiguity, traditionally displaced, and therefore rendered all-but-irresolvable. Gabriel and Satan, however vainly, must try to resolve it. We, congruently, must try to resolve their irresolution. Yet all we can be certain about, more-or-less as an hermeneutic principle, is that our efforts will fail. Reading the scales episode entails our submission to a Miltonic rule of uncertainty.

Such a view of Milton's hermeneutics is, first of all, intentionalist. It is a claim about what, and how, Milton means. As we have seen earlier in this book, all interpretation entails such a claim. Intentionalism is less a theory than it is a tautology. For that reason, critics who make a theoretical appeal to the concept of intention, as opposed to a critical description of written intentions, are making (as it were) a non-existent point. Now, uncertainty-critics claim to be describing an aspect of Milton's intentions, which is the kind of thing all critics must do. Specifically, uncertainty-critics claim to be showing us that Milton's intentions are uncertain. This, however, is not a critical description of Milton's intentions in any particular aspect. It is, rather, a theoretical assertion that Milton has expressed intentions *per se*. For intentions are always, and by definition, uncertain. They can only be recovered from the text; and yet the text is exactly what seems to lack them. Every act of reading, precisely because it must involve intentions, devolves on an interpretative standard of uncertainty. This standard, therefore, is theoretically universal – and critically insignificant. Uncertainty is nothing more than the objectivist shadow of intention, serving only to point out something that could not not be there.

We might claim, of course, that Milton's intentions are unusually uncertain. Perhaps, for example, Milton's writings contain more uncertainty than most. Perhaps, alternatively, Milton means something special by his uncertainty. Quantification of uncertainty, however, would seem inconsistent with uncertainty. Even if it could be carried out, it would amount to little more than a proof that Milton has intended more than most other writers – in other words, that his writings are unusually rich. But this, I think, is obvious. As for the possibility that Milton means something special by his uncertainty, this special something can be general or specific. If general, it is perhaps a deconstructive claim that our understanding is always-already vitiated by uncertainty – including, presumably, our understanding of this claim. The argument

---

[12]   See Chapter Two.

consumes itself. If specific, the special something of Milton's uncertainty is perhaps some kind of encoding, worked out with regard to secret referents. Versions of this idea (as discussed in my Introduction), have been very popular in Milton studies. The problem with encoding, however, is that it depends, not only on a secret referent, but also on a secret intention (as opposed to a merely uncertain one). The problem with secret intention, in turn, is that there can never be any evidence for it. Once evidence is identified, the intention is no longer secret; it remains uncertain, but only in the tautological manner of all intentional expression. Absent the identification of evidence, meanwhile, the claim of secret intention is hermeneutically terminal.

To sum up: the mere claim that Milton's intentions are uncertain boils down to a claim that he has expressed intentions. The special claim that Milton's intentions are very uncertain boils down to a claim that he has expressed lots of intentions. Finally, the special claim that Milton's intentions are secret boils down to a claim that he has not expressed his intentions. In no case does an hermeneutic of uncertainty appear to take us very far.

One aspect of our target issue, nonetheless, remains useful. It is Milton's representation of the conditions that produce our interest in uncertainty. Throughout *PL*, we find ourselves interpreting episodes of interpretation. These range from Satan's account of the "new Laws" (5.679), to Adam's analysis of the heavens (8.1–40), to Eve's deconstruction (second-hand though it be) of the paradisal prohibition (9.745–779). In the scales episode, we are trying to interpret Gabriel and Satan, not just fighting or parting, but trying to interpret the scales as a message telling them to fight or part. In our conventional terms, the archangel and the ex-archangel are trying to recover the intention with which God hung out the scales. The intention remains with God; yet the scales are the only evidence for it. Therefore these readers, like all readers, have to adduce meaning on a basis of uncertainty. Or perhaps we should just say, they have to adduce meaning. As I have argued, uncertainty attaches, willy-nilly, to this activity. What we hope to learn about, however, is the hermeneutic significance of its attachment. Milton has given us an opportunity to learn in his representations of reading and meaning.

Interpretation and Application

The first thing we learn, somewhat surprisingly, is that uncertainty does not matter very much. At least, it is not anything that Milton has taken care to emphasize. True, in the current episode Milton omits to tell us how Satan reads the scales. But by that token, he does not tell us that Satan is uncertain about how to read the scales. If anything, Milton represents Satan as certain, knowing – at least in his own mind, which is what we are wondering about. Gabriel, for his part, gives an extremely assured reading. As I have suggested, we may doubt its correctness. Our doubt, however, is ours, not Gabriel's. Neither do we have any reason to think that it is Satan's. Despite all indications, despite all expectations, hermeneutic uncertainty does not come into the scene. It is not mentioned, it is not urged, by characters or narrator. To be sure, the episode prompts our uncertainty very effectively, but what emerges here is precisely a *difference* between us and what we are reading. We may care about uncertainty a great deal, seeing it as an indispensable and profound conundrum. Gabriel and Satan, by contrast, seem not to care about uncertainty at all.

Do they care about the hermeneutic quantity that generates uncertainty? Do they care about the intention with which God hung out the scales? Well, they care about the meaning of the scales, which means, by definition, what God means by them. Neither Gabriel nor Satan seems to suppose, however, that one ought to pause over this consideration. They show no inclination to wonder about the correctness of their respective readings. Neither do they show any inclination to speculate about a special or secret intention reserved behind the scales. They simply read the scales. As I have noted, elsewhere in the poem, Satan exhibits a much more fraught interpretative practice. The elevation of the Son and the paradisal prohibition strike him as the cover for divine conspiracies. The temptation of Eve succeeds through esoteric re-ascription of God's prohibitive intention. In an episode toggled with the current one, Satan enters the created world immediately above the constellation Libra, and immediately below the stairs or ladder "scal'd by steps of Gold to Heav'n Gate" (3.541). Satan considers himself tantalized by that latter *scala*, precisely because he reads it as leading up to an absent intention: it is "to dare / The Fiend by easie ascent, or aggravate / His sad exclusion from the dores of Bliss" (3.523–525).[13] But when God hangs out his later scales, which really are intentional, Satan's interpretative reflex is overwhelmed. He does not stop to question or re-ascribe God's intention – much as the scales' ambiguity would seem to invite him. Rather, Satan allows himself to be addressed by the scales. He accepts their meaning, whatever it is, as something for him. He reads them, and moves on.

Moving-on, indeed, is a key interpretative response. The scales appear at a narrative crossroads. Because they appear, one possible outcome (fight) does not happen; another possible outcome (parting) does. God's text transforms the narrative, winnowing actuality out of possibility. Now, the narrative is nothing other than the lives of its members. God's text, therefore, transforms their lives. This transformation, moreover, is not consequent or adjunctive to the narrative members' understanding of the scales. It is their understanding. Satan's flight, as much as Gabriel's speech, is interpretative. In this respect, the conclusion of the scales episode is like many other moments in *PL*, from Abdiel's retort (6.131–203) to Raphael's blush (8.614–620) to Satan's punishment "in the shape he sin'd" (10.516). Understanding is an event, happening to the understander. It is not primarily an objective analysis of what is to be understood.

God's scales remain a peculiarly useful instance, because they make clear, like the oracular utterances they resemble, the full hopelessness of objectivist interpretation. The objective core of the scales' meaning could only be God's intention for them.

---

13   See Mindele Anne Treip, "'Reason Is Also Choice': The Emblematics of Free Will in *Paradise Lost*," *SEL* 31.1 (1991): 147–177.

Yet to seek this object, as we have seen, is to enter a garden of forking paths. It is to follow (as Milton might say) a marsh fire. The hermeneutic implication is not (as for Derrida, and uncertainty) that interpretation is an interminable search after an ephemeral trace. It is, rather (as for Gadamer, and pragmatism), that interpretation is not a search at all. Interpretation is an encounter; it is an attempt to recognize. The understanding that results is an experience of mattering that occurs within, and transforms, a certain life-situation.

Gerald Bruns, a major exponent of Gadamer, explains this idea via Plato's Socrates.[14] The latter is named by the Delphic oracle as the wisest man alive. Thus informed, the nominee is flummoxed. As far as he can tell, he knows nothing. The oracle is an enigma – as oracles usually are. Nonetheless, the intentionalist and/or objectivist procedure would be to go to the oracle and ask: what do you mean? Presumably, the oracle is determined by its intention. Asking the oracle for its intention, however, can only mean receiving another intention. It can only mean (oracles being what they are) glossing an enigma with an enigma. Objectivist hermeneutics, if applied to the oracle, would result only in deconstructive interminability. Yet for that very reason, oracular utterances, under objectivism, indicate the limits of hermeneutics. They indicate the ludic and irresolvable core of all interpretanda, *per se*. Oracles, on this view, constitute an hermeneutic embarrassment, and help to establish the epistemological turn to a non-hermeneutic objectivism.

Socrates does not turn that way. He does not shrug his shoulders at the oracle's arcaneness. Neither does he journey to Delphi, to interrogate the priestess. Rather, Socrates turns to his contemporaries, and tells them his situation. "The oracle at Delphi calls me wisest," he says (in effect). "And yet it seems to me that I know nothing. Do you know anything?" The question, eventuating from Socrates' self-presentation, elicits his interlocutors' accounts of what they think they know. Gratified, Socrates asks further questions about the proffered knowledge, until it breaks down into an ignorance like his own. He then moves on to other interlocutors, in other dialogues, and repeats the procedure. He tries and fails, again and again, to falsify the oracle. This is dialectic; it is Socrates' life in philosophy. *But his life in philosophy is precisely his attempt to interpret and understand the oracle.* Socrates hears the oracle as bidding him to a certain activity, in which he is to consider a certain subject-matter. His is the subject-matter of subject-matters: the whole question of knowledge. The model of his response, however, holds for all subject-matters. The response is philosophically hermeneutic, rather than objectivist. Socrates does not seek to go behind the oracle, but to place himself in front of it. He does not seek its meaning in its generative intention, but "if anywhere, in time."[15] Socrates takes the oracle, this enigmatic text, and asks his peers to help him understand what it means, for him and for them. The dialogue that results is not peripheral or epiphenomenal to the business of understanding the oracular text. It is the business of understanding that text.

---

14   Bruns, *Hermeneutics, Ancient and Modern*, pp. 39–45.
15   Bruns, *Hermeneutics, Ancient and Modern*, p. 41.

The name for this sort of thing, in philosophical hermeneutics, is application.[16] The concept has two aspects. First is reflexive application, whereby the meaning of a text is identified with its meaning for an understander. This is not licence to relativize or misconstrue the text, but – exactly to the contrary – an attempt to find in what way the text is binding upon the understander. A text becomes binding when it makes clear to its potential understander that its meaning is a game in which he is involved. Under these conditions, asking what the text means in and of itself can only mean avoiding its meaning. At the same time, asking what the text means for its reader is not the same as asking what meanings the reader can make from it. Meaning is something that happens to a reader. It is not something that a reader makes happen. Gadamer speaks of the text giving its reader some "offense"– using a wonderful word, *Anstoss*, that means both "insult" and "kickoff."[17] To be addressed by the text, to become involved in its game, is to find oneself suddenly losing, and wounded in the prejudices. To win, one must remain in the game, playing with those prejudices. This becoming and remaining involved, thereby improving in health and skill, is understanding.

The second aspect of application is transitive. Here, the meaning of a text for an understander is identified with its meaning in a certain set of circumstances. The model is jurisprudential. A judge, Gadamer notes, does not mechanically apply an objectively-understood law to a particular case. He does not understand the law as an ideal template on which to measure its putative scenarios. Rather, the judge's understanding of a law consists in his application of that law. Application of the law, in turn, determines the meaning of the law. It also establishes a precedent, which, perforce, becomes law. This is why judges have to explain their judgments, in and through and as their judgments. When they do not – when a judge simply says "I am the law" – we think there is something wrong.[18] Gadamer does not make jurisprudence paradigmatic for all interpretation, but he does link all interpretation with jurisprudence. Literary study, scriptural exegesis, and legal judgment are the main modes of an ontological continuity, in which application has universal play.

In *PL*, application is an unfallen norm. As is typical, the norm is illuminated by the fall. For Eve, the productive question is not what God meant by the Paradisal prohibition – and again, it is precisely Satan who encourages her to open up the intentionalist tautology – but what meaning she is prepared to experience as binding in that prohibition. Her failure to be guided by God's evident intention is a failure to mind the insult that it is giving her as she reaches for the fruit. Similarly, Satan does not fall because he misconstrues God's intention in elevating the Son. Rather, he misconstrues God's intention because he has refused the prior responsibility, or rather privilege, of setting God's intention into its appropriate motion. Satan denies himself to be a player in God's game. He thinks this denial gives him intentional

[16] See *TM*, pp. 307–340; John M. Connolly, "*Applicatio* and *Explicatio* in Gadamer and Eckhart," in Malpas, Arnswald, and Kertscher (eds), *Gadamer's Century*, pp. 77–96; and Bruns, *Hermeneutics, Ancient and Modern*, pp. 60–75.
[17] *WM*, p. 272. The translation "being pulled up short" is given in *TM*, p. 268.
[18] *TM*, pp. 324–340.

originality (the mind as its own place), and that intentional originality is a Godlike power of meaning (making, if necessary, a heaven of hell, a hell of heaven). But meaning, in *PL*, is not a matter of power – not even for God. Meaning is a matter of departing from power. It is a matter of grace. Satan's theory of interpretation as intentionalist scepticism is basically a refusal to accept God's applicative gift. It is a refusal to accept that God's meanings are not in the first place God's, but are always-already a move in the arena where God's creatures are empowered.

Adam and Eve, in the unfallen garden, know nothing of Satan's scepticism. They do not know that it is possible not to be subsumed in understanding. True, Raphael's theory of accommodation, prefaced to his account of Satan's rebellion, indicates that Adam may misunderstand the original intensions, and interpretative extensions, of heavenly utterances (5.563–576). As a Miltonic posit, this is not very remarkable; every exegete since Christ himself has said something similar. What is remarkable about Raphael's version in *PL*, however, is that it immediately cancels itself out. For "what if Earth / Be but the shaddow of Heav'n, and things therein / Each to other like, more then on Earth is thought?" (5.574–576). Far from being subjected to accommodation, Adam is given dominion over it. His application of meanings extends to application of a theory of meanings. This is precisely because Raphael declines to define accommodation as a consistent penetration or reversal of appearance. That would be too simple. It would also allow a reliable projection, through a mere negative logic, of heavenly originals. Raphael's self-cancelling accommodation, however, means that there is no clear content to the idea of such originals. They are neither here nor there. There is no intelligible difference between Adam's attempt to understand Raphael's story, and the validity of that attempt.

Appropriately, Adam is explicitly encouraged to application. He is encouraged to find the meaning of Raphael's history in its effect on his own subsequent conduct, "least wilfully transgressing he pretend / Surprisal" (5.244–245). So God to Raphael; so Raphael to Adam. "For thy good / This is dispenc't" (5.570–571); "let it profit thee to have heard" (6.909). Raphael applies, as he understands them, God's hermeneutic instructions to Adam's case. To be sure, the heavenly messenger seems not to understand that case in very much detail. He includes nothing in his history, because his history does not include (*inter alia*), jailbreaks, weird dreams, or talking snakes. Yet his is the history that God sends down. We are forced to conclude, therefore, (1) that Adam's activity is genuinely interpretative: he is trying to understand a story that is not his; (2) that the understanding Adam achieves *is* his – it is for his good; and (3) that the model of interpretation that Milton has placed in the garden is one in which interpretation *per se* is something for the interpreter's good. Interpretation in the garden is applicative. Again, the point is not to indicate an hermeneutic extra or bonus, over and above the normative determination of meaning. The point, rather, is to indicate what is involved in the normative determination of meaning. To revert to the Hirschean terms that occupied us in Chapter Two, the meaning of Raphael's narrative is indistinguishable from its significance to Adam. That is not to say that significance trumps meaning, but that the meaning / significance distinction is irrelevant to the hermeneutic scene as Milton represents it.

Where does that leave uncertainty? Nowhere. The argument here is analogous to, and a local version of, the argument about universal interpretativity, and its lack of consequences. Uncertainty is irrelevant because certainty is irrelevant. Certainty would only be relevant if Adam's interpretation were under objectivist instructions: if he were directed to understand his understanding as an attempt to recover an original state of affairs. This would be the war in heaven, as it was in itself. As we have seen, however, Adam is directed to understand his understanding as something that occurs without reference to such a state of affairs. He is directed to understand his understanding as something that occurs in and to himself. Raphael's narrative is set before Adam in much the same way as the scales are set before Raphael and Satan: as radically ambiguous, and isolated from generative or original objects. In a word, these texts are oracular – and that is their value to Milton. They predicate representations of interpretative activity, not as an objectivist process of discovery, but as an applicative process of dialogic transformation. These representations, as challenging as they are manifest, constitute the exoteric business of *PL*.

The Way of the Question

Adam's understanding of Raphael's narrative leads their dialogue beyond that narrative. This happens because Adam's understanding eventuates in questions. First he asks about creation (7.70–109), then about astronomy (8.1–40). The first question tropes Adam, "yet sinless," as a dialectic drinker, "whose drouth / Yet scarce allay'd still eyes the current streame" (7.66–67). The second question demonstrates Adam's unfallen knowledge, precisely by being a question. "When I behold this goodly Frame," he says,

> this World
> Of Heav'n and Earth consisting, and compute,
> Thir magnitudes ... reasoning I oft admire,
> How Nature wise and frugal could commit
> Such disproportions, with superfluous hand
> So many nobler Bodies to create,
> Greater so manifold to this one use,
> For aught appears, and on thir Orbs impose
> Such restless revolution day by day
> Repeated, while the sedentarie Earth,
> That better might with farr less compass move,
> Serv'd by more noble then her self, attaines
> Her end without least motion. (8.15–17, 25–35)

Adam is asking the question of heliocentrism – which will not be asked again until Copernicus (via Pythagoras). His unfallen knowledge leaps over medieval and

Renaissance astronomy, to arrive at, and express itself through, the foundational question of modern science. Raphael approves Adam's question as such, while distinguishing it from objectivist attempts to stabilize answers. "To ask or search I blame thee not," the archangel says; but "this to attain, whether Heav'n move or Earth, / Imports not, if thou reck'n right" (8.66, 70–71). The objectivist idea that answers matters more than questions is associated by Raphael with Adam's geocentric descendants. These will "model Heav'n / And calculate the Starrs," with "Cycle and Epicycle, Orb in Orb," moving God's "laughter" at their "quaint Opinions" (8.79–80, 84, 78). Adam, Raphael says, is to understand that the questions matter more. Asking questions is the way to "admire" God's creation, without in any way impinging on God's "secrets" (8.75, 74).

Adam, accordingly, finds a question in place of an answer. He asks whether Raphael has heard the story of Adam's own creation (8.203–216). Unusually among Adam's inquiries, this one concerns a topic that he knows something about. Yet Adam introduces the topic via the one aspect of it that he knows nothing about: namely, whether or not his interlocutor knows anything about it. "Now hear mee relate," he says, "My Storie, which perhaps thou hast not heard" (8.204–205). Dialogism, guaranteed by that subordinate clause, is extended into Adam's claim that his monologue will be a kind of post-prandial tactic, delivered only "in hope" of the archangel's reply (8.209). Adam then commences his story with an invocatory formula that disclaims the knowledge he is about to provide ("For Man to tell how human Life began / Is hard" [8.250–251]), while echoing the quasi-epic formula with which his interlocutor began the story of the heavenly war ("O prime of men, / Sad task and hard" [5.563–564]).

In short, the unfallen Adam is preternaturally dialogic (in Gadamer's sense). Even his signature monologue of being the only man alive presupposes conversation. Appropriately, it is also about conversation. Newly-created, Adam recalls, he tried to talk to the first interlocutor he found:

> Thou Sun, said I, faire Light,
> And thou enlight'nd Earth, so fresh and gay,
> Ye Hills and Dales, ye Rivers, Woods, and Plaines,
> And ye that live and move, fair Creatures, tell,
> Tell, if ye saw, how came I thus, how here?
> Not of my self; by some great Maker then,
> In goodness and in power praeeminent. (8.273–279)

His memory recalls, for the reader, Satan's nostalgic apostrophe to the sun at the beginning of his book 4 soliloquy:

> O thou that with surpassing Glory crownd,
> Look'st from thy sole Dominion like the God
> Of this new World; at whose sight all the Starrs
> Hide thir diminisht heads; to thee I call,
> But with no friendly voice, and add thy name

O Sun, to tell thee how I hate thy beams
That bring to my remembrance from what state
I fell, how glorious once above thy Spheare. (4.32–39)

Satan curses where Adam rejoices, and that is important. It is more fundamentally important, however, that Satan tells, where Adam asks to be told. Satan's basic utterance is the statement; Adam's, the question.

Now, questions can be divided, hermeneutically speaking, into two kinds: leading (or rhetorical), and real (or productive). Leading questions are those to which the questioner knows the answer. Real questions are those to which the questioner does not. Plainly, real questions are uniquely consistent with the hermeneutic conditions of dialogue, following from the full expression of what we (think we) know. Somewhat less plainly, but very importantly, real questions are extremely difficult to ask.[19] Anybody who has ever set an exam, or an essay topic, knows this painful truth. Real questions constitute the leading edge of knowledge – with the paradoxical result that asking them entails departing from knowledge. It entails not telegraphing answers, but trying to find things out. At the same time, the real question cannot merely be a shot in the dark. Rather, it must be formed and targetted in such a way that it can open up a subject-matter, on the basis of some fore-understanding. The latter's theoretical validity, finally, remains more-or-less opaque. We do not know, perhaps cannot know, how we come to know what we know. For we are "searching what we know not by what we know" (*CP* 2.541) – putting the latter at the service of the former. Our ability to do so, which we can only learn by doing, is the *phronesis*, or practical wisdom, that is inculcated by dialogue.

Gadamer follows this chain of ideas, as he frequently does, back to Plato. "It is among the greatest insights afforded us by the Platonic representation of Socrates," Gadamer writes,

> that questioning – entirely contrary to the general opinion – is more difficult than answering. When the members of the Socratic conversation, exasperated from answering Socrates' annoying questions, attempt to turn the tables and claim for themselves the apparently advantageous role of the questioner – then, and by that means, they really start to go wrong.[20]

Gadamer is glossing over, to some extent, irregularities in Plato's representation of Socrates. The radically-dialectic questioner of the early dialogues, seeking only to falsify his own ignorance, becomes a rhetorical seminar-leader in Plato's middle period. True, in the late dialogues, Socrates reverts to the pristine *docta ignorantia*. But in between is the Plato of *logos* and objectivism. This shift is itself consistent with Gadamer's point. Not even Plato could hold to the insight he had achieved. This was the insight of dialogue, in its full productivity, guaranteed by the real questions that are its basic play. Method, like a malevolent planet, turns dialogue into

---

[19] *TM*, pp. 362–369.
[20] *WM*, pp. 368–369. My translation. See *TM*, pp. 362–363.

stage-management. This degradation can be observed, and frequently is, in a choice of leading over real questions.[21]

To make that choice, however, is to deny it. The Socratic interlocutors described by Gadamer do not believe in real questions as an option they are forgoing. They believe that all questions are leading or rhetorical. This is the corollary of their tendency to disbelieve Socrates' protestations of ignorance, and to believe in their own secure sense of knowing what they know. In a word, these interlocutors are objectivists. As such, they question questions. Objectivism behaves on this point – and only on this point – quasi-hermeneutically. Conversely, hermeneutics behaves quasi-objectively, on the same point. Typically, objectivism seeks to found and hold distinctions: between interpretative and non-interpretative, meaning and significance, analytic and synthetic, etc. Typically, hermeneutics seeks to deny distinctions, treating them as objectivist paralogisms. For that very reason, however, hermeneutics must binarize questions into real (hermeneutic) and leading (paralogistic). Conversely, denial of the real / leading binary is what allows objectivism to claim that it is defending itself against sophistry. The question of the question emerges, in sum, as the fulcrum on which objectivism and hermeneutics pivot.

Clearly, Adam's questions to Raphael are real. They are questions to which Adam does not know the answer. To be sure, this is a function of Adam's paradisal ignorance – but an ignorance encountered at the margins of tremendous knowledge. Fulsomely praising Eve, the only woman in the universe, Adam elicits a stern lecture from Raphael about patriarchy and sexual temperance (8.560–594). "What admir'st thou," the archangel demands, "what transports thee so,"

> An outside? fair no doubt, and worthy well
> Thy cherishing, thy honouring, and thy love,
> Not thy subjection: weigh with her thy self;
> Then value. (8.568–571)

Adam's reply is one of the most remarkable moments in the poem. "Half abash't" (8.595), he defends his passion for Eve politely, but firmly (8.595–611). After all, the angel does not really know what he is talking about. Or does he? This is the stunning question that follows Adam's expression of his own position:

> To Love thou blam'st me not, for Love thou saist
> Leads up to Heav'n, is both the way and guide;
> Bear with me then, if lawful what I ask;
> Love not the heav'nly Spirits, and how thir Love
> Express they, by looks onely, or do they mix
> Irradiance, virtual or immediate touch? (8.612–617)

Raphael replies "with a smile that glow'd / Celestial rosie red, Loves proper hue" (8.618–619). Is he blushing? The line asks us. Certainly he departs within a dozen

---

21   See Davidson, "Gadamer and Plato's *Philebus*."

lines of this one. Before going, Raphael's reply to Adam is fairly vague – "Let it suffice thee that thou know'st / Us happie, and without Love no happiness" (8.620–621) – even as it concedes that angelic sex is not really (corporeal) sex at all. It is "Easier then Air with Air, if Spirits embrace," encountering no "obstacle ... / Of membrane, joynt, or limb" (8.626, 625). Meanwhile, in the background is the homonormativity and/or gender polymorphousness of Milton's angels, who can (at least on the hellish account) assume whichever sex they please (1.423–431), but are almost always assumed and presented by the narrative as male. All of which is to say that, in addressing himself to Adam's corporeal and heterosexual life, the angel really didn't know what he was talking about. Eve, and Adam's feelings for and about her, place the angel at the margins of his own knowledge. There, his appropriate utterance would have been a real, productive question, rather than a didactic and terminal lecture. This is the lesson that Adam gives him.

Not all questions in Paradise are equally productive. Most, probably, are leading or rhetorical. As we have seen, however, the ability to choose between real and rhetorical questions (rather than reducing all questions to the rhetorical) is precisely characteristic of genuine dialogic engagement. Moreover, in all of Milton's paradisal dialogues, the interlocutor who speaks for dialogue – who tries to open up its possibilities, rather than shutting them down – is typically the one who gets, and keeps, the upper hand. In accordance with the binary of real and rhetorical questions, therefore, there emerges another and greater binary of dialogue and non-dialogue. Dialogue is to non-dialogue as real is to rhetorical. The attempt to ask real questions within dialogue points and serves, and stands for, the larger attempt to open up and continue dialogue *tout court*.

Adam's remarkable colloquy with God, for example, is a volley of largely rhetorical questions in which a dialogic advantage, nonetheless, is evident. Remarkably, the advantage is with Adam. The conversation's main points are as follows. Adam (having just named the animals, who go "two and two" [8.350]): "In solitude / What happiness, who can enjoy alone?" (8.364–365). Where is my other me? God: "What call'st thou solitude?" (8.369). Just talk to the animals, if you want to talk. Adam: "Among unequals what societie?" (8.383). I need another me like me. God: "How have I then with whom to hold converse?" (8.408). Is there another me like me? Adam:

> To attaine
> The highth and depth of thy Eternal wayes
> All human thoughts come short, Supream of things;
> Thou in thy self art perfet, and in thee
> Is no deficience found; not so is Man,
> But in degree, the cause of his desire
> By conversation with his like to help,
> Or solace his defects. (8.412–419)

By his own account, God is behaving pedagogically: "Thus farr to try thee, *Adam*, I was pleas'd" (8.437). He can hardly behave otherwise. Since God, by definition, knows all questions and answers in advance, conversation with him constitutes a special case (a point to which we will return). God is testing Adam, knowing all along that it was "not good for Man to be alone" (8.445). Precisely for the conversation to achieve that point, however, Adam has to persist. He has to keep asking questions. That is how he gets the Eve he wants. The outcome of the conversation accords with the agenda of the interlocutor (Adam) who is trying to keep it going through questions, rather than with the agenda of the interlocutor (God) who is, ostensibly, trying to complete it with answers.

The God-Adam dialogue, on the morning of Adam's creation, is mirrored by the Adam-Eve dialogue, on the morning of the fall. Here, it is Eve who questions, and Adam who tries to terminate questioning. Eve wins. Her initial proposal for working apart having been rejected by her husband, on the grounds of "doubt" that she might be harmed by their "malicious Foe [Satan]" (9.251, 253), Eve turns doubt sweetly against this doubt:

> Ofspring of Heav'n and Earth, and all Earths Lord,
> That such an Enemie we have, who seeks
> Our ruin, both by thee informd I learne,
> And from the parting Angel over-heard
> ... But that thou shouldst my firmness therfore doubt
> To God or thee, because we have a foe
> May tempt it, I expected not to hear.
> ... Thoughts, which how found they harbour in thy brest,
> *Adam*, missthought of her to thee so dear? (9.273–276, 279–281, 288–289)

That is the least of her questions. All are more-or-less rhetorical, as is appropriate to a marital spat (albeit an unfallen one). Yet Eve is able to develop her interrogative attack into a veritable logic of Paradise:

> If this be our condition, thus to dwell
> In narrow circuit strait'nd by a Foe,
> Suttle or violent, we not endu'd
> Single with like defence, wherever met,
> How are we happie, still in fear of harm? (9.322–326)

The question gives the answer – "we are not happy, under such conditions." This is leading or rhetorical. The answer to which Eve points, however, is the very question of Paradise. Eve wins the argument by aligning her position with the dialectic condition of her and Adam's freedom.

Eve lives to regret her rhetorical success. The freedom that she re-asserts by working alone predicates the temptation, and failure, that Adam feared. What is worse (for our purposes): Eve's encounter with Satan, through which she falls, takes the form of a dialogue. Insofar as Eve falls through dialogue – insofar as dialogue itself is productive of the fall – then dialogue, arguably, emerges as Satanic in this case. Indeed, Satan is the one who initiates the conversation with Eve, playing "uncall'd" before her until gaining her attention (9.523). Satan, too, is the one who keeps the conversation going (as we will see), finding rhetorical ways around its potential termini. Finally, Satan is encouraging Eve to question God's commands – up to and including a unique command, the prohibition on the tree, that God has placed, rather non-dialogically, beyond question. Is Satan, here, not gaining and holding dialogic advantage?

If so, Eve's obedience to God would appear to entail a refusal to countenance Satan's questions. Eve would not have fallen, presumably, if she had walked away from the snake – or refused to answer it, or mocked its "gay rhetorick"(*Comus* 790), or told it to shut up. Eve would not have fallen, in other words, if she had behaved more like Milton's other Lady. As a matter of fact, Eve makes a couple of moves in this direction. Early in the temptation, she chides the serpent for "overpraising" the tree (9.615); later, she tidily repeats God's prohibition of it (9.659–663). More of the same would have produced dialogic termination – and dialogic termination, surely, would have prevented loss of paradise. In short, my whole argument in this chapter (and a large part of my argument in this book) is at issue in Eve's fatal encounter with the snake.

It is important to recognize, in this regard, that Satan never really joins a dialogue with Eve. Dialogue, as we have seen, presupposes openness. It presupposes its members' unreserved joining-in, based in their full and free intentional expression. Only in this way can real questions emerge; only through real questions can interlocutors learn. Now, Eve is open to the snake, both conversationally and physically. Precisely this openness, with its fatal result, can suggest a direct relationship between her willingness to engage in dialogue, and her fall. Against this suggestion, however, is the countervailing insight that Satan, the agent of the fall, is not open at all. He is faking. He is masked, hidden, dissembling in the snake. He is not expressing his actual intentions in any significant part, but is telling a story that is, from start to finish, a lie. (He is not a snake, has not learned to talk by eating the fruit, has not eaten the fruit at all, etc.) The very openness that Eve models in her encounter with the snake, therefore, illuminates the secrecy (from the reader's perspective) that the snake is modelling for her. It is through this secrecy, inimical to dialogue, that Satan tempts Eve.

In a word, Satan uses method. He uses anti-dialogic manipulation and falsification. This is evident, first of all, in Satan's overwhelming rhetoricality. Like "som Orator renound / In *Athens* or free *Rome*" (9.670–671), he asks question after leading question, building his argument out of them. His initial approach to Eve is through the Ciceronian *interrogatio* "one man except, / Who sees thee? (and what is one?)" (9. 545–546). His final approach is through an *anthypophora* (an inquiry to the audience), the rhetoricality of which is over-emphasized by its being, in addition, a distorted repetition of something Eve has just told him (and which he, and we, already know to be true). "Of this Tree we may not taste nor touch," she has just said (9.651). "Indeed?" he replies (like her, quoting Genesis). "Hath God then said that of the Fruit / Of all these Garden Trees ye shall not eate?" (9.656–657). Eve's correction involves her, willy-nilly, in the serpent's enervating rhetoric, as the crucial point in question is reduced to mere repetition:

> Of the Fruit
> Of each Tree in the Garden we may eate,
> But of the Fruit of this fair Tree amidst
> The Garden, God hath said, Ye shall not eate
> Thereof, nor shall ye touch it, least ye die. (9.659–663)

The childish simplicity with which Eve is forced to explain the matter then forms the backdrop for Satan's elaborate performance as impassioned *rhetor*.

To be sure, rhetoricality can be (as we have seen) a legitimate part of dialogue. To function in this way, however, it must remain subordinated to non-rhetoricality (the asking of real questions). Pure rhetoricality – rhetoricality as interrogative norm – is the opposite of dialogue. Pure rhetoricality is the discursive corollary of objectivism. If knowledge is considered fundamentally non-interpretative, then questions, which call for interpretative work, must be considered fundamentally trivial as a response to what is known. Questions can be substantial, under objectivism, only as a response to what is *not* known. Conversely, an objectivist knower's question *about something he (thinks he) knows* can consist only in an artificial withholding or manipulation of that knowledge. The rhetorical questions that result, to the extent that they suggest their own discursive normativity, also suggest objectivism.

In this respect, it is important that Satan presents his most crucial and characteristic question *as a statement*. "The Gods are first," Satan says,

> and that advantage use
> On our belief, that all from them proceeds;
> *I question it*, for this fair Earth I see,
> Warm'd by the Sun, producing every kind,
> Them nothing. (9.718–722, my emphasis.)

Satan is expressing an empiricist scepticism that he has previously deployed against Abdiel. At issue, more or less, is the core question of (dis)obedience: the question of whether God is God, and whether or not, and how, one can know. In its earlier version, Satan's question was plainly rhetorical: "who saw / When this creation was", etc. (5.856–857). It was a question to which he (thought he) knew the answer ("nobody"). In this later version, the question has become purely or normatively rhetorical. It is no longer – or not even – a rhetorical question, but merely the rhetorical figure of a question. A question has become, for Satan, something to be mentioned, rather than used.

In this way, Satan projects rhetorical normativity. He therefore suggests or projects objectivism. Since Satan is, in the relevant passage, arguing for empiricist scepticism – and since the latter is itself a main form of objectivism – his talk is attaining a high degree of formal coherence. More importantly, however, his talk is leading toward objectivism as the only valid mode of talk, and one that produces alienation from theocentric obedience. If God created all things, Satan asks, where's the proof? How do we know that divine creation is a non-interpretative fact? To be sure, the same sorts of questions could be asked about the aetiologies that Satan proposes in lieu of God. Neither Eve nor Satan, for example, has irrefutable evidence (proof) that the sun's warmth really produces anything. Where is the stop-action photography? they might ask. How do we *know* that the sun is really the source of its apparent warmth? Satan, however, does not ask these questions. His scepticism, like most, is both selective and transitive. He applies the standard of non-interpretativity, so fragile and hopeless an account of facts, only and exclusively to what he opposes.

Satan's opposition of God to objectivism may seem a curious move. After all (and as discussed at the outset of this chapter), God is the conventional, even the necessary posit of the idealisms that have traditionally supported objectivism. Satan is not claiming, however, that "God" and "objectivism" don't make mutual sense. He is claiming – exactly to the contrary – that "God" and "objectivism" *only* make mutual sense: that God, as focus of Eve's obedience, has to be understood as an objectivist posit. Satan's claim to Eve, formally refined since he made it to Abdiel, is that God's claim to be God must stand or fall on objectivist standards. As we have seen, it is in the nature of these standards to fail on their own terms. Deconstructive doubt then replaces objectivist facticity. This outcome, however, is exactly what Satan wants. He is a uniquely clear-eyed deconstructionist: one who recognizes his aims to be fundamentally objectivistic. Satan encourages Eve to take up objectivist standards by way of finding her obedience wanting on those standards.[22]

Accordingly, Satan backs up his empirical scepticism with logical reduction. He vigorously attempts to show, à la Derrida, contradiction within God's prohibitive coherence.[23] If "the gods" created all things, the deconstructive snake argues, "who enclos'd / Knowledge of Good and Evil in this Tree, / That whoso eats thereof, forthwith attains / Wisdom without their leave?" (9.722–725) This argument is not very powerful – it founders on God's promise of his creatures' freedom – but one only sees that by unwinding its coils. More impressive is the preceding inquiry into the kind of knowledge that God has forbidden. If it is knowledge "of good," the snake demands, how can it be "just" of God to forbid it (9.698)? If, on the other hand, God forbids knowledge "of evil ... why not known, since easier shunnd?" (9.698–699) "God therefore cannot hurt ye, and be just," the snake concludes: "Not just, not God; not feard then, nor obeyd: / Your feare it self of Death removes the feare" (9.701–702). Again, the argument founders on its major premise. There is not really knowledge of anything inside the tree's fruit; there is only an interpretative condition, as Milton puts it in *Areopagitica*, of "knowing good *by* evil." (*CP* 2.514). The current point, however, is simply that Satan deconstructs God's prohibition.

---

22   For a related discussion, see Daniel Fried, "Milton and Empiricist Semiotics," *MQ* 37.3 (2003): 117–138 – despite Fried's tendency to align Milton's own semiotics with Satan's empiricism.

23   See Thomas L. Martin, "On the Margin of God: Deconstruction and the Language of Satan in *PL*," *MQ* 29.2 (1995): 41–47.

He does so by appealing to an objectivist, even positivist logic in which the mere possibility of contradiction indicates vitiation.

Above all, Satan appeals to an object. He appeals to the tree. "O Sacred, Wise, and Wisdom-giving Plant," he apostrophizes, commencing the final phase of his temptation:

> Mother of Science, Now I feel thy Power
> Within me cleere, not onely to discerne
> Things in thir Causes, but to trace the wayes
> Of highest Agents, deemd however wise. (9.679–683)

Satan posits "Science," knowledge, as a matter of sudden, non-dialogic access. It is solitary and subjective revelation, guaranteed by objective origin. This is consistent with the snake's (fictitious) account of his own cognitive breakthrough. Having eaten the fruit, he claims,

>   ere long I might perceave
> Strange alteration in me, to degree
> Of Reason in my inward Powers, and Speech
> Wanted not long, though to this shape retain'd.
> Thenceforth to Speculations high or deep
> I turnd my thoughts, and with capacious mind
> Considerd all things visible in Heav'n,
> Or Earth, or Middle, all things fair and good. (9.598–605)

Knowledge is not the product, but the pre-requisite, of talking and learning. It is because (allegedly) the snake has eaten facts that he can talk about them. Conversely, talking about facts, without the basis of an objective and non-dialogic encounter, is a waste of time. Reversing and completing Comus' urging to "be wise, and taste," Satan urges Eve to "taste, and be wise." Without the taste, without the object, there can be no wisdom.

Of course, a connection of some kind between gustation and intellection is a genuine feature of Paradise. Raphael tells Adam and Eve that they may, just by ingesting the "corporal nutriments" of their unfallen environment, "at last turn all to Spirit, / Improv'd by tract of time" (5.496, 497–498). That possibility, however, is an organic aspect of their lives. Satan proposes, instead, an artificial transcendence of their lives. He is like a drug manufacturer who proposes pills as a short-cut to food. In such propositions, such claims of essential distillation, consists the objectivist temptation to dialogic complexity. Raphael's teaching about "one first matter all" (5.472) is delivered, not incidentally, in and through a dialogue. The latter is itself (or so I have argued) largely about the epistemological priority of dialogue. In urging Eve to the tree, by symmetrical contrast, Satan is urging her to the epistemological subordination of dialogue. He is urging her to see talk, even insofar as it may occur or be offered at all, as a mere epiphenomenon and appendage of objects.

And he succeeds. "Great are thy Vertues, doubtless, best of Fruits," Eve muses to the tree, "Though kept from Man, and worthy to be admir'd" (9.745–746). She accepts, with very little demur, Satan's objectivist narrative. Having accepted it, having fallen, Eve *condescends* to dialogue. "But to *Adam* in what sort / Shall I appeer?" she asks herself.

> shall I to him make known
> As yet my change, and give him to partake
> Full happiness with mee, or rather not,
> But keep the odds of Knowledge in my power
> Without Copartner? (9.816–821)

She dresses (metaphorically speaking) for talk with her husband, just as Satan dressed for talk with her. Meanwhile, Eve falls into an inner monologue (as I noted in this book's Introduction) that mimics Satanic secrecy, and replaces talking to her other half (Adam) with talking to herself as other. Eve thinks she has gained the objectivist answer, the epistemological product, that talk serves only to retail. But that is to say that she is alien to dialogue from the moment she eats the fruit – and that alienation from dialogue is what the fruit provides. Eve falls, not through dialogue, but through loss of dialogue.

That things might have been different – that Eve might have denied Satan, and how – is indicated by that word "doubtless." "Doubt" is what Eve previously turned against Adam's didactic authority (9.279). "Doubt" resulted from the serpent's hyperbolic praise (9.615). Now, however, Eve doubts doubt. That is to say, she fails to question. To be sure, her pro-lapsarian apostrophe is replete with *rhetorical* questions:

> what forbids [God] but to know,
> Forbids us good, forbids us to be wise? (9.758–759)

> How dies the Serpent? hee hath eat'n and lives,
> And knows, and speaks, and reasons, and discerns. (9.764–765)

> what hinders then
> To reach, and feed at once both Bodie and Mind? (9.778–779)

But these are paralogisms that have lost all dialogic contact. They are addressed to the tree (which cannot answer) and/or to Eve herself (who is the one doing the addressing). They are also copied, almost verbatim, from Satan's preceding diatribe. Eve allows the serpent to act on her as the tree, supposedly, acted on the serpent: as cognitive dictation, prior to discussion and beyond question. As a result, she takes on the content of the serpent's dictation – which is precisely objectivism, focussed on the tree.

Had Eve asked (real) questions – had she pressed her dialogic engagement – she could have recognized the serpent's fallaciousness. Indeed, she could have recognized the serpent's fallaciousness *only* by dialogic means. Walking away, or stopping her ears, would not have sufficed. As Milton argues in *Areopagitica*, withdrawing truth from falsehood simply indicates lack of confidence in the truth. Moreover, recognizing the serpent's fallaciousness, at least in some degree, would have been pre-requisite to Eve's terminating their encounter. It would hardly have been appropriate for an unfallen person to run away from a creature she had no reason to run away from. Yet if Eve had recognized the serpent's fallaciousness, she would not have needed to run away from it. The recognition itself would have been prophylactic. We have here a paradox of method – the method that Eve would have been employing, if she had consciously avoided dialogue with the snake. Since method is (as we have seen) the leitmotif of objectivism, a prophylactic turn to method (enacted in a turn away from dialogue) would have been inappropriate, as well as paradoxical. For Eve would then have been turning to objectivism in order to avoid objectivism.

Recognition through dialogue, by contrast, would have been neither paradoxical, nor inappropriate. And this because it would have involved no method. As we see from Adam's encounter with Raphael, it requires an effort *not* to keep asking questions in Paradise. Dialogue is just what the unfallen Adam and Eve do. It is their practice, their daily bread, their form of life. It would have been no *special* move, in other words, for Eve to urge dialogue with the snake. She would have needed no technique, nor even any suspicion that anything untoward was going on, in order to ask real questions. She would simply have needed to do what comes naturally to her. Why she does not – why she is persuaded by the snake to make the objectivist turn – is a point that Milton leaves obscure. That Eve makes the turn, however, and falls through it, is a point that Milton makes clear.

And what of Adam? He meets his intoxicated wife, bearing armfuls of the deadly fruit (9.848–853). She tells him, ecstatically, what she has done (9.856–885). He is horrified (9.888–894). Yet after a soliloquy, he eats and falls (9.895–1005). It is extremely characteristic of Milton's dialogic paradise that Adam does *not* try to talk the situation over with Eve. Having fallen, she is beyond dialogic recovery. Sure, Adam talks *to* her, lamenting and remonstrating; but he does not talk *with* her, with a view to learning anything that he, or she, does not already know. For that matter, Adam knows exactly what he (thinks he) knows, in this case, from the moment he opens his mouth. This is the point that Milton achieves (as discussed in this book's Introduction) by making Adam's speech to Eve follow, and repeat, an "inward" monologue (the first, as far as we are aware, that he has ever had) (9.886–959). Milton thereby re-aligns the boundary between unfallen and fallen states with the boundary between dialogue and non-dialogue. Adam perceives that he is going to choose, "not decea v'd," to cross that boundary (9.998); even as he perceives that Eve is already across it. On both counts, Adam eschews transitive dialogue, while turning to reflexive non-dialogue.

My point in this section has not been, however, that Milton represents dialogue as unique to the unfallen state. Such a claim would be frankly false as an account of *PL*: after the fall, its characters still talk, and some of these talks – between Adam and Michael, for example (to which I will turn in a moment) – surely attain or at least approach the status of Gadamerian dialogue. Moreover, representing dialogue as solely unfallen would be theoretically impossible, since Milton's text, with all its intensions, including the concept of dialogue, is fallen. My point, rather, has been that Milton represents the fall, in part, as a theoretical turn from dialogue to objectivism. This is not a turn that is inaccessible to us, or lost with the fall. Quite the contrary: the turn from dialogue to objectivism is supremely accessible – which is exactly why Milton's tragic topos functions for us an ongoing and urgent concern. Like the unfallen Adam and Eve, we have to do our best to remain within the ambit of dialogue, and not to allow our thirst for knowledge to be degraded by the temptation of method. Unlike the unfallen Adam and Eve, we are not necessarily doing what comes naturally when we do our dialogic best in this way.

Dialogue and Anti-Dialogue

This point is consistent with the second of Adam's archangelic tutorials. Michael, coming to instruct Adam in temporal history, begins with an objectivist expedient. From Adam's eyes, Michael removes a "Filme" left by the forbidden fruit (11.412). He then purges his pupil's "visual Nerve" with "Euphrasie and Rue," and instills "from the Well of Life three drops" (11.414–416). All this because Adam has "much to see" (11.415) – and of course it is not irrelevant that seeing, as opposed to talking, is the mode in which Michael begins. The archangel's turn to demonstration, in lieu of dialogue, manifests and is consequent on the objectivism into which Adam has sunk. The fallen Adam needs the movie, before he can understand the book. Accordingly, Michael's pharmacological and quasi-surgical interventions are of a kind with the interventions proposed and effected by Satan. If not "taste and be wise," Michael says, in effect, "take this, and be less stupid." The archangel is to the enemy as a doctor is to a drug-dealer.

Adam's initial responses to Michael's historical movie are voluble – and quite rhetorical. Presented with agonizing and, to him, incomprehensible visions, Adam asks leading questions, and/or guesses at answers. "Is Pietie thus and pure Devotion paid?" he wails at Abel's murder by Cain (11.452). "Why is life giv'n / To be thus wrested from us?" he later laments (11.502–503). Presented with the courtship between the sons of God and the daughters of Cain, Adam rushes to approve the scene: "Much better seems this Vision" (11.598). Michael slaps him down:

> Judg not what is best
> By pleasure, though to Nature seeming meet,
> Created, as thou art, to nobler end
> Holie and pure, conformitie divine. (11.603–606)

The reproof is all the more painful for its reprise of Raphael's prudishness (8.560–594). This time, no puckish question about angelic sex puts a flea in the teacher's ear. Michael's pedagogic authority is not to be subverted; Adam's interrogative abilities are not up to the subversion. On both counts, the fallen classroom is as dialogically disappointing as the unfallen one was exhilarating.

Nonetheless, Adam learns. That is to say, in part, that he gains knowledge; in part, that he gains judgment. Above all, though, it is to say that Adam learns how to ask questions. Both knowledge and judgment are thereby presupposed. Contemplating the rainbow that follows the flood, Adam asks,

> But say, what mean those coloured streaks in Heavn,
> Distended as the Brow of God appeas'd,
> Or serve they as a flourie verge to binde
> The fluid skirts of that same watrie Cloud.
> Least it again dissolve and showr the Earth? (11.879–883)

"To whom th' Arch-Angel. Dextrously thou aim'st" (11.884). This is the culmination, and indeed the termination, of Adam's hermeneutic remediation. Adam has asked a question to which he does not know the answer, and yet has thereby opened up the subject-matter that he is asking about. True, he includes a clumsy hypothesis, the rainbow as "flourie verge," that compares poorly with his unfallen abilities. To Raphael, we recall, Adam put the Galilean question of "celestial Motions" (8.Argument); to Michael, he suggests a folkish model of terrestrial meteorology. For that very reason, however, the angel's unequivocal approval stands out. Michael cannot be praising Adam's hypothesis, because the latter is not very dextrous. He must be praising Adam's question, because the latter is well-aimed. Adam has learned to ask, again.

Accordingly, at this point Michael "with transition sweet new Speech resumes" (12.5). Dialogue having become possible again, the archangel switches from showing to talking. He remains in the latter mode until the end of his mission, when he prophesies Christ, and expells Adam and Eve from Paradise. Milton gathers the poetic forces of his conclusion with an extraordinary epic simile:

> now too nigh
> Th' Archangel stood, and from the other Hill
> To thir fixt Station, all in bright array
> The Cherubim descended; on the ground
> Gliding meteorous, as Ev'ning Mist
> Ris'n from a River o're the marish glides,
> And gathers ground fast at the Labourers heel
> Homeward returning. (12.625–632)

This recalls and revises the simile via which Satan led Eve to the tree:

> Hope elevates, and joy
> Bright'ns his Crest, as when a wandring Fire,
> Compact of unctuous vapor, which the Night
> Condenses, and the cold invirons round,

Kindl'd through agitation to a Flame,
Which oft, they say, some evil Spirit attends,
Hovering and blazing with delusive Light,
Misleads th' amaz'd Night-wanderer from his way
To Boggs and Mires, and oft through Pond or Poole,
There swallow'd up and lost, from succour farr. (9.633–642)

The marsh-fire of the temptation, leading the wanderer into a bog, becomes the marsh-mist of the expulsion, chasing him back home. The effect is plangent and moving, as befits Milton's irenic treatment of the expulsion. It is also, in its theoretical applications, linguistic and dialogic. For the marsh-fire simile functions, during the temptation, as an emblem of the rhetorical and epistemological degradation to which Satan is leading Eve. It functions, that is, as an emblem of leading – of the leading questions that manifest dialogic termination and Satanic objectivism. At the expulsion, by contrast, that very emblem is dialogically redeemed. Satan's objectivist attempt at normative rhetoricality becomes the template for the dialogic "wandring" by which Adam and Eve go forward, "solitarie," together (12.648, 649).

Returning to Michael's transition from showing to talking, we find that the first thing he talks about is talk. After the Flood, Michael explains, humankind will live more-or-less without crisis until the rise of Nimrod, and the construction of the tower of Babel. The latter, designed to "reach to Heav'n" and get its makers "a name" (12.44, 45), gets them instead the famous punishment that makes the tower proverbial:

God who oft descends to visit men
Unseen, and through thir habitations walks
To mark thir doings, them beholding soon,
Comes down to see thir Citie, ere the Tower
Obstruct Heav'n Towrs, and in derision sets
Upon thir Tongues a various Spirit to rase
Quite out thir Native Language, and instead
To sow a jangling noise of words unknown:
Forthwith a hideous gabble rises loud
Among the Builders; each to other calls
Not understood, till hoarse, and all in rage,
As mockt they storm; great laughter was in Heav'n
And looking down, to see the hubbub strange
And hear the din; thus was the building left
Ridiculous, and the work Confusion nam'd. (12.48–63)

Language, garbled by God, turns dialogue into din. The latter characterizes the fallen world, precisely as a punitive consequence of the fall – and of its fallen and wilfull reiterations. The choice before fallen creatures is whether to ameliorate this consequence, as best they can; or worsen and repeat it, as well they may. The fomer choice is made by Adam and Eve, who pray, attend, and learn once more to learn. The latter choice, as Michael here makes clear, is made by some of their descendants. Having fallen out of a normative dialogue, and into a struggle with objectivism, people are free to keep falling, if they wish. They are free to choose the "ridiculous" and deconstructive ruin that always follows objectivist attempts to "obstruct Heav'n Towrs."

But this we already know. We readers of *PL*, now in its final book, have already seen the original of Babel: "Th'ascending pile" that Satan and his followers build in Hell (1.722), and call Pandaemonium. We have also seen the pile of snakes, incoherently hissing, that Satan and his followers become through God's punishment, casting "shame / ... on themselves from thir own mouths" (10.545–546). We have seen, finally, the kind of talk that Satan's pile is supposed to be for. In the great consult that opens book two, the newly-fallen angels debate possible responses to their defeat. The fiercest proposal, for immediate counter-attack, is made first by Moloch (2.43–105), but is quickly and effectively followed by Belial's rebuttal (2.119–225). Into this impasse comes Mammon's observation that

> This Desart soile
> Wants not her hidden lustre, Gemms and Gold;
> Nor want we skill or Art, from whence to raise
> Magnificence; and what can Heav'n shew more?
>   ... All things invite
> To peaceful Counsels, and the settl'd State
> Of order, how in safety best we may
> Compose our present evils. (2.270–273, 278–281)

Milton compares the resulting applause to the sound of a storm in a cave (2.284–292). The fallen angels dread "another Field" of battle with God "worse then Hell" (2.292–293). Satan, and his henchman Beëlzebub, therefore have a problem. To them, "warr" must be "resolv'd" (1.661, 662); but there can be no war without an army. The dialogic format of Pandaemonium, where "who can advise, may speak" (2.42), seems to be getting away from them.

Beëlzebub, accordingly, rises. He proposes "an easier enterprise" than Moloch's counter-attack (2.345). The new plan is high-value, and low-risk. The target is "expos'd," "left / To their defence who hold it" (2.360, 361–362). But these are "punie habitants," whom the devils will be able to drive off or "seduce" (2.367, 368). The whole operation will "surpass / Common revenge" (2.370–371). "Advise if this be worth / Attempting," Beëlzebub laconically concludes, "or to sit in darkness here / Hatching vain Empires" (2.37–378). His listeners take the bait. "With full assent / They vote" (2.388–389). Then Satan's first minister offers his follow-up. "But first whom shall we send" he asks,

> In search of this new world, whom shall we find
> Sufficient? who shall tempt with wandring feet
> The dark unbottom'd infinite Abyss
> And through the palpable obscure find out
> His uncouth way, or spread his aerie flight

Upborn with indefatigable wings
Over the vast abrupt, ere he arrive
The happy Ile; what strength, what art can then
Suffice, or what evasion bear him safe
Through the strict Senteries and Stations thick
Of Angels watching round? Here he had need
All circumspection, and we now no less
Choice in our suffrage; for on whom we send,
The weight of all and our last hope relies. (2.402–416)

Like all effective politicians, Satan and his lieutenant know their audience.[24] They know that none of the fallen angels, save one, will think himself "indefatigable" enough, possessed of enough "strength," "art," "evasion" and "circumspection," for the proposed mission. Yet in case this point be missed, Beëlzebub's question is overwhelmingly rhetorical – both in the sense that it is not a real question (he already knows the answer), and in the sense that its epithets are crassly deictic. They point toward the hellish chief like a spotlight in the big top. Moreover, the narrator tells us that Beëlzebub's whole speech was "first devis'd / By *Satan*, and in part propos'd" (2.379–380). We have been watching, not an outcome of dialogue, but the stage-management of such an outcome. Beëlzebub's rehearsed question allows a rehearsed answer from Satan, in a simulacrum of dialogue from which nobody learns anything.

Accepting the proferred mission, Satan promises "Deliverance for us all" (2.465). He adds: "this enterprize / None shall partake with me" (2.465–466). The narrator comments: "Thus saying rose / The Monarch, and prevented all reply" (2.466–467). The moment recalls Gadamer's observation that reaching an understanding in dialogue "is not merely a matter of putting oneself forward and successfully asserting one's own point of view." It is, rather, a transformative communion "in which we do not remain what we were."[25] Milton's Satan, uniquely, fears transformation, because being Milton's Satan is all he knows how to do. Accordingly, he only ever enters dialogue in order to assert his own view – both because he thinks he is always right, and because he thinks he has nothing to learn from dialogue (other than the rightness of his own view). It is disturbing to note how many of our own real-world discursive models – when we interrogate, attack, or rhetorically ambush our interlocutors – are consistent with this degraded attitude. In any case, it is not enough for Satan and Beëlzebub to snuff out their followers' discussion, by pre-arrangement, when it begins to seem dangerously productive. Even their falsification of dialogue must be further falsified, as Satan hastily rises in order to have the last word.

Gadamer quotes Rainer Maria Rilke, on the frontispiece of *Truth and Method*, to the effect that whatever is "self-thrown" is not really worth catching.

---

[24] For period constructions of Satan as political operator, see Diana Treviño Benet, "Hell, Satan, and the New Politician," in Benet and Lieb (eds), *Literary Milton*, pp. 91–113.
[25] *TM*, p. 379.

only when you're the sudden catcher
of an eternal partner's ball
thrown to you, in your center, with exact
and measured swing, a certain arch
out of God's great bridge-building:
only then is catch-as-catch-can a power –
not yours, a world's.[26]

Satan's lack of a world is his inability to catch. It is inability to engage in dialogue. This is a point that takes us right back to the early-modern discourses of casuistry. As discussed in the opening chapters of this book, the conscience joins the creature's mind to God's, in an hypostatic communication. Satan, by claiming his mind as its own place, tries to shut down this communication. Although he cannot really succeed – God will always be privy to his thoughts – he can, and does, suffer as though he had succeeded. His is the nauseating regress of mirror-monologue. As he approaches Eve in book nine, Satan is suddenly and unexpectedly ravished by her beauty. For a moment, the "Evil one" is "stupidly good" (9.463, 465). Then he recollects himself:

Thoughts, whither have ye led me, with what sweet
Compulsion thus transported to forget
What hither brought us, hate, not love, nor hope
Of Paradise for Hell, hope here to taste
Of pleasure, but all pleasure to destroy,
Save what is in destroying, other joy
To me is lost. (9.473–479)

Satan's soliloquizing, persistent throughout *PL*, degrades into the absurdity of self-copying. "Me" + "thoughts" = "us." The final form of Satan's casuistical degradation, from dialogue into monologue, is a further degradation of monologue into false dialogue. Satan thinks that he is talking to his conversational other precisely, and perhaps uniquely, when he is talking to himself. Thus Satan's psychic structure mimics, but totally falsifies, the dialogic structure of conscience. Satan embodies anti-dialogue.

Now, the pendant to Beëlzebub's question in Hell is God's in Heaven. Having agreed with the Son that fallen humanity shall find grace, God maintains that a sacrifice will nonetheless be necessary to "pay / The rigid satisfaction, death for death" (3.211–212). Otherwise, forgiving Adam and Eve for freely falling would mean revoking their freedom (3.125–128). God therefore asks his assembled angels: "Which of ye will be mortal to redeem / Mans mortal crime, and just th' unjust to save, / Dwels in all Heaven charitie so deare?" (3.214–216) As in Hell, the answer is silence, until broken by the Son:

---

[26]   *WM*, p. xii. My translation.

Behold mee then, mee for him, life for life
I offer, on mee let thine anger fall;
Account mee man; I for his sake will leave
Thy bosom, and this glorie next to thee
Freely put off, and for him lastly dye. (3.236–240)

Morally, the difference between the hellish and heavenly exchanges is, of course, that the Son goes to suffer and save, while Satan goes to indulge and destroy. Hermeneutically, however, the difference between the two exchanges is that the hellish one is designated by Milton as fake, while the heavenly one is not so designated. Dialogue is in heaven, as it is not in Hell. To adopt Rilke's sporting metaphor, so productive for Gadamer: when the ball is thrown in heaven, and the Son steps up to catch, we are not told – we are given no reason to think – that the whole play is fixed.

Perhaps we don't need to be told. Perhaps all questions are leading, from God's point of view. Arguably, all talk in which he engages fails to teach him anything. For he knows everything and sees everything, "past, present [and] future" (3.78). To some extent, this view of the matter could be countered by invoking Arian theology. This is suggested at several points of *PL* – for example, when God begets the Son, apparently, in time (5.600–608) – and is asserted in Milton's *De Doctrina Christiana*.[27] In Arianism, the Son is not coessential or coeternal with the Father. In the classic formulation (as discussed in my Introduction), God differs from the Son only by an iota. Yet in that iota, the indivisibility and infinity of the Father re-asserts itself. On an Arian reading, then, God's soteriological question need not be leading to the Son. It would, however, remain leading to the Father. Moreover, even if we read *PL* as Arian, we can hardly be certain about the extension of the Father/Son iota. In other words, even if the Son and the Father do not share everything, it does not follow that God's soteriological question is part of what they do not share. An Arian Son, despite his ontological limitations, might still be privy to his Father's plan for his own sacrifice.

On balance, this is all to the good. The significance of God's question – the significance of his *asking* the question – is, if anything, stronger on an orthodox view of the relationship between Son and Father. On such a view, questioner and answerer both know that both question and answer are coming. They know who will ask, and who will answer; they know the issue, and the response. The question, therefore, is leading, the talk inauthentic. Yet under these circumstances, what is notable is not that God in his several persons has no use for dialogue. What is notable, rather, is that *God sees fit to use dialogue anyway*. Here the exceptionality of God, so emphasized by Milton in his deployment of the "secret" keyword (see pp.6–16), is absolutely probative. God is the one being in the universe who has no use for dialogue. Yet he is the one being in the universe who freely chooses to constitute himself through dialogue. In this respect, as in many others, God is the being that Satan (thinks he) wants to be. If Satan were God, he would not make God's free choice of dialogue. God's free choice, however, is definitive of God. Conversely, Satan's free choice to

---

27   See Bauman, *Milton's Arianism*.

wish that he were a God who could make a free choice against dialogue is definitive of Satan. As we have already noted, the hermeneutic distinction between real and rhetorical questions tends to align with a congruent and greater distinction between dialogue and non-dialogue. Milton's God, who dwells in the latter, chooses the former. This is the hermeneutic miracle that *PL* relates.

Thus God is dialogue, as much as Satan is anti-dialogue. And thus dialogue, in and of its self, emerges in the poem as uniquely praiseworthy. To participate in dialogue is to participate in God. This, surely, is the reason there is so much talk in Milton's paradise before it is lost; and so much talk, after it is lost, about the kinds of talk that recall it, and/or deny it. Dialogue, in and of itself, is soteriological. As such, it is also epistemological. It is the activity by which we "repair the ruins of our first parents, by regaining to know God aright" (*CP* 2.366–367). This is not to say (returning to the theoretical opening of this chapter), that Milton is ludically disinterested in knowledge. It is to say, rather, that he is seriously interested in the hermeneutic game by which knowledge becomes possible. The game that we have to play, if we are to know, turns out to be the game that God chooses to play, because he knows. It is, therefore, not helpful to our prospects, but utterly detrimental, to think that our knowledge might know a better activity – the work of facts – than the game of words.

In conclusion, let us return to the scales of *PL* book four. These, I suggest, are typical of Milton's hermeneutics, not as uncertain statement, but as productive question. God is asking Gabriel and Satan what they will do next. Of course God knows the answers, as he knows the mechanisms that will produce them: application of his text, and dialogue about it. The normativity of these mechanisms, however, is the point. It is very much to Gabriel's credit that he hears God's call to dialogue, and tries to engage Satan in an impromptu seminar. It is very much to Satan's discredit that he declines to be engaged. Satan, the embodiment of anti-dialogue, correctly perceives his own antithesis in the dialogic invitation. As suggested above, the invitation is all the more apotropaic, from Satan's perspective, to the extent that it appears genuine – whether in Raphael's construction, or God's inscription. Satan does not want to talk. He does not want to learn. He does not want to open himself, through expression and questioning, to the possibility that he might become more than he is. Satan wants only to think what he thinks, and know what he knows – certain or uncertain, "nor more."

Conclusion

Secrecy Again?

In the opening and titular essay of his *The World, the Text and the Critic* (1983), Edward Said compares two medieval schools of Koranic interpretation. One, the Batinist (from the Arabic for "internal"), held that "meaning in language is concealed within the words." Promulgating a grammatical art that reserved understanding for initiates, Batinists valorized the secret, in an elaborate hermeneutics of discovery. The other school, the Zahirite (from the Arabic for "clear, apparent, and phenomenal"), arose against the Batinists to argue that "words had only a surface meaning." Zahirites disputed that the sacred Koran provided any warrant for an "inward-tending exegesis." Instead, they argued that God's word favored (what I would call) an hermeneutics of recognition. By predicating their work on a questioning of Batinist assumptions, Zahirites moved from textual criticism to philosophical hermeneutics. They secured this advance by a very simple and yet totally momentous interpretative contribution: as Said puts it, their work "dispells the illusion that a surface reading ... is anything but difficult."[1]

It is difficult. And this for two main reasons. First: the attempt to achieve an hermeneutic alignment with the surface – an exoteric hermeneutics – must combat the almost reflexive assumption that interpretation *per se* entails (esoteric) depth and discovery. Said himself serves as an example of how hard a fight this is: having introduced, with his usual erudition, the amazing phenomenon of Zahiritism – this utter confound to the ideological claim of continuity between reading and esoteric reading – Said doesn't know what to do with it. All he retains from his 12th-century exotericists, all he applies to his wider argument, is a vague standard of literary "worldliness." Said's failure to *grasp* his own discussion is all the more striking given his construction of the Zahirites as anti-Orientalists, true Koranists. In this regard he compares them favorably with the Batinists, who seem to have been influenced by the Christian idea of revelation. Yet having got that far – theoretical water, preciously, in hand – Said drops it to the ground. For the rest of his book he aligns himself, hermeneutically speaking, with the very same idea. He makes no attempt to take seriously the Zahirite "ambition" of surface reading, but constantly assumes that a text is the mere trace of deep and surprising origins; that expression consists in a paradoxical failure to express a determinative intention; that the meanings of words are always-already annihilated by the absent presence of authorial mind, etc.[2]

---

[1] Edward Said, *The World, the Text, and the Critic* (Cambridge, MA, 1983), pp. 36–39, 45.
[2] Said, pp. 128–133.

The reason this matters – the reason esotericism is an error – is also the second reason that exoteric reading is difficult. It is difficult because reading is difficult; and exoteric reading is nothing other than the necessary mode of reading. After all, a text is "the verbal realization of a signifying intention," as Said puts it (*qua* Zahirite). "Now the signifying intention," he goes on, "is synonymous not with a psychological intention but exclusively with a verbal intention" – what I have called, in accordance with modern semantic usage, a (secondary) intension. But if (secondary) intension is what we are trying to recover by reading; and if (secondary) intension is exclusively realized in text, composed of words; then it follows that to read is to turn, and return, exclusively, to "the phenomenal words themselves." Very unsurprisingly, reading must be about words.[3] But words are only words because of their exoteric or surface form: their pre-constitution, by language, as special units of intention. They are not words – *contra* some versions of strong intentionalism – just insofar as they have been imprinted by someone's intention.

To posit, therefore, "a hidden level beneath words," is not to posit a better way of reading. It is to posit a non-reading. As I have suggested intermittently throughout this book, the latter activity has had many proponents in the history of understanding. Perhaps most relevant among them, as I bring my discussion to a conclusion, is Stanley Fish. A Miltonist of unparalleled influence both within and beyond his discipline, Fish has spent his career developing and advocating a paradigm of unknowing. He has placed textuality at the center of this paradigm, and has constructed Milton as the exemplar of (his version of) textuality. Briefly, Fish's claim is that one has nothing to learn from exoteric textuality; except that one has nothing to learn from exoteric textuality. Under a critical handling that usually includes vigorous esotericization, "good" texts teach this lesson, while "bad" texts teach what happens if one does not learn it. And what happens? Basically, one fails to recognize the priority – ethical, epistemological, and interpretative – of social-psychological immanentism and semiotic-semantic intentionalism. One fails to learn, in other words, that the pre-determination of minds matters, more than the work of expression; and that the projective power of intentions matters, more than the work of words. Since both positions are consistent with what I have been calling *logos*-philosophy, it is evident that Fish is arguing in this broad and orthodox tradition. And since the idea of the *logos* is, more or less, the idea that one has nothing to learn from exoteric textuality, it is evident that the circularity and vacuity of Fish's system – and these, I think, are compliments in his terms – are complete.[4]

Milton, for Fish, is the great poet of the *logos*. His are words in lieu of non-words, and expressions as poor substitutes for intentions. Fish's Milton is the epic trickster directing us to attend, not so much to his text, as to our intentional reactions to his

---

   3   Said, p. 38.
   4   See Fish, *Self-Consuming Artifacts: The Experience of Seventeenth-Century Literature* (Berkeley, 1972); *"Is There a Text in this Class?"*; *Doing What Comes Naturally*; and *The Trouble with Principle*.

text.[5] He is the pastoral utterer systematically evacuating his utterance of all reference and all subjectivity, in order to demonstrate the objective and non-referential vacuity of all utterance.[6] He is the Biblical exegete refusing to commit to exegesis, except insofar as his commentary can be about the pointlessness of exegesis; and then he is the hermeneutic Biblicist, more daringly logistic, who refuses to accept the surface integrity of the Biblical text itself.[7] In the fullest and most recent articulation of his "Miltonic paradigm," Fish places everything proper to literary textuality – action, speech, plot, understanding, and intelligibility – under the heading of "temptations." All we get from any of them, he claims, is a missing of the point. The point, for Fish, is to "believe" – in God's will, or the truth, or (as he puts it) the "really real."[8] But believing is an internal matter, and can never really be effected or determined by anything other than itself. Least of all text. For belief, an absolutely arbitrary and determinative intentional state, always retains the right and tendency to pre-determine what all texts mean (regardless of what they seem, exoterically, to mean). For Fish's Milton, belief trumps meaning, and meaning can never really effect belief. His oeuvre gigantically paraphrases and repetitively represents Louis Armstrong's definition of jazz: "if you don't know, I can't tell you."

Obviously, my own account of Milton differs diametrically. My Milton is committed to the efficacy of telling, and to the transformative possibility of understanding. My Milton is the great poet of the exoteric word. On *Lycidas* and the *Second Defense*, I have argued that Milton is trying to textualize a conscience that he perceives, in the first place, to be a textualization. This is not a deconstructive deferral of understanding, but is instead the very recognitive structure of understanding. On *Comus*, I have argued that the Lady's abjuration of expression, in favor of an esoteric and immanent intention, is inimical to her own interests and to the masque's exoteric imperatives. *Samson Agonistes*, then, counters the masque's anti-heroine with a hero who abjures intention in favor of expression – even to the extent that he models an intension (in the semantic sense) divorced from intentional origin, and left as real meaning in the world. Finally, I have argued that *Paradise Lost* is centrally about the real-world activity that is thereby enabled. Dialogue, as our paradisal inheritance, is what the poem both represents and teaches.

Above all, I have argued that Milton is hostile to any hermeneutics, and to any epistemology, that devolves on the category of secrecy. That most hermeneutics – some people would say all hermeneutics – does so devolve is what makes Milton's (anti)secrecy a matter of some moment. In my Introduction, I tried to support Milton's attitude with some general and all-too-brief comments about early-modern exotericism, and via theoretical connection with Gadamer's hermeneutics of recognition. (It seems to me that Said, although he never mentions Gadamer, would

---

5   Fish, *Surprised by Sin*.

6   Fish, *"Lycidas*: A Poem Finally Anonymous," in *How Milton Works*, pp. 256–280.

7   Fish, "Wanting a Supplement: The Question of Interpretation in Milton's Early Prose," in *How Milton Works*, pp. 215–255.

8   *How Milton Works*, pp. 307–476; 41; and 572.

have found in him a fellow Zahirite *manqué*.) Yet the whole business remains tricky. It would be quite surprising if Milton did not sometimes fall into esoteric patterns, or if my own comments on him did not sometimes fall similarly.

The Plain Sense

Perhaps the most hazardous areas, for Milton and for me, are theology and cosmology. As I pointed out in my Introduction, the secrecy of God is a Christian commonplace that Milton places at the center of his ethical and hermeneutic thinking. Because God is secretive, the rest of us must not be. Furthermore, because God must be assumed to *control* the discovery and concealment of creation – "and not divulge / His secrets to be scann'd by them who ought / Rather admire" (*PL* 8.73–75) – we must be extremely wary of our own tendency to unilateral and intemperate investigation. Thus we are directed toward an exoteric encounter with the universe, and an attempt to understand understanding as an exclusive function of this encounter. Yet the secrecy of God, being a universal postulate, tends to subvert, as well as to support, this direction. For it means that the way things seem to us, much as we must accept them, is not the way things are in their ultimate and divinely-guaranteed reality. It further means that a secret explanation is always, potentially, available, whenever an obvious or intelligible one is lacking.

In short, the plane of recognition, where we know we dwell, rests on a vast area of discovery where we know we do not. Hamlet defies "augury," the ancient Roman method of divination by bird-watching, but not because he denies the secret meaning of ordinary signs. Rather, Hamlet is asserting that the secret meaning is the real meaning, and is also really secret – inaccessible, and overriding. Explaining that "there is special providence in the fall of a sparrow" (5.2.217–218), he founds a higher augury on Matthew 10:29. Calvin makes much of the same scriptural chapter, with its apocalyptic assurances (10:26), and provides the necessary gloss on Shakespeare's theology. In the Augustinian tradition, "special providence" differs from the "general providence" by which God makes and maintains all things.[9] "Special" providence designates direct and targetted divine intervention; for Calvin, as for Hamlet, it means that accidents do not happen. "Carnal reason" may be impressed by the unreason of events, "but anyone who has been taught by Christ's lips that all the hairs of his head are numbered will look farther afield for a cause."[10] Like many early-modern thinkers, the Genevan reformer usually has a naïve semiotics: he looks for, in Bacon's words, "proportion betweene the similitude and the thing signified."[11] Yet the occlusion of God's purposes occludes, potentially,

---

[9]   Calvin, *Institutes*, pp. 202–203.

[10]   Calvin, *Institutes*, p. 199. Matthew 10:29 was ubiquitous among Protestants: see Wright, "The World's Worst Worm," p. 115.

[11]   Bacon, *Wisdome*, Preface.

all such normative relations. God's will, as interpretative background, produces the universe as conspiracy theory.

These cosmological tensions are reflected, arguably, in reformed Biblical interpretation. Plain or literal readings of the sacred text, already preferred in the Catholic tradition, are raised by Protestantism to the status of a first principle, joining exegesis to soteriology. To be taught *sola scriptura* – by scripture alone, unmediated by other interpretative authority – is to be saved *sola fide* (only by faith), even as it is to be prepared for both processes *sola gratia* (only by grace). Literalism, the self-conscious rejection of extra-scriptural interpretative control, is the way to guarantee that one is learning exclusively from scripture. Yet this means learning some pretty strange things, when it comes to the Bible's strange and/or contradictory passages. Protestantism, accordingly, retains two major techniques of pre-Reformation non-literalism: the doctrine of accommodation, and the theory of typology. The former proposes that God does not express himself to us as he really is, but only as he knows we will be able to understand him. The latter reads the New Testament as both transcending and fulfilling the Old, in a mysterious network of characterological prefigurations and narratological interrelations.[12] These techniques allow Protestantism to explain difficult passages of the Bible; even as they allow, somewhat more importantly, a general explanation or theory of Biblical difficulty. God's secrecy, accepted as the premise of exegetic literalism, also underwrites the necessary exceptions to that literalism. Yet Protestantism is thereby opened to a charge of hermeneutic incoherence. For if non-literalism intervenes whenever it is needed – esotericizing a Biblical text that fails, repeatedly, at the exoteric level – how can Protestants claim anti-authoritarianism and anti-esotericism as their overarching interpretative standards?

Milton, as an exegetic theorist, is an extreme Protestant. That is to say, he takes an anti-authoritarian and anti-esoteric approach to the interpretation of the Bible – and takes that approach far enough to be offensive to many of his fellow Protestants. In *Of Reformation*, for example, Milton aggressively rejects the notion – cited on the Geneva Bible's very title page, and held in trust by the reformers whom Milton excoriates as lukewarm – that "the Scriptures are difficult to be understood." "Ever that which is necessary to be known is most easie," Milton says; "and that which is most difficult, so far expounds it selfe ever as to tell us how little it imports our *saving knowledge*" (*CP* 1.566). The scripture, on Milton's account, does not only have an obvious meaning. It also makes obvious, helpfully and recursively, that none of its meaning is in its own non-obvious portions. Indeed, Milton's anti-prelatical and anti-patristic Bible is sometimes so radically obvious that it becomes a "mirror of Diamond" irradiating "not only the *wise*, and *learned*, but the *simple*, the *poor*," and even "the *babes*." Here the poet is waxing millenial, but he rationally explains

---

12   For accommodation and typology as exceptions to Protestant literalism, see Peter Harrison, *The Bible, Protestantism, and the Rise of Natural Science* (Cambridge and New York, 1998). For the literal understanding as primary even in pre-Reformation exegesis, see D.C. Allen, *Mysteriously Meant*.

that "the Scriptures themselves pronounce their own plainness" (ibid.). The only exegetic theory he will accept is just that (non)theory of exoteric statement and luminous transparency.

That does not mean, for Milton, that the Bible does not require interpretation. Milton's exegetic plainness is not the ultra-denotation sometimes imagined by *logos-philosophy* – words objectively and unmistakably standing for intentions and/or for references. But neither is Milton's concept of interpretation the obverse of logistic denotation – the swamp of subjective connotation, the consequence and sign of linguistic unreliability. Rather, Miltonic interpretation is true understanding through *Gespräch*. It is the necessary, difficult, and inexhaustible activity of the good-faith human attempt to enter into dialogue with words. This is the activity of the "plain upright man that all his dayes hath bin diligently reading the holy Scriptures." It is the activity of the so-called "heretic" (a word that Milton re-etymologizes to mean something like "chooser"), "who holds in religion that belief or those opinions which to his conscience and utmost understanding appear with most evidence of probability in the scripture" (*CP* 7.251).[13]

Most memorably, Miltonic interpretation is the activity of the many "pens and heads," "sitting by their studious lamps, musing, searching, revolving new notions and ideas ... others as fast reading, trying all things, assenting to the force of reason and convincement" (*CP* 2.554). These students, these citizens of *Areopagitica*, know that "truth is compared in Scripture to a streaming fountain; if her waters flow not in a perpetuall progression, they sick'n into a muddy pool of conformity and tradition." They know that they must take "charge and care of their Religion," and that "our faith and knowledge thrive by exercise, as well as our limbs and complexion." Above all, they know that the right kind of exercise is not to "stand in watch" over "certain common doctrinal heads" – stabilized in "interlinearies, breviaries, synopses, and other loitering gear" – but to allow their "old collections" to be "sedu'ct" by a "bold book" (*CP* 2.547). After reading the bold book, they will find it necessary to liberate and re-read the old collections – viz., the scriptures. There, they will be surprised at what they find; but not necessarily because they find anything new. Rather, they will necessarily experience anew the truth of the text, in the light of all their reading. Precisely because the text is completely evident, completely open, it is completely illuminable and re-illuminable by new thinking.

In short, Milton is a Zahirite. He believes in reading. Specifically, he believes in a reading that is not subordinated, theoretically speaking, to non-reading. Expressions, more than intentions; words, more than minds; these are the hermeneutic phenomena that matter. Milton posits an encounter with text, and especially with sacred text, that moots and jeopardizes all the reader's knowledge in the reading process itself. To cop a phrase from Donald Davidson, Milton subordinates prior theory (ideas about language and understanding that provide the grounds for a conversation) to

---

13   For Milton's radical retheorization, see Janel Mueller, "Milton on Heresy," in Dobranski and Rumrich (eds), *Milton and Heresy*, pp. 21–38.

passing theory (ideas about language and understanding that are produced by that very conversation).[14] It follows that Miltonic exegesis is non-objectivistic: it assumes understanding as a function of text and language, the *copia* of which can never be fully controlled or pre-determined. At the same time, however, Miltonic exegesis is non-relativistic: it denies that text or language are themselves functions of the understanding – if they were, how would there be anything to read? – and therefore removes both words, and the subject-matters they render accessible, from a merely subjective determination.

True, reading means working toward a textual understanding that is implicated in, and (partly) constituted by, all manner of circumstantiality. A given interpretation is temporal, it is historical, it is local, it is pscyhological, editorial, emotional, etc. Given the inexhaustible range of possible circumstantialities, it follows that there is an inexhaustible range of possible interpretations – even of the same text, even when the text is considered entirely as an exoteric or surface-function. But *that is precisely the richness of text*, its metastability and superabundance as a site of recognition. Reading is not lost labor, but is the undiscovered labor before us: "had we but eyes to lift up, the fields are white already" (*CP* 2.554).

Of Christian Doctrine

John Savoie has recently pointed out that in a passage of his theological treatise, the *De doctrina Christiana*, Milton suggests subordinating scripture to inward interpretative authority. Reading, in other words, seems to fall to non-reading here. Considering the transmission and editting of the New Testament by "a variety of hands, some more corrupt than others," Milton writes: "I do not know why God's providence should have committed the contents of the New Testament to such wayward guardians, unless it was so that this very fact might convince us that the Spirit which is given to us is a more certain guide than scripture, and that we ought to follow it" (*CP* 6.589). Savoie concludes, therefore, that Milton "prefers spirit to letter and internal illumination to external text."[15]

Savoie's (Fishy) claim is well-argued. It is not, however, well-supported by the passage under consideration. Milton's concern here is precisely with the transmission and integrity of the external text. First, he contrasts the doubtful redaction of the New Testament with the reliable provenance of the Old, holding up as an exegetic ideal the inviolability of the latter. ("In every period the priests considered it a matter of supreme importance that no word should be changed, and they had no theories which might have made them alter anything.") Turning to the gospels, Milton's point is to establish textual authority as unique, *despite* everything that might be said against it. ("Clearly the editors and interpreters of the Greek Testament, which is of prime

---

[14]   See Davidson, "A Nice Derangement of Epitaphs."
[15]   John Savoie, "The Point of the Pinnacle: Son and Scripture in *Paradise Regained*," *ELR* 34.1 (2004): 83–124; 119.

authority, rest all their decisions upon the weight and reliability of the manuscript evidence.") In cases of evident textual corruption, Milton's position is that we simply have no recourse. ("If the reliability of the manuscripts varies or is uncertain, these editors must be at a loss.") Moreover, while we may have doubts about believing everything in scripture, we must be absolutely certain that we can believe nothing that is *not* in it. ("Least of all can a magistrate impose rigid beliefs upon the faithful, beliefs which are either not found in scripture at all, or [are] only deduced from scripture by a process of human reasoning which does not carry any conviction with it.") Finally, the spirit with which Savoie associates Milton's exegesis – the "internal scripture of the Holy Spirit," "the pre-eminent and supreme authority," which "guides man to truth" and "inwardly persuades every believer" – this spirit, in relation to the external text, has not an hierarchical but an ameliorative function. The spirit is what allows us to "believe in the whole scripture," and not just "in a general or overall way," but in all its details. Milton's spirit affirms and reaffirms, it does not supplant or subvert, the authority of the "external text" (ibid.).

This is all very much consistent with Milton's literalism. The *De doctrina* offers his version of Biblical orthodoxy through a very simple, and overwhelmingly exoteric, methodology: he quotes scripture, seeking to "cram" his pages with it, "even to overflowing" (*CP* 6.122). Of course this means reproducing exegetic conundra, but this is a difficulty that Milton welcomes. For it allows him to assert that exegetic conundra are not to be ingeniously or esoterically resolved. On Genesis 6:6 and Judges 2:18, for example, where the emotion of repentance is attributed to God, Milton departs from the ubiquitous view that scripture is lying – or, rather, that it is accommodating itself to our understanding. The latter view is shared by both Augustine and Calvin, and is duly cited in the Geneva Bible glosses on the relevant passages.[16] Milton will have none of it. "We ought not to imagine," he writes, "that God would have said anything or caused anything to be written about himself unless he intended that it should be a part of our conception of him ... If Jehovah repented that he had created man, and repented because of their groanings, let us believe that he did repent" (*CP* 6.134). It follows, if not that God has "lack of foresight," at least that he is mutable and narratable. It is "not beneath God to feel what grief he does feel, to be refreshed by what refreshes him, and to fear what he does fear" (*CP* 6.135). This is exactly the kind of anthropomorphic or at least naïve inference that the whole Christian exegetic tradition, Reformed and otherwise, finds intolerable. But for Milton, it is even *more* intolerable to esotericize the scriptural text. He proposes, therefore, that we simply work with the strangeness of the exoteric reading.

As I have noted, the doctrine of accommodation is a major exception to Protestant literalism. Milton, however, follows through the logic of accommodation in such a way that it ceases to be such an exception, but becomes profoundly consistent with literalism. "They understand best what God is like," he writes, "who adjust their understanding to the word of God, *for he has adjusted his word to our understanding*"

---

16   Calvin, *Institutes*, pp. 225–227.

(*CP* 6.136, my emphasis).[17] Milton has cottoned on to the strange redundancy of much accomodationist doctrine. God speaks so that we can understand him, the doctrine says – and therefore we must take care not to understand what he speaks. We must suppose, with Calvin, that he is "lisping" to us. But if God has tailored his utterances to fit us, why must we re-fit them? Why must scripture be *twice* accommodated? This, Milton says, is simply frustrating God of his purpose: "as if, indeed, we wished to show that our concept of God was not too debased, but that his concept of us was" (*CP* 6.136). Like Nicholas of Cusa, Milton supposes that language and text are imperfect intellectual vehicles – but that their imperfection perfectly accords with the imperfection of human understanding. Nothing is to be gained, therefore, by doubting or disassembling the linguistic vehicle. Everything is to be gained, insofar as anything is to be gained, by climbing aboard it, as is.[18]

The problem with this sort of strategy is that the linguistic vehicle has a tendency to lead to uncomfortable places. Ultimately, it can lead to exegetic car-crash: the intra-scriptural contradiction that St. Augustine so feared.[19] In order to avoid that result, Augustine introduced what became the basic principle of all Christian non-literalism: the principle of charity, which asserts the internal consistency of scripture *a priori*. Milton, however, has an exoteric fondness for intra-scriptural contradiction. In *The Doctrine and Discipline of Divorce* (1644), for example, his notorious attempt to derive a liberal divorce law from scriptural sources, Milton is faced with the little problem that Christ speaks explicitly against divorce at Matthew 19:9. Now, Stanley Fish has argued (very influentially) that Milton subverts Christ's injunction by an esotericist invocation of the rule of charity.[20] But Fish is wrong. Milton *contradicts* Christ's injunction by an exotericist examination of the *text* of charity. First, Milton aligns Christ's statement in Matthew with the hardness of the Mosaic law, and contains its interpretative writ (in speech-act fashion) as a "slighting answer" to the Pharisees. Then he goes on to observe Christ overthrowing the Law (and here Milton works from Mark) in his defense of healing on the Sabbath. Finally, he tries to overpower the statement in Matthew by arguing that it is inconsistent with the new dispensation. Milton's is a trumping strategy, adventurous and provocative, but it is not "intentional" or "circular" as Fish claims. Matthew 19:9 retains, for Milton, the clear meaning of Matthew 19:9. It just so happens that Mark 2:27 – "the Sabbath was made for man, and not man for the Sabbath" – is, in Milton's claim, stronger (*CP* 2.281–284).

No doubt such an argument, such a procedure, is very strange. But it is strange precisely because it is a surface procedure, and an argument that refuses to retreat from the exoteric level. It has absolutely nothing to do with esoteric penetration or pre-determination of the text; but follows, on the contrary, from a resolute anti-esotericism. "It is amazing what nauseating subtlety," Milton writes in *De Doctrina*

---

[17] *Contra* Silver, *Predicament*, pp. 26 and 48–49 – passages against which Milton might be polemicizing.
[18] See *TM*, pp. 425–456.
[19] Augustine, *On Christian Doctrine* (Indianapolis, 1978), Book I, section xxxvii.
[20] Fish, "Wanting a Supplement."

Christiana (*DDC*), "not to say trickery, some people have employed in their attempts to evade the plain meaning of these scriptural texts. They have left no stone unturned; they have followed every red herring they could find; they have tried everything" (*CP* 6.218). Milton's vituperation of interpretative discovery, his utter rejection of mystery and secrecy as hermeneutic standards, extends to a general loathing of paradoxes, supported with "strange terms and sophistries." It is in this spirit that Milton offers his long, patient, and logical rejection of the consubstantiality of Son and Father (*CP* 6.211–212). Even grammar must be saved from esoteric abuse: "nor should we believe in something which has to be lured out from among articles and particles by some sort of verbal bird-catcher, or which has to be dug out from a mass of ambiguities and obscurities like the answers of an oracle. Rather, we should drink our fill from the clearest fountains of truth. For this open simplicity, this promised clarity of doctrine is what makes the gospel superior to the law" (*CP* 6.246).

Ultimately, Milton's exegetic emphasis on openness and plainness extends to the secrecy of God himself. It extends, that is, not just to our perception of God – to what he has told us, or has "caused ... to be written about himself" – but to God's actual being. Commenting on the doctrine of predestination, which he constructs from scriptural sources as clearly Arminian (and thus as only semi-predestinarian), Milton writes:

> Without doubt the decree as it was made public was consistent with the decree itself. Otherwise we should have to pretend that God was insincere, and said one thing but kept another hidden in his heart. This is, indeed, the effect of that academic distinction which ascribes a twofold will to God: the revealed will, by which he instructs us what he wants us to do, and the will of his good pleasure, by which he decrees that we will never do it. As good split the will in two and say: will in God is twofold – a will by which he wishes, and a will by which he contradicts that wish! (*CP* 6.177)

Milton is contradicting (and to some extent parodying) the ubiquitous Reformed position that God's will differs from our experience of God's will. He is contradicting the idea, in other words, that God's deepest plan for us remains mysterious to us. For Milton, in *DDC*, a split manifestation of God's will in the world could only mean a split manifestation of God's will in God. After all, God's will could only be manifested as split in the world if God so willed it to be manifested. But that would mean, assuming unity of will in God, that God willed a lie; which would amount, paradoxically and unacceptably, to God's will being really split. In the end, not even Milton's God can support a reflexive differentiation between intention and expression, self and speech-act. Not even God can escape the exoteric imperatives of Milton's secrecy, which makes uttering the measure of meaning, and demands that all meaning be uttered.

In Secret Done

Arguably, Milton's (anti)secrecy therefore eats up itself. For it seems to dictate that not even God can be secret. But the secrecy of God is what started things off in the first place. If it dissolves, there is no particular reason (presumably) for God's creatures not to be secretive. Perhaps a fully open God, a knowable and narratable and exoteric God, produces the imperatives of anti-secrecy anyway. Just as a secret God forbids secrecy by making it his fief, so an anti-secret God forbids secrecy by placing it beyond the pale. Be that as it may, the problem of secrecy, which demarcates Milton's hermeneutic system, would seem to have reappeared at its centre.

Perhaps this is why, in the opening lines of his late work *Paradise Regained* (1671), Milton pledges to tell "of deeds / Above Heroic, though in secret done" (1.14–15).[21] At first glance those lines appear to continue, via "though," the disapprobation of secrecy that has been so definitive of Milton's work. The deeds he describes will be above heroic, *despite* their secret execution. Yet even this reading indicates an important re-evaluation. It is hard to imagine, on the apotropaic coding of the keyword elsewhere in Milton's work, how "deeds above heroic" could be done "in secret" at all. Now it appears that they can – at least in the person of the hero of the new poem. The hero in question is the incarnate Christ. *Paradise Regained* describes his temptation in the desert. Why does Milton see fit to call "secret" Christ's resistance to Satan?[22]

Further qualifications make the problem worse. Milton says that Christ's "deeds," done "in secret," have been "unrecorded left through many an Age," though they were "worthy t'have not remain'd so long unsung" (1.16–17). Both characterizations are odd. The temptation in the desert is detailed in three of the four Gospels, and formed a not unpopular subject for medieval and Renaissance retelling.[23] In telling the story yet once more, Milton cannot be claiming to offer an "unrecorded" tale. Neither does he seem to be claiming any new or dense narrative articulation. When he gets a chance to explain how Christ passed the forty days before the temptation, for example, Milton says simply that such details are "not reveal'd" (1.307). If "secret" means hidden or withheld, then merely re-telling the gospel story of the temptation is telling nothing secret. Yet when the poet of *Paradise Regained* considers aspects of the story that are omitted from the gospels, he denies any knowledge of them.

The deeds of the temptation, as recounted by Milton, appear to be "secret" only in the social-psychological sense that they involve the workings of Jesus' conscience. This hero enters the desert in response to an internal "Guide" (*PR* 1.336), resembling the "guide" of conscience that God promised to place "within" (see *PL* 3.194–198). He engages in long internal monologues by day (*PR* 1.196–294, 2.244–262), and dreams, "as appetite is wont to dream" (2.264), despite himself, by night. "O what

---

21   Milton, *Paradise Regaind. A poem. In IV books. To which is added Samson Agonistes* (London, 1671). All further citations to this edition, parenthesized by book and line number in body of my text.
22   See Christopher, "Secret"; and Savoie.
23   See Watson Kirkconnel (ed.), *Awake the Courteous Echo: The Themes and Prosody of* Comus, Lycidas, *and* Paradise Regained *in World Literature with Translations of the Major Analogues* (Toronto, 1973), pp. 249–312.

a multitude of thoughts at once / Awakn'd in me swarm," the savior complains at one point,

> while I consider
> What from within I feel my self, and hear
> What from without comes often to my ears,
> Ill sorting with my present state compar'd. (1.197–199)

He goes full of "deep thoughts" (1.190), "musing and much revolving" (1.185). As that last line indicates, this "secret" protagonist is in some ways a descendant of Milton's great "secret" antagonist: the Satan of *Paradise Lost*, whose "revolving" indicates his self-division (*PL* 4.31). We find the same emphasis on inner experience, the same self-division and radical aloneness. This Christ has his expectations violated ("I as all others to his Baptism came / Which I believ'd was from above; but he / Strait knew me" [*PR* 1.273–275]); he experiences doubt ("where will this end" [2.245]); and he is led by a "strong motion" that he experiences as a self apart from himself (1.290). He even dissembles, telling Satan that he is not hungry after we have just learned to the contrary (see 2.318, 260–284). The interiority of Jesus goes (arguably) "unrecorded" in the Gospels, and any secrecy other than the Satanic has long been absent from the narrative poetry of John Milton. And yet it was – Milton now seems to recognize – "worthy t'have not remain'd so long unsung."

It is hard not to see this recognition as a retrenchment. The exoteric imperatives of all Milton's major works (as I have read them) would appear to be trumped, in *PR*, by an esoteric and inward Christ. Satan, for his part, is quite unable to draw his intended victim out of the latter's social-pychological fortress. In one of the poem's most famous images, the frustrated tempter is compared to "a swarm of flies in vintage time," which,

> Beat off, returns as oft with humming sound;
> Or surging waves against a solid rock,
> Though all to shivers dash't, the assault renew,
> Vain battry, and in froth or bubbles end. (4.15–20)

The hopelessness of Satan's assault implies the security of Christ's fortifications. More importantly, it implies that Christ's resistance to Satan's temptation – regaining Paradise, somehow, "in the wast Wilderness" (1.7) – consists precisely in his sequestration of "minde" from "rinde." Milton's Christ would seem to be the latest incarnation of Milton's strong-intentionalist Lady. Unlike her, moreover, he would seem to suffer no ill-effects from his intentional retreat.

At the end of *Paradise Regained*, Christ returns home "to his mother's house private" (4.639). "Private" modifies "house" as much as it modifies the following verb "return'd."[24] "Private house," Gary Hamilton argues, is Restoration usage for

---

24   See Gary D. Hamilton, "*Paradise Regained* and the Private Houses," in P.G. Stanwood (ed.), *Of Poetry and Politics: New Essays on Milton and His World* (Binghamton,

"conventicle," the class of private chapel or meeting banned by statute in 1664 (with the legislation strengthened in 1670). As Puritanism became Dissent in the late seventeenth century, the godly way increasingly became one *of separation* [*secretionis*]. In the great Restoration debauch, the defeated saints had to "come out from among them," in the words of St. Paul, "and be ... separate ... and touch not the unclean *thing*" (2 Corinthians 6.17).[25] In this context, arguably, Christ's return to the house private is a political act; and this because *Paradise Regained* reflects "the politics of inwardness."[26]

And yet: this is a pattern more familiar than strange. Christ's return to his privacy, after the successfully-resisted temptation, is exactly congruent to Milton's own return home after the Italian journey – a journey that Milton constructs, in the *Second Defense*, as (in part) a successfully-resisted temptation. As I have argued, Milton's London privacy becomes the rhetorical springboard for his noble and uncompelled entry into public controversy. It is the abjuration of privacy that he offers, the wilfull inversion of his justly-won secrecy. The maneuver is predicated on occupying the position that the occupier then renounces. In Milton's polemical self-presentation, the renunciation has to be iterated and re-iterated. Milton must go on, after describing his triumphant renting, to describe his publications and other political engagements. In *PR*, however, it is hardly necessary for Milton to point out what follows the private house. What follows is the ministry; what follows is the fulfillment of scripture through preaching. The private house is simply a pause before Christ moves, gloriously and astonishingly, to the exoteric imperatives of prophecy. The private house is the necessary spot from which to start. Christ has been trying to *start*, to get out of the private via the private, since the beginning of the poem. The whole reason he entered the desert was in order to figure out "which way first" to "*publish* his God-like office" (1.188, my emphasis). Wandering into the desert, while wondering how to lead humanity into the kingdom of heaven, Christ is not being esoterically absent-minded, but is finding the exoteric path.

Moreover: Satan is wrong to think he has to break into Christ's head. Christ has been freely opening it to him, all along. Unlike Milton's Lady, Milton's Christ does not say to his tormentor "I could refute you if I wanted" (or words to that effect). Rather, Christ refutes Satan, in speech after long speech.[27] The remarkable thing about Christ's loquacity in *PR* is that it seems quite unnecessary – if our measure of the necessary is immanentist and intentionalist. Christ does not need to learn (contrary to

---

NY, 1995), pp. 239–248.

[25]   For late seventeenth-century Puritanism, see John Spurr, "From Puritanism to Dissent, 1660–1700," in Christopher Durston and Jacqueline Eales (eds), *The Culture of English Puritanism, 1560–1700* (New York, 1996), pp. 234–265.

[26]   Hamilton, 240–241. For a similar reading, see Andrew Shifflett, *Stoicism, Politics, and Literature in the Age of Milton: War and Peace Reconciled* (Cambridge, 1998), pp. 129–154.

[27]   See Steven Goldsmith, "The Muting of Satan: Language and Redemption in *Paradise Regained*," *SEL* 26 (1986): 125–140.

perennial critical assumptions) that he is the son of God, or what this identity means. He knows these things already. He does not need to learn what his mission on earth is, or how he will fulfill it, or what is meant by his kingdom. He knows these things already. Christ's job in the desert, his heroic action "in secret done," is not knowing but speaking. By speaking, he both demonstrates and actualizes his knowing.

In the end, Milton's Christ regains paradise through speech-action. The Austinian category appears here in its full significance. By standing on the pinnacle, by performing what he says, Christ unifies intention and expression from the side of expression. He shows that utterance is not an epiphenomenon of thought, but that thought is an item of a unified theory of action. "Also it is written, / Tempt not the Lord thy God, he said and stood" (4.560–561). This is performance-art as moral lecture. It is ending by beginning, achieving by trying. Christ says and stands his resistance to temptation. He says and stands his fulfillment of prophecy. He defeats Satan neither by resting in his perfect mind, nor by manifesting the incongruity of his imperfect embodiment; but by comporting himself, perfectly, as the imperfect and incarnate word.

I have been arguing throughout this book that Milton redirects our hermeneutic attention from intentions to expressions, minds to texts. This is supported by subsidiary redirections, from the esoteric to the exoteric, and from discovery to recognition. The upshot of it all is neither strange nor trivial, but radically pragmatic. Milton illuminates understanding as what we naturally do – but only insofar as we are able to see ourselves as the natural elements of understanding. Christ, the exemplar, cannot help but be the word. He always was, and is, and always will be, what is spoken. It follows that he is at home in conversation, but not in charge of it. This is the essence of the hermeneutic attitude.

Now, understanding, as I have been trying to show, produces an inertia called method. This is the idea of controlled conversation. It is the idea that understanding is something we effect (or perhaps affect), rather than something we suffer. Ultimately, method is the idea that we understand understanding. At least, it is the idea that we understand any understanding that is worthy of that name. Method is so pervasive, so immanent within our intellectual activities, that it unifies deconstruction with objectivism, and scientific ideology with aesthetic consciousness. It even persists apotropaically (by being warded off). For the attempt to understand without method, as Milton's Eve learns to her cost, can come to look suspiciously like a method – in which case, method wins.

That is to say, however, that genuine understanding – hermeneutic, dialogic, questioning understanding – involves and mandates and absolutely demands a re-iterative recognition and rejection of method. This is worthy, endless work. It is true hermeneutic work. The rejection of method amounts to saying, on the analogy of liberal economics, "allow to do": let conversation work. No imperative could be less substantial. Yet – as the history of the liberal idea makes clear – none could be more burdensome or challenging, either.[28] *Milton's Secrecy* has, in this respect, been about the iteration and reiteration of hermeneutic *laissez-faire*. This is what Milton does. It is a thing needful to be done, precisely because the disallowance of method so incessantly and automatically interferes with the natural and illimitable productivity of thought.

Finally: if method is the idea that we understand understanding, philosophical hermeneutics is the idea that we do not. Visited upon us through *Gespräch*, understanding is, by definition, beyond us and in control of us. That is why we are able, from time to time, to say with confidence and sincerity that we understand a given subject-matter. We will never be able to say, at least not with the same confidence or sincerity, that we understand understanding *per se*. Understanding enables our grasp of subject-matters, and is itself beyond that grasp, because it is the ultimate and transcendent subject-matter. As such it is what Milton, "with no middle flight" (*PL* 1.14), chooses to write about.

---

[28]   See Tom G. Palmer, "The Hermeneutical View of Freedom: Implications of Gadamerian Understanding for Economic Policy," in Lavoie (ed.), *Economics and Hermeneutics*, pp. 299–318.

Works Cited

Abrams, M.H., *The Mirror and the Lamp: Romantic Theory and the Critical Tradition* (New York: Oxford University Press, 1953).

Achinstein, Sharon, *Milton and the Revolutionary Reader* (Princeton, NJ: Princeton University Press, 1994).

Albert, Hans, "Critical Rationalism and Universal Hermeneutics," in Malpas, Arnswald, and Kertscher (eds), *Gadamer's Century*, pp.15–24.

Alberti, Leon Battista, *Momus*, trans. Sarah Knight, eds Virginia Brown and Sarah Knight (Cambridge, MA: Harvard University Press, 2003).

Alexander, Thomas M., "Eros and Understanding: Gadamer's Aesthetic Ontology of the Community," in Hahn (ed.), *The Philosophy of Hans-Georg Gadamer*, pp. 323–348.

Allen, Don Cameron, *Mysteriously Meant: The Rediscovery of Pagan Symbolism and Allegorical Interpretation in the Renaissance* (Baltimore: Johns Hopkins University Press, 1970).

——, "Milton's 'Comus' as a Failure in Artistic Compromise," *ELH* 16 (1949): 104–119.

Alpers, Paul, *What is Pastoral?* (Chicago and London: University of Chicago Press, 1996).

Ambrosio, Francis J., "The Figure of Socrates in Gadamer's Philosophical Hermeneutics," in Hahn (ed.), *The Philosophy of Hans-Georg Gadamer*, pp. 259–274.

Ames, William, *Conscience with the Power and Cases thereof* (London, 1643).

Armitage, David, and Armand Himy and Quentin Skinner (eds), *Milton and Republicanism* (Cambridge: Cambridge University Press, 1995).

Armstrong, Nancy, and Leonard Tennenhouse, *The Imaginary Puritan* (Berkeley and Los Angeles: University of California Press, 1992).

Arnswald, Ulrich, "On the Certainty of Uncertainty: Language-Games and Forms of Life in Gadamer and Wittgenstein," in Malpas, Arnswald, and Kertscher (eds), *Gadamer's Century*, pp. 25–44.

Arthos, John, *Milton and the Italian Cities* (London: Bowes and Bowes, 1968).

Augustine, *On Christian Doctrine*, trans. D.W. Robertson (Indianapolis: Prentice Hall, 1978).

Austin, J.L., *How to Do Things with Words* (New York: Oxford University Press, 1965).

Bacon, Francis, *The New Organon*, eds Lisa Jardine and Michael Silverthorne (Cambridge: Cambridge University Press, 2000).

——, *The Essayes or Counsels, Civill and Morall*, ed. Michael Kiernan (Oxford: Clarendon Press, 1985).

——, *The Wisdome of the Ancients, written in Latine by the Right Honourable Sir Francis Bacon Knight*, trans. Sir Arthur Gorges (London, 1619).

Ball, Terence, "Constitutional Interpretation and Conceptual Change," in Gregory Leyh (ed.), *Legal Hermeneutics: History, Theory, and Practice* (Berkeley: University of California Press, 1992), pp. 129–146.

Barton, Carol, "'In This Dark World and Wide': *Samson Agonistes* and the Meaning of Christian Heroism," *Early Modern Literary Studies: A Journal of Sixteenth- and Seventeenth-Century English Literature* 5.2 (1999). (Available online at: http://extra.shu.ac.uk/emls/05-2/05-2toc.htm)

Bath, Michael, *Speaking Pictures: English Emblem Books and Renaissance Culture* (London and New York: Longman, 1994).

Bauman, Michael, *Milton's Arianism* (New York: Peter Lang, 1986).

Baumlin, James S., "Willam Perkins's *Art of Prophesying* and Milton's 'Two-Handed Engine'," *MQ* 33.3: 66–71.

Beiner, Ronald, "Gadamer's Philosophy of Dialogue and Its Relation to the Postmodernism of Nietzsche, Heidegger, Derrida, and Strauss," in Krajewski (ed.), *Gadamer's Repercussions*, pp. 145–157.

Belsey, Catherine, *John Milton: Language, Gender, Power* (Oxford and New York: Blackwell, 1988).

Benet, Diana Treviño, and Michael Lieb (eds), *Literary Milton: Text, Pretext, Context* (Pittsburgh: Duquesne University Press, 1994).

——, "Hell, Satan, and the New Politician," in Benet and Lieb (eds), *Literary Milton*, pp. 91–113.

——, "The Escape from Rome: Milton's *Second Defense* and a Renaissance Genre," in di Cesare (ed.), *Milton in Italy*, pp. 29–51.

Bernstein, Richard J., *Beyond Objectivism and Relativism: Science, Hermeneutics and Praxis* (Philadelphia: University of Pennsylvania Press, 1983).

Biagioli, Mario, *Galileo's Instruments of Credit: Telescopes, Images, Secrecy* (Chicago and London: University of Chicago Press, 2006).

Blake, William, *The Marriage of Heaven and Hell*, in *Romanticism: An Anthology*, ed. Duncan Wu (Oxford: Blackwell, 1996), pp. 79–97.

Bok, Sissela, *Secrets: On the Ethics of Concealment and Revelation* (New York: Pantheon, 1982).

Bork, Robert, *The Tempting of America: The Political Seduction of the Law* (London: Collier Macmillan, 1990).

Brown, Cedric C., *John Milton's Aristocratic Entertainments* (Cambridge and New York: Cambridge University Press, 1985).

Bruns, Gerald, *Hermeneutics, Ancient and Modern* (New Haven: Yale University Press, 1992).

Burke, Seán, *The Death and Return of the Author: Criticism and Subjectivity in Barthes, Foucault and Derrida* (Edinburgh: Edinburgh University Press, 1998).

Burton, Robert, *The Anatomy of Melancholy*, eds Thomas C. Faulkner, Nicolas K. Kiessling and Rhonda L. Blair (Oxford: Clarendon Press, 1989).

Calvin, John, *Institutes of the Christian Religion*, ed. John T. McNeill, trans. Ford Lewis Battles (Philadelphia: Westminster Press, 1960).

Campbell, Gordon, *A Milton Chronology* (New York: St. Martin's Press, 1997).

Carew, Thomas, *Thomas Carew: Poems 1640, together with Poems from the Wyburd Manuscript* (Menston, England: Scolar Press, 1969).

Carey, John, "A work in praise of terrorism?" *Times Literary Supplement*, September 6, 2002.

———, *Milton* (London: Evans Bros., 1969).

Carrithers, Gale H. and James D. Hardy, Jr., *Milton and the Hermeneutic Journey* (Baton Rouge: Louisiana State University Press, 1994).

Castiglione, Baldesar, *The Book of the Courtier*, trans. and introd. George Bull (Harmondsworth, Middlesex: Penguin, 1976).

di Cesare, Mario (ed.), *Milton in Italy: Contexts, Images, Contradictions* (Binghamton, NY: Medieval and Renaissance Texts and Studies, 1991).

Chambers, A.B., *Andrew Marvell and Edmund Waller: Seventeenth-Century Praise and Restoration Satire* (University Park: Pennsylvania State University Press, 1991).

Champagne, Claudia, "Adam and his 'Other Self' in *Paradise Lost*: A Lacanian Study in Psychic Development," in William Zunder (ed.), *Paradise Lost* (New York: St. Martin's Press, 1999), pp. 117–135.

Chaney, Edward, *The Grand Tour and the Great Rebellion: Richard Lassels and "The Voyage of Italy" in the Seventeenth Century* (Moncalieri: Biblioteca del Viaggio in Italia, 1985).

Chartier, Roger (ed.), and Arthur Goldhammer (trans.), *A History of Private Life III: Passions of the Renaissance* (Cambridge, MA, and London: Belknap Press of Harvard University Press, 1989).

Chernaik, Warren, "Books as Memorials: The Politics of Consolation," *Yearbook of English Studies* 21 (1991): 207–217.

Christopher, Georgia B., "The Secret Agent in *Paradise Regained*," *Modern Language Quarterly* 41.2 (1980): 131–150.

Cicero, *Letters to Atticus*, ed. and trans. D.R. Shackleton Bailey (6 vols, Cambridge, MA: Harvard University Press, 1999).

Cinquemani, A.M., *Glad to Go for a Feast: Milton, Buonmattei, and the Florentine Accademia* (New York: Peter Lang, 1998).

Colie, Rosalie, Paradoxia Epidemica: *The Renaissance Tradition of Paradox* (Princeton, NJ: Princeton University Press, 1966).

Connolly, John M., "*Applicatio* and *Explicatio* in Gadamer and Eckhart," in Malpas, Arnswald, and Kertscher (eds), *Gadamer's Century*, pp. 77–96.

Corns, Thomas, "'Some Rousing Motions': the Plurality of Miltonic Ideology," in Thomas Healey and Jonathan Sawday (eds), *Literature and the English Civil War* (Cambridge and New York: Cambridge University Press, 1990), pp. 110–126.

———, "John Milton: Italianate Humanist, Northern European Protestant, Englishman," in di Cesare (ed.), *Milton in Italy*, pp. 1–8.

Crawford, Julie, *Marvelous Protestantism: Monstrous Births in Post-Reformation England* (Baltimore and London: Johns Hopkins University Press, 2005).

Culler, Jonathan, *On Deconstruction* (Ithaca: Cornell University Press, 1982).

Curry, Walter Clyde, *Milton's Ontology, Cosmogony, and Physics* (Lexington: Kentucky University Press, 1957).

Daly, Peter M., *Literature in the Light of the Emblem* (Toronto and London: University of Toronto Press, 1998).

——, and John Manning (eds), *Aspects of Renaissance and Baroque Symbol Theory, 1500–1700* (New York: AMS Press, 1999).

Damrosch, Leo, *God's Plot and Man's Stories: Studies in the Fictional Imagination from Milton to Fielding* (Chicago: University of Chicago Press, 1985).

Dasenbrock, Reed Way, *Truth And Consequences: Intentions, Conventions, And The New Thematics* (University Park: Pennsylvania State University Press, 2001).

Davidson, Donald, *Essays on Actions and Events* (Oxford: Clarendon, 2001).

——, *Inquiries into Truth and Interpretation* (Oxford: Clarendon, 2001).

——, "Actions, Reasons, and Causes," in *Essays on Actions and Events*, pp. 3–19.

——, "Intending," in *Essays on Actions and Events*, pp. 83–102.

——, "Theories of Meaning and Learnable Languages," in *Inquiries into Truth and Interpretation*, pp. 1–16.

——, "Truth and Meaning," in *Inquiries into Truth and Interpretation*, pp. 17–36.

——, "On Saying That," in *Inquiries into Truth and Interpretation,* pp. 93–108.

——, "Thought and Talk," in *Inquiries into Truth and Interpretation*, pp. 155–170.

——, "On the Very Idea of a Conceptual Scheme," in *Inquiries into Truth and Interpretation*, pp. 183–198.

——, "Gadamer and Plato's *Philebus*," in Hahn (ed.), *The Philosophy of Hans-Georg Gadamer*, pp. 421–432.

——, "A Coherence Theory of Truth and Knowledge," in Lepore (ed.), *Truth and Interpretation*, pp. 307–319.

——, "A Nice Derangement of Epitaphs," in Lepore (ed.), *Truth and Interpretation*, pp. 433–446.

——, "What Metaphors Mean," *Critical Inquiry* 5 (1978): 29–45.

Debus, A.G., *The Chemical Philosophy: Paracelsian Science and Medicine* (New York, 1977).

Derrida, Jacques, "Structure, Sign and Play in the Discourse of the Human Sciences," in Richard Macksey and Eugenio Donato (eds), *The Structuralist Controversy: The Languages of Criticism and the Sciences of Man* (Baltimore and London: Johns Hopkins University Press, 1972), pp. 247–264.

——, *Marges de la Philosophie* (Paris: Minuit, 1972).

——, and Maurizio Ferraris, *A Taste for the Secret*, trans. Giacomo Donis (Oxford: Polity, 2001).

Dobranski, Stephen, and John Rumrich (eds), *Milton and Heresy* (New York: Cambridge University Press, 1998).

Donne, John, "A Valediction: Upon My Name in the Window," in *John Donne's Poetry: Authoritative Texts, Criticism*, ed. Arthur L. Clements (New York and London: Norton, 1992), pp. 15–17.

Dostal, Robert J. (ed.), *The Cambridge Companion to Gadamer* (Cambridge and New York: Cambridge University Press, 2002).

Douglas, J.D. et al. (eds) *New Bible Dictionary* (Grand Rapids, MI: Eerdmans, 1971).

Draper, William H. (trans.), *Petrarch's Secret: Or, The Soul's Conflict with Passion, Three Dialogues between Himself and S. Augustine* (Westport, CT.: Hyperion Press, 1978).

Dummett, Michael, "'A Nice Derangement of Epitaphs': Some Comments on Davidson and Hacking," in Lepore (ed.), *Truth and Interpretation*, pp. 459–476.

——, "What Is a Theory of Meaning? (II)," in Evans and McDowell (eds), *Truth and Meaning*, pp. 67–137.

Duran, Angelica, "The Last Stages of Education: *Paradise Regained* and *Samson Agonistes*," *MQ* 34.4 (2000): 103–117.

Eamon, William, *Science and the Secrets of Nature: Books of Secrets in Medieval and Early Modern Culture* (Princeton, NJ: Princeton University Press, 1994).

Edwards, Karen, *Milton and the Natural World: Science and Poetry in* Paradise Lost (Cambridge: Cambridge University Press, 1999).

Elukin, Jonathan M., "Keeping Secrets in Medieval and Early Modern English Government," in Engel and Elukin (eds), *Geheimnis*, pp. 111–129.

Empson, William, *Milton's God* (London: Chatto & Windus, 1965).

Engel, Gisela, and Jonathan Elukin et al. (eds), *Das Geheimnis am Beginn der europäischen Moderne* (Frankfurt: Vittorio Klostermann, 2002).

Erasmus, Desiderius, *Collected Works of Erasmus*, eds Sir R.A.B. Mynors et al., trans. Margaret Mann Phillips et al. (43 vols, Toronto: University of Toronto Press, 1982).

Erastus, Thomas, *Disputationes de medicina noua Philippi Paracelsi* (Basil, 1572).

Erickson, Robert A., *The Language of the Heart, 1600–1750* (Philadelphia: University of Pennsylvania Press, 1997).

Evans, Gareth, and John McDowell (eds), *Truth and Meaning: Essays in Semantics* (Oxford: Clarendon Press, 1977).

Evans, J. Martin, "*Lycidas*," in Dennis Danielson (ed.), *The Cambridge Companion to Milton* (Cambridge: Cambridge University Press, 1999), pp. 39–53.

——, *The Miltonic Moment* (Lexington, KY: University Press of Kentucky, 1998).

Fallon, Robert, *Milton in Government* (University Park: Pennsylvania State University Press, 1993).

Fallon, Stephen M., "The Spur of Self-Concernment," *MS* 38 (2000): 220–242.

——, *Milton among the Philosophers: Poetry and Materialism in Seventeenth-Century England* (Ithaca, NY: Cornell University Press, 1991).

Ferry, Anne, *The "Inward" Language: Sonnets of Wyatt, Sidney, Shakespeare, Donne* (Chicago and London: University of Chicago Press, 1983).

Ficino, Marsilio, *Platonic Theology: Volume I, Books I–IV*, eds James Hankins and William Bowen, trans. Michael J.B. Allen and John Warden (Cambridge, MA, and London: Harvard University Press, 2001).

Fish, Stanley, *How Milton Works* (Cambridge, MA: Belknap Press of Harvard University Press, 2001).

——, *The Trouble with Principle* (Cambridge, MA: Harvard University Press, 1999).

——, *Professional Correctness: Literary Studies and Political Change* (New York: Clarendon Press, 1995).

——, *Doing What Comes Naturally: Change, Rhetoric, and the Practice of Theory in Literary and Legal Studies* (Durham and London: Duke University Press, 1989).

——, *"Is There a Text in this Class?": The Authority of Interpretive Communities* (Cambridge, MA: Harvard University Press, 1980).

——, *Self-Consuming Artifacts: The Experience of Seventeenth-Century Literature* (Berkeley: University of California Press, 1972).

——, *Surprised by Sin: The Reader in* Paradise Lost (Berkeley: University of California Press, 1971).

——, "Wanting a Supplement: The Question of Interpretation in Milton's Early Prose," in *How Milton Works*, pp. 215–255.

——, "*Lycidas*: A Poem Finally Anonymous," in *How Milton Works*, pp. 256–280.

——, "With the Compliments of the Author: Reflections on Austin and Derrida," in *Doing What Comes Naturally*, pp. 37–67.

——, "Working on the Chain Gang: Interpretation in Law and Literature," in *Doing What Comes Naturally*, pp. 87–102.

——, "Don't Know Much About the Middle Ages: Posner on Law and Literature," in *Doing What Comes Naturally*, pp. 294–314.

Forsyth, Neil, *The Satanic Epic* (Princeton and Oxford: Princeton University Press, 2003).

Foucault, Michel, *The History of Sexuality, Volume I: An Introduction*, trans. Robert Hurley (New York: Vintage, 1990).

Fowler, Alastair (ed.), *John Milton:* Paradise Lost (London and New York: Longman, 1998).

Fraser, Russell, "Milton's Two Poets," *SEL* 34 (1994): 109–118.

Freedberg, David, *The Eye of the Lynx: Galileo, His Friends, and the Beginnings of Modern Natural History* (Chicago: University of Chicago Press, 2002).

Frege, Gottlob, "On Sense and Nominatum," in Garfield and Kiteley (eds), *Essential Readings*, pp. 35–52.

French, J. Milton (ed.), *The Life Records of John Milton* (5 vols, New Brunswick: Rutgers University Press, 1950).

Fried, Daniel, "Milton and Empiricist Semiotics," *MQ* 37.3 (2003): 117–138.

Gadamer, Hans-Georg, *Truth and Method*, trans. rev. Joel Weinsheimer and Donald G. Marshall (New York: Continuum, 2003).

———, *Wahrheit und Methode: Grundzüge einer philosophischen Hermeneutik* (Tübingen: J.C.B. Mohr, 1990).

———, "From Word to Concept: The Task of Hermeneutics as Philosophy," in Krajewski (ed.), *Gadamer's Repercussions*, pp. 1–12.

———, "Reply to Stanley H. Rosen," in Hahn (ed.), *The Philosophy of Hans-Georg Gadamer*, pp. 219–222.

———, "Reply to Davidson," in Hahn (ed.), *The Philosophy of Hans-Georg Gadamer*, pp. 433–436.

———, "Text and Interpretation," in Michelfelder and Palmer (eds.), *Dialogue and Deconstruction*, pp. 21–51.

———, *Philosophical Hermeneutics*, trans. and ed. David E. Linge (Berkeley: University of California Press, 1976).

Gardiner, Anne Barbeau, "Milton's Parody of Catholic Hymns in Eve's Temptation and Fall: Original Sin as a Paradigm of 'Secret Idolatries'," *Studies in Philology* 91.2 (1994): 216–231.

Garfield, Jay L., and Murray Kiteley (eds), *Meaning and Truth: Essential Readings in Modern Semantics* (New York: Paragon House, 1991).

Gay, David, *The Endless Kingdom: Milton's Scriptural Society* (London: Associated University Press, 2002).

Goldberg, Jonathan, *James I and the Politics of Literature: Jonson, Shakespeare, Donne and their Contemporaries* (Baltimore and London: Johns Hopkins University Press, 1983).

Goldsmith, Steven, "The Muting of Satan: Language and Redemption in *Paradise Regained*," *SEL* 26 (1986): 125–140.

Goulemot, Jean-Marie, "Literary Practices: Publicizing the Private," in Chartier (ed.) and Goldhammer (trans.), *Passions of the Renaissance*, pp. 362–396.

Graff, Gerald, *Professing Literature: An Institutional History* (Chicago: University of Chicago Press, 1987).

Graham, Jean E., "Virgin Ears: Silence, Deafness, and Chastity in Milton's *Maske*," *MS* 36 (1998): 1–17.

Greenblatt, Stephen, "Invisible Bullets: Renaissance Authority and Its Subversion, Henry IV and Henry V," in Jonathan Dollimore and Alan Sinfield (eds), *Political Shakespeare: New Essays in Cultural Materialism* (Manchester: Manchester University Press, 1985), pp. 18–47.

Gregerson, Linda, *The Reformation of the Subject: Spenser, Milton, and the English Protestant Epic* (Cambridge and New York: Cambridge University Press, 1995).

———, "The Secret of Princes: Sexual Scandal at the Tudor Court," in Engel and Elukin, *Geheimnis*, pp. 130–141.

Grice, H. Paul, *Studies in the Way of Words* (Cambridge, MA: Harvard University Press, 1989).

Groebner, Valentin, "Invisible Gifts: Secrecy, Corruption and the Politics of Information at the Beginning of the 16th Century," in Engel and Elukin, *Geheimnis*, pp. 98–110.

Grossman, Marshall, *The Story of All Things: Writing the Self in English Renaissance Narrative Poetry* (London: Duke University Press, 1998).

Habermas, Jürgen, *The Structural Transformation of the Public Sphere*, trans. Thomas Bürger (Cambridge, MA: MIT Press, 1989).

Hahn, Lewis Edwin (ed.), *The Philosophy of Hans-Georg Gadamer* (Chicago: Open Court, 1997).

Haji, Ishtiyaque, "On Being Morally Responsible in a Dream," in Gareth B. Matthews (ed.), *The Augustinian Tradition* (Berkeley and London: University of California Press, 1999), pp. 166–182.

Hall, David H. (ed.), *The Antinomian Controversy, 1636–1638* (Durham and London: Duke University Press, 1990).

Hamilton, Gary D., "*Paradise Regained* and the Private Houses," in P.G. Stanwood (ed.), *Of Poetry and Politics: New Essays on Milton and His World* (Binghamton, NY: Medieval and Renaissance Texts and Studies, 1995), pp. 239–248.

Hanson, Elizabeth, *Discovering the Subject in Renaissance England* (Cambridge: Cambridge University Press, 1998).

Harrison, Peter, *The Bible, Protestantism, and the Rise of Natural Science* (Cambridge and New York: Cambridge University Press, 1998).

Hart, D. Bentley, "Matter, Monism, and Narrative: An Essay on the Metaphysics of *PL*," *MQ* 30.1 (1996): 16–26.

Harvey, William, *Exercitatio Anatomica de Motu Cordis*, trans. Chauncey D. Leake (Springfield, IL: Charles C. Thomas, 1958).

——, *Anatomical Exercitations Concerning the Generation of Living Creatures* (London, 1653).

Haskin, Dayton, *Milton's Burden of Interpretation* (Philadelphia: University of Pennsylvania Press, 1994).

Hawkes, David, *Idols of the Marketplace: Idolatry and Commodity Fetishism in English Literature, 1580–1680* (New York: Palgrave, 2001).

Heidegger, Martin, *Sein und Zeit* (Tuebingen: M. Niemeyer, 1967).

Herman, Peter C., *Destabilizing Milton:* Paradise Lost *and the Poetics of Incertitude* (New York: Palgrave, 2005).

——, "*Paradise Lost*, the Miltonic 'Or,' and the Poetics of Incertitude," *SEL* 43.1 (2003): 181–211.

Hiltner, Ken, *Milton and Ecology* (Cambridge and New York: Cambridge University Press, 2003).

Hirsch, E.D., *Validity in Interpretation* (New Haven: Yale University Press, 1967).

Hoy, David C., "Post-Cartesian Interpretation: Hans-Georg Gadamer and Donald Davidson," in Hahn (ed.), *The Philosophy of Hans-Georg Gadamer*, pp. 111–130.

——, "Legal Hermeneutics: Recent Debates," in Wright (ed.), *Festivals of Interpretation*, pp. 111–135.

Hutchison, Keith, "What Happened to Occult Qualities in the Scientific Revolution?" in Peter Dear (ed.), *The Scientific Enterprise in Early Modern Europe: Readings from* Isis (Chicago and London: University of Chicago Press, 1997), pp. 86–106.

Iseminger, Gary, (ed.) *Intention and Interpretation* (Philadelphia: Temple University Press, 1992).

James I, *The True Law of Free Monarchies* and *Basilikon Doron*, eds Daniel Fischlin and Mark Fortier (Toronto: Centre for Reformation and Renaissance Studies, 1996).

Jones, David Martin, *Conscience and Allegiance in Seventeenth Century England: The Political Significance of Oaths and Engagements* (Rochester, NY: University of Rochester Press, 1999).

Kahn, Victoria, *Machiavellian Rhetoric from the Counter-Reformation to Milton* (Princeton, NJ: Princeton University Press, 1994).

Kelley, Mark R., and Joseph Wittreich (eds), *Altering Eyes: New Perspectives on* Samson Agonistes (London: Associated University Press, 2002).

Kermode, Frank, *The Genesis of Secrecy: On the Interpretation of Narrative* (Cambridge, MA: Harvard University Press, 1979).

Kerrigan, William, *The Sacred Complex: The Psychogenesis of* Paradise Lost (Cambridge, MA: Harvard University Press, 1983).

——, "The Irrational Coherence of *Samson Agonistes*," *MS* 22 (1986): 217–232.

Kertscher, Jens, "'We understand differently when we understand at all': Gadamer's Ontology of Language Reconsidered," in Malpas, Arnswald, and Kertscher (eds), *Gadamer's Century*, pp. 135–56.

Kilby, Richard, *The Burthen of a Loaded Conscience* (Cambridge, 1608).

Kirconnell, Watson (ed.), *Awake the Courteous Echo: The Themes and Prosody of* Comus, Lycidas, *and* Paradise Regained *in World Literature with Translations of the Major Analogues* (Toronto: University of Toronto Press, 1973).

——, (ed.), *That Invincible Samson: The Theme of* Samson Agonistes *in World Literature with Translations of the Major Analogues* (Toronto: University of Toronto Press, 1964).

Knapp, Steven, and Walter Benn Michaels, "Against Theory," *Critical Inquiry* 8 (1982): 723–742.

——, "Against Theory 2: Hermeneutics and Deconstruction," *Critical Inquiry* 14 (1987): 49–68.

——, "The Impossibility of Intentionless Meaning," in Iseminger, (ed.), *Intention and Interpretation*, pp. 51–64.

Kolbrener, William, *Milton's Warring Angels* (Cambridge: Cambridge University Press, 1997).

Krajewski, Bruce (ed.), *Gadamer's Repercussions: Reconsidering Philosophical Hermeneutics* (Berkeley: University of California Press, 2004).

Krier, Theresa M., *Gazing on Secret Sights: Spenser, Classical Imitation, and the Decorums of Vision* (Ithaca: Cornell University Press, 1990).

Krouse, Michael F., *Milton's Samson and the Christian Tradition* (Princeton, NJ: Princeton University Press, 1949).

Lavoie, Don (ed.), *Economics and Hermeneutics* (London and New York: Routledge, 1991).

Lee, Hansoon, *Kunsttheorie in der Kunst: Studien zur Ikonographie von Minerva, Merkur und Apollo im 16. Jahrhundert* (Frankfurt am Main: Peter Lang, 1996).

Leonard, John, *Naming in Paradise: Milton and the Language of Adam and Eve* (New York: Oxford University Press, 1990).

——, "Milton's Vow of Celibacy: A Reconsideration of the Evidence," in P.G. Stanwood (ed.), *Of Poetry and Politics: New Essays on Milton and His World* (Binghamton, NY: Medieval and Renaissance Texts and Studies, 1995), pp. 187–202.

——, "Saying 'No' to Freud: Milton's *A Mask* and Sexual Assault," *MQ* 25.4 (1991): 129–140.

——, "'Trembling ears': The Historical Moment of *Lycidas,*" *Journal of Medieval and Renaissance Studies* 21 (1991): 59–81.

Lepore, Ernest (ed.), *Truth and Interpretation: Perspectives on the Philosophy of Donald Davidson* (Oxford and New York: Basil Blackwell, 1986).

Levin, Richard A., *Shakespeare's Secret Schemers: The Study of an Early Modern Dramatic Device* (Newark, DE: University of Delaware Press, 2001).

Lewalski, Barbara, *The Life of John Milton: A Critical Biography* (Oxford, and Malden, MA: Blackwell, 2000).

——, "How Radical Was the Young Milton?" in Dobranski and Rumrich (eds), *Milton and Heresy*, pp. 49–72.

——, "Milton's *Comus* and the Politics of Masquing," in David Bevington et al. (eds), *The Politics of the Stuart Court Masque* (Cambridge: Cambridge University Press, 1998), pp. 296–320.

——, "Milton: Political Beliefs and Polemical Methods," *PMLA* 74 (1959): 191–202.

Lieb, Michael, "'A Thousand Foreskins': Circumcision, Violence, and Selfhood in Milton," *MS* 38 (2000): 198–219.

——, "'Our Living Dread': The God of *Samson Agonistes,*" *MS* 33 (1997): 3–25.

Linche, Richard, *The Fountaine of Ancient Fiction* (London, 1599).

Lindberg, David C., and Robert S. Westman (eds), *Reappraisals of the Scientific Revolution* (Cambridge and New York: Cambridge University Press, 1990).

Loar, Brian, "Two Theories of Meaning," in Evans and Mcdowell (eds), *Truth and Meaning*, pp. 138–161.

Long, Pamela O., *Openness, Secrecy, Authorship* (Baltimore and London: Johns Hopkins University Press, 2001).

Loxley, James, *Royalism and Poetry in the English Civil Wars: The Drawn Sword* (London and New York: St. Martin's Press, 1997).

Luxon, Thomas, *Literal Figures: Puritan Allegory and the Reformation Crisis in Representation* (Chicago: University of Chicago Press, 1995).

Lyons, William, *Approaches to Intentionality* (Oxford: Clarendon Press, 1995).

MacLaren, I.S., "Milton's Nativity Ode: The Function of Poetry and Structures of Response in 1629," *MS* 15 (1981): 181–200.

Madison, G.B., *The Hermeneutics of Postmodernity: Figures and Themes* (Bloomington and Indianapolis: Indiana University Press, 1990).

——, "Getting beyond Objectivism: The Philosophical Hermeneutics of Gadamer and Ricoeur," in Lavoie (ed.), *Economics and Hermeneutics*, pp. 34–58.

Malpas, Jeff, Ulrich Arnswald and Jens Kertscher (eds), *Gadamer's Century: Essays in Honor of Hans-Georg Gadamer* (Cambridge, MA: MIT Press, 2002).

Marcus, Leah S., *The Politics of Mirth: Jonson, Herrick, Milton, Marvell, and the Defense of Old Holiday Pastimes* (Chicago: University of Chicago Press, 1989).

——, "The Earl of Bridgewater's Legal Life: Notes toward a Political Reading of *Comus*," in J. Martin Evans (ed.), *John Milton: Twentieth-Century Perspectives, Volume 2: The Early Poems* (New York: Routledge, 2003), pp. 297–307.

Marmor, Andrei, *Interpretation and Legal Theory* (Oxford: Clarendon Press, 1992).

Marshall, Donald G., "On Dialogue: To Its Cultured Despisers," in Krajewski (ed.), *Gadamer's Repercussions*, pp. 123–144.

——, "Dialogue and Ecriture," in Michelfelder and Palmer (eds), *Dialogue and Deconstruction*, pp. 206–214.

Martin, Catherine Gimelli, "'What If the Sun Be Centre to the World?': Milton's Epistemology, Cosmology, and Paradise of Fools Reconsidered," *Modern Philology* 99.2 (2001): 231–265.

Martin, Thomas L., "On the Margin of God: Deconstruction and the Language of Satan in *PL*," *MQ* 29.2 (1995): 41–47.

Maus, Katharine Eisaman, *Inwardness and Theater in the English Renaissance* (Chicago: University of Chicago Press, 1995).

McCrea, Adriana, *Constant Minds: Political Virtue and the Lipsian Paradigm in England, 1584–1650* (Toronto: University of Toronto Press, 1997).

McDowell, John, "Gadamer and Davidson on Understanding and Relativism," in Malpas, Arnswald, and Kertscher (eds), *Gadamer's Century*, pp. 173–194.

Mcgrath, Elizabeth, "Rubens' Musathena," *Journal of the Warburg and Courtauld Institutes* 50 (1987): 233–245.

McGuire, Maryann, *Milton's Puritan Masque* (Athens, GA: University of Georgia Press, 1983).

Michelfelder, Diane P., and Richard E. Palmer (eds), *Dialogue and Deconstruction: The Gadamer-Derrida Encounter* (Albany: State University of New York Press, 1989).

Millen, Ron, "The Manifestation of Occult Qualities in the Scientific Revolution," in Margaret J. Osler and Paul Lawrence Farber (eds), *Religion, Science, and Worldview: Essays in Honor of Richard S. Westfall* (Cambridge and New York: Cambridge University Press, 1985), pp. 185–216.

Milton, John, *Complete Prose Works of John Milton*, eds Don M. Wolfe et al. (8 vols, New Haven and London: Yale University Press, 1953–1982).

——, *The Works of John Milton*, eds Frank Allen Patterson et al. (18 vols, New York: Columbia University Press, 1931–1938).

——, *Paradise Lost. A Poem in Twelve Books* (London: Samuel Simmons, 1674).

——, *Poems, etc. upon Several Occasions* (London: Thomas Dring, 1673).

——, *Paradise Regaind. A poem. In IV books. To which is added Samson Agonistes* (London: John Starkey, 1671).

Mirowski, Philip, "The Philosophical Bases of Institutionalist Economics," in Lavoie (ed.), *Economics and Hermeneutics*, pp. 76–112.

More, Henry, A *Platonick Song of the Soul*, ed. and introd. Alexander Jacob (Lewisburg, PA, and London: Associated University Press, 1998).

Morgan, Edmund S., *Visible Saints: The History of a Puritan Idea* (Ithaca and London: Cornell University Press, 1963).

Mueller, Janel, "Milton on Heresy," in Dobranski and Rumrich (eds), *Milton and Heresy*, pp. 21–38.

Naffine, Ngaire, and Rosemary Owens and John Williams (eds), *Intention in Law and Philosophy* (Aldershot, Hants: Ashgate, 2001).

Newman, William, "The Alchemical Sources of Robert Boyle's Corpuscular Philosophy," *Annals of Science* 53 (1996): 567–585.

Norbrook, David, *Writing the English Republic: Poetry, Rhetoric, and Politics, 1627–1660* (New York: Cambridge University Press, 1999).

——, "Republican Occasions in *Paradise Regained* and *Samson Agonistes*," *MS* 42 (2002): 122–148.

——, "The Politics of Milton's Early Poetry," in Annabel Patterson (ed.), *John Milton* (London and New York: Longman, 1992), pp. 46–64.

——, "The Reformation of the Masque," in David Lindley (ed.), *The Court Masque* (Manchester: Manchester University Press, 1984), pp. 94–110.

O'Keefe, Timothy J., *Milton and the Pauline Tradition: A Study of Theme and Symbolism* (Washington: University Press of America, 1982).

Oram, William A., "The Invocation of Sabrina," *SEL* 24 (1984): 121–139.

Palmer, Tom G., "The Hermeneutical View of Freedom: Implications of Gadamerian Understanding for Economic Policy," in Lavoie (ed.), *Economics and Hermeneutics*, pp. 299–318.

Parker, William Riley, *Milton: A Biography*, ed. Gordon Campbell (2 vols, Oxford: Clarendon Press, 1996).

Patrides, C.A. (ed.), *Milton's* Lycidas*: The Tradition and the Poem* (Columbia, MO: University of Missouri Press, 1983).

Patterson, Annabel, *Reading between the Lines* (Madison, WI: University of Wisconsin Press, 1993).

——, (ed.), *John Milton* (London and New York: Longman, 1992).

——, *Censorship and Interpretation* (Madison, WI: University of Wisconsin Press, 1984).

——, "Intention," in Frank Lentricchia and Thomas McLaughlin (eds), *Critical Terms for Literary Study* (Chicago: University of Chicago Press, 1995), pp. 136–146.

——, "'Forc'd fingers': Milton's Early Poems and Ideological Constraint," in Claude J. Summers and Ted-Larry Pebworth (eds), *"The Muses Common-Weale": Poetry and Politics in the Seventeenth Century* (Columbia, MO: University of Missouri Press, 1988), pp. 9–22.

Perkins, William, *A Discourse of Conscience*, in Thomas F. Merril (ed.), *William Perkins 1558–1602: English Puritanist* (Nieuwkoop: B. De Graaf, 1966).

Poole, William, "Milton and Science: A Caveat," *MQ* 38.1 (2004): 18–34.

Posner, Richard A., *Law and Literature: A Misunderstood Relation* (Cambridge, MA: Harvard University Press, 1988).

Potter, Lois, *Secret Rites and Secret Writing: Royalist Literature, 1641–1660* (Cambridge and New York: Cambridge University Press, 1989).

Prineas, Matthew, "'Yet once, it is a little while': Recovering the Book of Haggai in 'Lycidas'," *MQ* 33.4 (1999): 114–123.

Rambuss, Richard, *Spenser's Secret Career* (Cambridge and New York: Cambridge University Press, 1993).

Ranum, Orest, "The Refuges of Intimacy," in Chartier (ed.) and Goldhammer (trans.), *Passions of the Renaissance*, pp. 207–264.

Revard, Stella P., *Milton and the Tangles of Neaera's Hair: The Making of the 1645 Poems* (Columbia, MO: University of Missouri Press, 1997).

Revel, Jacques, "The Uses of Civility," in Chartier (ed.) and Goldhammer (trans.), *Passions of the Renaissance*, pp. 167–206.

Ricoeur, Paul, *Hermeneutics and the Human Sciences: Essays on Language, Action, and Interpretation*, ed. and trans. John B. Thompson (New York: Cambridge University Press, 1981).

Risser, James, *Hermeneutics and the Voice of the Other: Re-Reading Gadamer's Philosophical Hermeneutics* (Albany: State University of New York Press, 1997).

Rogers, John, "The Secret of *Samson Agonistes*," *MS* 33 (1996): 111–132.

Rosen, Stanley, "*Horizontverschmelzung*," in Hahn (ed.), *The Philosophy of Hans-Georg Gadamer*, pp. 207–222.

Rosendale, Timothy, "Milton, Hobbes and the Liturgical Subject," *SEL* 44.1 (2004): 149–172.

Ross, Alexander, *Arcana microcosmi, or, The hid secrets of man's body discovered* (London, 1652).

Rudrum, Alan, "Milton Scholarship and the Agon over *Samson Agonistes*," *Huntington Library Quarterly: Studies in English and American History and Literature* 65 (2002): 465–488.

——, "Discerning the Spirit in *Samson Agonistes*: The Dalila Episode," in Charles W. Durham and Kristin A. Pruitt (eds), *All in All: Unity, Diversity, and the Miltonic Perspective* (London: Associated University Press, 1999), pp. 245–258.

Rumrich, John, *Milton Unbound: Controversy and Reinterpretation* (Cambridge: Cambridge University Press, 1996).

Russell, Bertrand, "Mr. Strawson on Referring," in Garfield and Kiteley (eds), *Meaning and Truth*, pp. 130–135.

Russell, Daniel S., "Perceiving, Seeing and Meaning: Emblems and Approaches to Reading in Early Modern Culture," in Daly and Manning (eds), *Aspects of Renaissance and Baroque Symbol Theory*, pp. 77–92.

Said, Edward, *The World, the Text, and the Critic* (Cambridge, MA: Harvard University Press, 1983).

Samuel, Irene, "*Samson Agonistes* as Tragedy," in Joseph Anthony Wittreich (ed.), *Calm of Mind: Tercentenary Essays on* Paradise Regained *and* Samson Agonistes*, in honor of John S. Diekhoff* (Cleveland: Press of Case Western Reserve University, 1971).

Sauer, Elizabeth, "The Politics of Performance in the Inner Theater: *Samson Agonistes* as Closet Drama," in Dobranski and Rumrich (eds), *Milton and Heresy*, pp. 199–215.

Savoie, John, "The Point of the Pinnacle: Son and Scripture in *Paradise Regained*," *ELR* 34.1 (2004): 83–124.

Sawday, Jonathan, "The Transparent Man and the King's Heart," in Claire Jowitt and Diane Watt (eds), *The Arts of 17th-Century Science: Representations of the Natural World in European and North American Culture* (Aldershot, Hants: Ashgate, 2002), pp. 12–24.

Schneider, Robert A., "Disclosing Mysteries: The Contradictions of State in 17th-Century France," in Engel and Elukin (eds), *Geheimnis*, pp. 159–178.

Schultz, Howard, *Milton and Forbidden Knowledge* (New York: MLA, 1955).

Schwartz, Regina, *Remembering and Repeating: Biblical Creation in* Paradise Lost (Cambridge and New York: Cambridge University Press, 1988).

Searle, John, *Consciousness and Language* (New York: Cambridge University Press, 2002).

——, *Intentionality: An Essay in the Philosophy of Mind* (Cambridge: Cambridge University Press, 1983).

——, *Speech Acts: An Essay in the Philosophy of Language* (London: Cambridge University Press, 1969).

——, "Literary Theory and its Discontents," in Dwight Eddins (ed.), *The Emperor Redressed: Critiquing Critical Theory* (Tuscaloosa and London: University of Alabama Press, 1995), pp. 166–198.

——, "The Word Turned Upside Down," *The New York Review of Books* (October 1983): 12–16.

Shakespeare, William, *The Complete Works of Shakespeare*, ed. David Bevington (New York: Longman, 1997).

Sharpe, Kevin, *Reading Revolutions: The Politics of Reading in Early Modern England* (New Haven and London: Yale University Press, 2000).

——, *Remapping Early Modern England: The Culture of Seventeenth-Century Politics* (Cambridge: Cambridge University Press, 2000).

Shawcross, John, *The Uncertain World of* Samson Agonistes (Rochester, NY: D.S. Brewer, 2001).

——, *Milton: The Self and the World* (Lexington, KY: University Press of Kentucky, 1993).

——, *Intentionality and the New Traditionalism: Some Liminal Means to Literary Revisionism* (University Park: Pennsylvania State University Press, 1991).

Sherry, Beverly, "A 'Paradise Within' Can Never Be 'Happier Far': Reconsidering the Archangel Michael's Consolation in *PL*," *MQ* 37.2 (2003): 77–91.

Shifflett, Andrew, *Stoicism, Politics, and Literature in the Age of Milton: War and Peace Reconciled* (Cambridge: Cambridge University Press, 1998).

Shoaf, R.A., *Milton, Poet of Duality: A Study of Semiosis in the Poetry and the Prose* (New Haven, CT: Yale University Press, 1985).

Shuger, Debora, "'Gums of Glutinous Heat' and the Stream of Consciousness: The Theology of Milton's *Maske*," *Representations* 60 (1997): 1–21.

Silver, Victoria, *Imperfect Sense: The Predicament of Milton's Irony* (Princeton, NJ: Princeton University Press, 2001).

———, "'Lycidas' and the Grammar of Revelation," *ELH* 58 (1991): 779–808.

Simonds, Peggy Muñoz, "Some Images of the Conscience in Emblem Literature," in Stella P. Revard, Fidel Rädle and Mario di Cesare (eds), *Acta Conventus Neo-Latini Guelpherbytani: Proceedings of the Sixth International Congress of Neo-Latin Studies* (Binghamton, NY: Medieval and Renaissance Texts and Studies, 1988), pp. 314–330.

Slights, Camille Wells, *The Casuistical Tradition in Shakespeare, Donne, Herbert and Milton* (Princeton, NJ: Princeton University Press, 1981).

———, "Notaries, Sponges, and Looking-glasses: Conscience in Early Modern England," *ELR* 28.2 (1998): 231–246.

Slights, William W.E., *Ben Jonson and the Art of Secrecy* (Toronto: University of Toronto Press, 1994).

Sokolowski, Robert, "Gadamer's Theory of Hermeneutics," in Hahn (ed.), *The Philosophy of Hans-Georg Gadamer*, pp. 223–236.

Spenser, Edmund, *The Yale Edition of the Shorter Poems of Edmund Spenser*, eds William Oram et al. (New Haven and London: Yale University Press, 1989).

———, *The Faerie Queene*, ed. Thomas P. Roche (London and New York: Penguin, 1978).

Spurr, John, "From Puritanism to Dissent, 1660–1700," in Christopher Durston and Jacqueline Eales (eds), *The Culture of English Puritanism, 1560–1700* (New York: St. Martin's Press, 1996), pp. 234–265.

Stoljar, Natalie, "Postulated Authors and Hypothetical Intentions," in Naffine, Owens and Williams (eds), *Intention in Law and Philosophy*, pp. 271–290.

Strauss, Leo, *Persecution and the Art of Writing* (Glencoe, IL: Free Press, 1952).

Strawson, P.F., "On Referring," in Garfield and Kiteley (eds), *Meaning and Truth*, pp. 108–129.

Strier, Richard, *Resistant Structures: Particularity, Radicalism, and Renaissance Texts* (Berkeley: University of California Press, 1995).

Stubbes, Henry, *Conscience the Best Friend Upon Earth* (London, 1678).

Swaim, Kathleen M., "'Myself a True Poem': Early Milton and the Reformation of the Subject," *MS* 38 (2000): 66–95.

Targoff, Ramie, *Common Prayer: Models of Public Devotion in Early Modern England* (Chicago: University of Chicago Press, 2001).

——, "The Performance of Prayer: Sincerity and Theatricality in Early Modern England," *Representations* 60 (1997): 49–69.

Tayler, Edward, *Milton's Poetry: Its Development in Time* (Pittsburgh: Duquesne University Press, 1979).

Taylor, Charles, *Sources of the Self: The Making of the Modern Identity* (Cambridge, MA: Harvard University Press, 1989).

Taylor, Jeremy, *Ductor Dubitantium, or The Rule of Conscience In All her General Measures* (London, 1666).

Teigas, Demetrius, *Knowledge and Hermeneutic Understanding: A Study of the Habermas-Gadamer Debate* (Lewisburg and London: Associated University Press, 1995).

Tourneur, Cyril, *The Revenger's Tragedy*, ed. R.A. Foakes (Manchester and New York: Manchester University Press, 1996).

Treip, Mindele Anne, "'Reason Is Also Choice': The Emblematics of Free Will in *Paradise Lost*," *SEL* 31.1 (1991): 147–177.

Tully, James, and Quentin Skinner (eds), *Meaning and Context: Quentin Skinner and His Critics* (Cambridge: Polity Press, 1988).

Vergil, Polydore, *On Discovery*, ed. and trans. Brian P. Copenhaver (Cambridge, MA.: Harvard University Press, 2002).

Vinovich, J. Michael, "Protocols of Reading: Milton and Biography," *Early Modern Literary Studies* 1.3 (1995): 1–15.

Waldock, A.J.A., Paradise Lost *and its Critics* (Gloucester, MA: Peter Smith, 1959).

Warnke, Georgia, *Gadamer: Hermeneutics, Tradition and Reason* (Cambridge: Polity, 1987).

——, "Walzer, Rawls, and Gadamer: Hermeneutics and Political Theory," in Wright (ed.), *Festivals of Interpretation*, pp. 136–160.

Wecker, Jacob, *Eighteen Books of the Secrets of Nature ... now much Augmented and Inlarged by Dr R. Read* (London, 1660).

Weinsheimer, Joel, *Philosophical Hermeneutics and Literary Theory* (New Haven, CT: Yale University Press, 1991).

——, "Meaningless Hermeneutics?" in Krajewski (ed.), *Gadamer's Repercussions*, pp. 158–166.

Wilcher, Robert, *The Writing of Royalism, 1628–1660* (Cambridge and New York, 2001).

Wilding, Michael, "Milton's 'A Masque Presented at Ludlow Castle, 1634': Theatre and Politics on the Border," *MQ* 21 (1987): 35–51.

Williams, John, "Constitutional Intention: The Limits of Originalism," in Naffine, Owens and Williams (eds), *Intention in Law and Philosophy* (Aldershot, Hants: Ashgate, 2001), pp. 321–344.

Wilson, George M. "Again, Theory: On Speaker's Meaning, Linguistic Meaning, and the Meaning of a Text," *Critical Inquiry* 19 (1992): 164–193.

Wittreich, Joseph, *Shifting Contexts: Reinterpreting* Samson Agonistes (Pittsburgh: Duquesne University Press, 2002).

——, "'Reading' Milton: The Death (and Survival) of the Author," *Milton Studies* 38 (2000): 10–46.

——, *Interpreting* Samson Agonistes (Princeton, NJ: Princeton University Press, 1986).

Wood, Derek N.C., *"Exiled from Light": Divine Law, Morality, and Violence in Milton's* Samson Agonistes (Toronto: University of Toronto Press, 2001).

Woods, Suzanne, "'That Freedom of Discussion Which I Loved': Italy and Milton's Cultural Self-Definition," in di Cesare (ed.), *Milton in Italy*, pp. 9–18.

Wright, Jonathan, "The World's Worst Worm: Conscience and Conformity during the English Reformation," *Sixteenth Century Journal* 30.1 (1999): 113–133.

Wright, Kathleen (ed.), *Festivals of Interpretation: Essays on Hans-Georg Gadamer's Work* (Albany: State University of New York Press, 1990).

Young, R.V., *Doctrine and Devotion in Seventeenth-Century Poetry: Studies in Donne, Herbert, Crashaw, and Vaughan* (Rochester, NY: D.S. Brewer, 2000).

Zachman, Randall C., *The Assurance of Faith: Conscience in the Theology of Martin Luther and John Calvin* (Minneapolis: Fortress Press, 1993).

Zagorin, Perez, *Ways of Lying: Dissimulation, Persecution, and Conformity in Early Modern Europe* (Cambridge, MA: Harvard University Press, 1990).

Zalta, Edward N., *Intensional Logic and the Metaphysics of Intentionality* (Cambridge, MA: MIT Press, 1988).

Index

Agrippa, Cornelius 19, 22
Alpers, Paul 45
antinomianism 37, 72, 89
Austin, J.L. 37–8, 45, 66, 103, 172

Bacon, Sir Francis 17–20, 22, 54, 73, 75,
  162, 175–6
Bath, Michael 21–2
Bentley, Richard 6, 8
Bruno, Giordano 20, 22
Bruns, Gerald 150
Burton, Robert 20, 74–7, 79

Calvin, John 4, 50, 71, 82, 89, 162
  against Nicodemism 36
  on conscience 33, 35–7
  on public confession 36–7, 72
  on scriptural accommodation 166–7
  on secrecy of God 7
Calvinism ix, 14, 36–7, 50, 54, 72, 75, 87–8,
  107–8
Cardano, Girolamo 19–20
Carew, Thomas 20, 78–9, 177
Carey, John 58–61
casuistry ix, 33, 35, 37–40, 50, 54, 72, 82,
  93, 96, 98, 156
Charles I 17, 78–80
Cicero 20–21, 85
conscience 10, 14, 31, 33–9, 48–53, 55,
  67–9, 72, 74, 76–7, 79, 81–2, 87, 89,
  94, 96, 98, 100, 112, 129, 156, 161,
  164, 169
conspiracy theory 2, 163
Corns, Thomas N. 32

Davidson, Donald 110, 126, 164
deconstruction 25–6, 28, 35, 38–9, 47, 54,
  65–7, 84, 125–9, 134, 147, 172
Derrida, Jacques 3, 16, 18, 25–6, 31, 38–9,
  45, 47, 53, 65–6, 74, 88, 111, 115,
  136, 147

discovery
  assumed by Manoah 101
  as basis for knowledge 1
  controlled by God 162
  as interpretative model 1–4, 6, 93
  as Miltonic subject-matter 14
  opposed to recognition 28
  related to secrecy 3, 13
  as Satanic 9, 12–13
  as trope 1, 9, 12–13

Erasmus, Desiderius 35, 75–6, 79, 88
Evans, J. Martin 41–3

Fallon, Stephen 109
Ficino, Marsilio 20, 84–5, 87–8
Fish, Stanley 4, 13, 59–60, 65–7, 111, 125,
  160–61, 165, 167
Foucauldianism 3
Freedberg, David 1, 85
Frege, Gottlob 109–10, 125

Gadamer, Hans-Georg; see also
  hermeneutics, philosophical
  hermeneutics of 14–15, 25–9
  art ontologized in 27
  and authorial biography 42
  concept of experience in 28
  concept of incarnation in 114
  fusion of horizons in 128
  Gespräch in 119
  jurisprudence in 137
  play theorized in 26, 157
  opposed to Straussian discovery 28
  outside logic of object and subject 26
  related to pragmatism 127, 136
  repetition in 47
  role of Anstoss in 137
  significance of expression in 118
  significance of questioning in 120,
    130, 141–2

against method 123–4
against objectivism 127
intrigued by paralogism 125
on Plato 118, 141
quoting Rilke 155
Truth and Method 2, 15, 25–8, 42, 47,
    114–15, 119–20, 123, 125
as Zahirite *manqué* 161–2
Greenblatt, Stephen 3
Gregerson, Linda 16, 31, 39
Grice, H.P. 62–3

Hamilton, Gary 170
Harvey, William 79–80
Hermathena 20–22
hermeneutics
    conservative 116
    denying distinctions 142
    devolving on secrecy 161
    of discovery 2–3, 25; *see also* discovery
        and aesthetic differentiation 27
        associated with modern science 1–3,
            19, 26
        attending genesis of secrecy 11
        Batinists as practitioners of 159
        in early-modern period 4, 24–5
        as esoteric 159
        in Milton criticism 4–5, 32
        objectivism at stake in 124
        in *SA* 93, 105
    intentionalist, strong 61–2, 65–7, 82, 89,
        94–5, 98, 111, 115–16, 124–5, 160
    legal 63–6
    in Milton criticism 15
    Milton's 133, 158
    objectivist 133
    philosophical 1, 14, 33, 95, 101, 105,
        124, 127–8, 159; see also Gadamer,
        Hans-Georg
        aesthetic consciousness in 26–8, 172
        aesthetic differentiation in 26–7
        aesthetic non-differentiation in 27–8
        application in 134, 137–8
        dialogue in 15, 25, 28, 119, 121,
            127–9, 136, 141, 143, 145–6,
            151, 155, 157, 164
        logos in 115–16, 119–20, 141, 160,
            164

logos-philosophy in 115–16,
    119–20, 160, 164
method in x, 123–4, 127, 129, 145,
    150–51, 174–5
recognition in 28, 33, 47–8, 54, 95,
    101, 103, 105, 120, 124, 126,
    150, 159, 161–2, 165, 172
understanding in 15, 28, 117–20,
    123, 126–9, 136–7, 141, 155,
    164, 172–3
    of reference 110
    restricted by objectivism 124
    Satan's 12
    of suspicion 2
    as "taste for the secret" 66
Hirsch, E.D. 42, 60–62, 67, 110–11, 116, 125

interpretation; *see also* hermeneutics
    and application 134, 138
    author-centered 42
    Biblical 163–4
    decoding as model of 2, 23, 25, 68
    and "devil's party" thesis 13
    and dialogue 128
    in early-modern period 4
    of emblems 21
    as esoteric penetration 23
    intentionalist 61, 111, 133, 138
    Koranic 159
    from life-documents 32
    as matrix of understanding 123
    and method 123–4
    Milton's concept of 163–4
    opposed by objectivism 124
    in *PL* 133
    as pre-requisite of knowledge 1, 127
    and secrecy/discovery 13, 15, 159
    as "taste for the secret" 66

James I 17, 54, 71, 76

Kermode, Frank 24
Knapp, Steven 66–7, 116–17

Luther, Martin 36–7, 71

Maus, Katharine Eisaman 69–70
Michaels, Walter Benn 66–7, 116–17

Milton, John
  Arianism of 7, 157
  authorship, attitude to 32
  Biblical exegesis of 163–8
  biography of 40–44, 48–50
  conscience, attitude to 14, 33, 48–55,
    67, 93, 95, 161
  "devil's party," alleged to be of 13
  dialogue, attitude to 119, 121, 128–30,
    143–4, 149–51, 155–9, 161, 164,
    172
  divine surveillance, attitude to 10
  exhibitionism of, mental 73–5, 90
  interpretation, attitude to 13–14, 164–5
  language, attitude to 15, 67, 108, 112,
    114, 119, 129, 161, 167, 172
  literary techniques of 131
  new science, attitude to 5, 12
  on prime matter 7
  scholarship on
    biocritical 31–48
    intentionalist 60–62, 133
    Lacanian 39–40
  secrecy, attitude to 6–8, 13–14, 25, 29,
    161–2, 168–71
  uncertainty in writings of 5, 133–4
  works of
    Apology for Smectymnuus 49, 73–4
    Areopagitica 6, 9, 107, 119, 147,
      149–50, 164
    CP 7, 9–10, 32, 43, 48–9, 51–2,
      72–4, 107, 119, 128, 141, 147,
      158, 163–8
    Defense of Himself 49, 51, 53, 73
    De Doctrina Christiana 165–8
    *The Doctrine and Discipline of
      Divorce* 167
    Lycidas 14, 32, 40–48, 50–51, 53,
      161
    A Masque at Ludlow Castle (Comus)
      14, 68–70, 80–84, 88–91
    PL 5–14, 15, 28–9, 32, 39, 72,
      81, 89, 94–5, 101, 107, 121,
      129–58, 161–2, 169–70, 172–3
    PR 169–72
    The Reason of Church Government
      32, 48–9, 73–4
    Of Reformation 42, 163

*The Second Defense of the English
  People* 32, 43, 48–51, 53, 73,
  161, 171
SA 14–15, 57–61, 67, 72, 83, 90,
  93–109, 111–15, 120–21, 129, 161
Treatise of Civil Power 74
Momus 20, 22, 75–9
More, Alexander 49–50, 55, 73, 75, 90
More, Henry 86–7

objectivism 115, 124–5, 136, 141–2, 146–7,
  149–51, 153, 172
originalism 64–6

Neoplatonism ix, 9, 14, 54, 84–8
Nicodemism 35–6, 44

Paracelsus, Theophrastus 7–8, 22
Perkins, William 33, 36, 50, 69
Posner, Richard 65, 67
prejudice 1–2, 137
probabiliorism 35
probabilism 35, 108

Ricoeur, Paul 2, 124
Rudrum, Alan 60
Ruscelli, Girolamo 19

Said, Edward 159–61
Savoie, John 165–6
Scaliger, Julius Caesar 20
science
    and aesthetic consciousness 27–8
    and hermeneutics 123
    as interpretative model 1
    involving alienation 26
    and objectivism 124
    in *PL* 5, 8
    posited by Satan 148
Searle, John 37–9, 61–3, 66–7
secrecy
    abhorred by English church 70–71
    associated with the divine will 4–5, 7–8,
      10, 162–3, 168–9
    as breakdown of conscience 10
    and casuistry 72
    as category of interpretation 6, 161
    and "devil's party" thesis 13–14

disapproved of by James I 76
and discovery 13
in early-modern period 4, 16–25
esoteric 20–25
and exegesis 163
exoteric 22–5, 87
fall as choice of 11, 149
fetishization of 3
genesis of 11
as hiding-place of knowledge 2
inimical to dialogue 129, 145
and interpretation 13, 15, 159
inverted by Calvin 72
inverted by James I 77
inverted by Samson 14, 100–101, 106
of Jesus in *PR* 170
in Milton criticism 5
Milton's 6, 13, 25, 52, 168
  abjured or exposed 49, 72, 90, 171
  juxtaposed with openness 73–4
of Milton's opponents 52, 90
modern knowledge as function of 2
of Naziritism 103
and Nicodemism 36
normative in fallen state 107
as paradox 2–3, 17–18, 23–4
rejected by Milton 6, 161, 168–9
in Renaissance literary scholarship 5
Satan's 9–11, 145, 149
as separateness 8
in Sin's rhetoric 10
secrets
  abjured by James I 17, 54, 77
  abjured by Milton 6, 10, 67
  absent from Paradise 8–9
  and aesthetic differentiation 27
  ancient 19
  as annihilated by interpretation 3, 15, 19
  books of 4, 74

as conserved by interpretation 19
deplored by Momus 76
and discovery 3
in early-modern period 19–22
and emblems 21–2
eschewed by Adam 9, 140
as hermeneutic fuel 3
indulged in by Satan 11
in literature 6
in Milton's work, alleged 4–5
known by conscience 33
known by courtiers 17
of nature 4
as revealed by Samson 93–4, 100, 103–8
in Samson story 101
secretary as repository of 5
taste for 3
undiscoverable 18
Shakespeare, William 32, 71, 80, 162
Sharpe, Kevin 16–17, 76–7, 188
Shuger, Debora 88–9, 91, 98
Silver, Victoria 46, 167
Slights, Camille Wells 69–70
speech-acts 14, 37, 61–2, 67, 83, 89–90, 100, 103, 117, 120, 131, 167, 172
Spenser, Edmund 5–6, 12–13, 17, 32, 45–6, 83, 85–7
Strauss, Leo 2, 23–5, 28, 125
Strier, Richard 39

Targoff, Ramie 70–71, 74–5, 82, 88–9, 98
Taylor, Jeremy 33, 50, 69, 79
Tillyard, E.M.W. 40–41
tutiorism 35, 72

Wecker, Jacob 19–20

Young, R.V. 39